There is joy in healing relationships!

Dear Roz

Rich Levton

Dear Roz

✦

Finding the Truth about My Father in his Wartime Love Letters to My Mother

Richard Leitman
with Michael Hollander

iUniverse, Inc.
New York   Bloomington

Dear Roz

Finding the Truth about My Father in his Wartime Love Letters to My Mother

iUniverse books may be ordered through booksellers or by contacting:

iUniverse
1663 Liberty Drive
Bloomington, IN 47403
www.iuniverse.com
1-800-Authors (1-800-288-4677)

ISBN: 978-1-4401-7114-7 (pbk)
ISBN: 978-1-4401-7116-1 (cloth)
ISBN: 978-1-4401-7115-4 (ebk)

Printed in the United States of America

iUniverse rev. date: 10/5/2009

The Letters

My friend Rich is crawling in the darkest corners of his father's life
Like a deep mine spelunker
He is picking between the lines
of the letters his father wrote
during the second world war
Like the cave paintings of Lascaux,
the walls of his father's life
are filled with wild animals and mysteries wanting to be known
And to Rich, each of these letters brings him closer
to this man who, while alive, could only reach out from the shadows
of his own scarred -over wartime wounds
to try his very best at being a father, a husband, a man.
Closer to the one person from whom Rich wanted nothing
more than love and witness
Closer to what every boy wants,
to know the heart of his father
and to be known and held softly
in that very heart.

—Michael Hollander

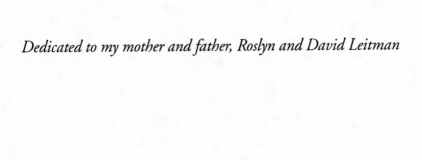

Dedicated to my mother and father, Roslyn and David Leitman

Contents

1.

Introduction

Today my father died. His passing was not easy and as we waited for his last breath to mercifully arrive, as I saw that frail and dying man lying before me, I experienced a deep longing for his eyes to really see me,

Dad and Mom on an army base.

his hands to touch me, and his heart to love me. My mind was filled with a whirlpool of memories that carried me back through 65 years of events, which eventually led to a reversal in the adult-child roles between us. Back to his strength, his laughter, his fearsome roar, his absence, and his sadness. I found myself wanting one more chance to ask him all the unasked questions that had followed me for a lifetime, only to realize that even if he were still alive I would first have to complete my transformation into an adult, and he would have to soften his heart if this quest for answers was to be successful.

I was born in New York City and my early childhood was formed in the shadow of World War II. The country was optimistic and the opportunity for personal achievement was palpable. My parents, like most, wanted their children to be the best, to grow and prosper. In my young mind, our home was a place to celebrate good grades and achievement. A place where to be loved was often to be judged, where failure carried the belief that one was less loved. This was a time when fathers who fought in WW II carried wounds too deep to permit an outward expression of love so fully needed by a sensitive young son.

As a boy I mostly succeeded; that was the message I wanted to give to my father. When success eluded me, I sometimes invented the success so that Dad would be happy and continue to be proud of me. I now understand that the possibility of either of us truly knowing each other was difficult or remote if, to meet his expectations, I had to be something other than what I really was.

My relationship with my father was not very healthy, although I did not acknowledge this until my own children were young adults. In earlier years I strived to live by the commandment "Honor thy father and mother." I would not allow myself to concede that Dad was anything but perfect, and I stuffed any negative feelings towards him deep into my gut. Slowly I began to erect a barrier between us, protecting me from his behavior; so I could be safe in my childhood beliefs of his perfection.

About fifteen years ago I began a program of self-growth and as a result began to acknowledge some of my truths about myself and others, including my father. I began to see things more realistically, and for the first time acknowledged how my father had hurt me and others. The barrier I had erected between us commenced to grow taller and wider as I attempted to block out decades of anger and frustration towards him. In time, however, this did not satisfy my core need to love and be close to my father, so I changed the direction of my personal work. My goal now was to find a place in my heart for my father. Writing this book is part of that work.

Dad died when he was 89; for several years prior he had become progressively weaker as his body tired and he was afflicted with some dementia. In the final two years of his life, my mother chose to have a full time aide live in their home to help care for him. While his physical deterioration was difficult to witness, it was the slow deterioration of his mind that became increasingly challenging to all of us and was particularly hard on my mother. Even as he approached death, he was unable to find ways to connect with and love those who cared the most. He needed my mother to sit next to him and hold his hand for hours at a time, and he became agitated, even hostile, if she was called away. As his concentration failed, he became more easily angered by the real or imagined world of his death.

During his last several months his children spent more time visiting with him and Mom. My wife and I stayed several nights at a time at their home. Once I remember sitting up with Mom all night when we thought Dad was at his end, holding his hand, caressing him and sending him love. True to form, Dad suddenly opened his eyes, told us to stop bothering him, turned over, and went back to sleep. Needless to say, I spent the rest of the night holding and comforting my mother. Was this to be the way I remembered my father, as a fierce, insensitive, and angry man?

Following Dad's funeral Mom gave me a special family treasure and for the past months I have been mining it for pieces of gold that might begin to give me the father I had lost amongst his and my unseen and unspoken shadows. That treasure is an intricately detailed five-year written record of his journey through the Second World War, in letters he wrote to my mom, Roz. A treasure that has held the truth of my father's heart for a half century waiting for the moment of his passing to give him back to me. I went from being a man who occasionally thought of his father to a son who can't get thoughts of him out of his head. I am so much more for having traveled to that place. Like an archeologist I have found in the bones of his writing a man who touched me deeply, a person I wish I had known more fully when he

3

was alive, and a father who will forever hold me as I now hold him in my heart.

This book is documentation of my journey to find my father, and at the same time, to find pieces of myself which lay hidden in my collective shadows, most notably anger and fear. It documents my search for the truth by reading Dad's letters and speaking to him through letters of my own; letting my sorrow, fear, joy, anger and a host of other emotions flow freely from me to paper. Since this is my search for the truth to foster my own growth and healing, this was not the place to put on the proverbial rose colored glasses and present Dad, or myself, as more or less than we were.

The emotions and thoughts presented in this book, especially about my dad, are mine and I own them. I have not attempted to represent how my brother Mark, or my sisters, Susan and Sally feel, or reacted to any situation I discuss. That would be a subject for their own personal explorations and I encourage them to do so.

My mom is now living in a beautiful assisted living home where she gets excellent care but misses my father very much. I have discussed some of the facts and questions I encountered in my journey of discovery with Mom, but her memory is becoming weaker and her emotions are too raw for me to push the discussions too far with her. I do know that she is happy that Dad's wish that the letters be published is fulfilled and I believe she is proud of me for undertaking my own journey of discovery. Mom has read many portions of this manuscript and has told me I captured Dad's spirit very well. She has pressured me to allow her to read more and I walk a delicate balance wire, providing a section to her and scanning her eyes for signs that the memories are too strong for her to handle now.

I leave this document as a record for my children, their children and future generations of Leitmans so they will have a better understanding of who they are and where they came from. I hope they will learn from the mistakes I made in putting up barriers between my father and myself based on my insecurities and childish angers and not giving my father a chance to show me who he really was.

Life goes by very quickly. The infant boy, Dick, that my father asked about in his letters is now 65 years old with a family of his own, and an eye on the next twenty or so years that will be granted to him. I believe the most significant lesson I learned through this journey, and by taking many, many breaths on this earth, is that the time to love is now and the time to say I love you was yesterday.

The Letters

In October of 1940, Dad's draft lottery number, # 158, was picked by Secretary of War Henry Stimson, putting Dad in the first group of men to be drafted into the US army. On January 18, 1941 he officially entered military service for what was to be a one year stint. He committed to Mom that he would write a letter to her every day that he was away. The letters began on January 18 and the first was dated, Day 1, and continued consecutively as he counted down the 365 days his service commitment was to last. The last letter to be dated in this way was Day 244, when he learned his commitment to the army was extended, just before Pearl Harbor shocked the nation, and he began to put the actual dates on the letters. The last letter I found was dated November 6, 1945. Dad was released from service on December 13, 1945, marking a period of service of four years, eleven months. Some days he could not write but on others he wrote two or even three letters to Mom. During 1943 and early 1944 Dad was stationed in Freehold, New Jersey which was close to home. He did not write to Mom as much during this period as he was able to see her quite often.

The letters were written on any stationary he could obtain and he used fountain pens, pencils and sometimes a typewriter for inscription. At the time, there existed a form of communication called V mail in which a letter was written on a special form and photo reduced. The reduced copy was sent to the recipient. When Dad received a V mail letter from Mom he felt gypped because the writing space was limited and they were very difficult to read because of the size reduction.

Mom saved every letter that Dad wrote, tying them up in bundles with a piece of colored ribbon. When he came home from the war they were placed in his army foot locker and stored there, rarely touched. Occasionally the foot locker was opened and we were shown the letters. Once in awhile someone would read a few and put them back. Their limited handling assured that they would be preserved without too much deterioration over the years.

A few years ago my daughter, Jennifer Mirman, read some of the letters and was astounded to see the quality of the information they contained. She began a project to organize them by date and put them in protective sheets, and then in binders. She told me that I just had to read them as they were fascinating and, since I was born during this period, I was discussed in most of them.

After Dad passed away, my wife and I took up the task of completing the organization of the letters into binders. I decided to scan the letters into our home computer so they would be preserved for future generations to read. While scanning them it became necessary to read many of the pages so that they could be electronically filed in the proper sequence. In doing so I too became fascinated with their content.

Dad used to ask which one of us was going to make a book out of them. As he got older and feebler he asked more often but no one took his request seriously at the time. However, after seeing how beautifully he had written these letters and their fascinating content I decided to take him up on his request.

As I wrote this journey, and as I explored my deepest feelings and thoughts, I often felt that my work on the letters, the words I typed and the organization of subject matter was not my creation but rather the result of energy channeled from my father to me. Once I began, I was powerless to stop until I had peeked into every corner and examined every barrier that stood between us. The letters provided an insight into the man I called my father, in the years before I knew him. They speak the words of an innocent young boy as he was forced to take on the responsibilities of an adult. I chose to explore the letters he wrote during the period of August 11, 1944 (just before he went overseas) through August 23, 1945 (when he returned to the States). I was born in July 1944, one month before he left home aboard the *Ile de France* for England.

I searched the letters to see what I recognized in this young man that seemed out of character with my father as I remembered him. What could these letters tell me about the experiences he went through that could have contributed to shaping his future attitudes and reactions towards life? I struggled to envision what my life, and my own personality, would have been like if Dad did not have to endure the traumas of war. Most importantly, I hoped to approach the barriers we both erected between us, with hammer and chisel, and begin chipping away at those walls, even at this late date.

This book is in honor of 1st Lieutenant David Leitman, U.S, Army Infantry and his wife Roslyn, my dad and mom.

The Well of Grief

Those who will not slip beneath
the still surface on the well of grief

turning down to its black water
to the place that we can not breathe

will never know
the source from which we drink
the secret water cold and clear

nor find in the darkness
the small gold coins
thrown by those who wished for something else

— David Whyte

2.

From My Heart

Dear Dad,

Thank you for the historical gift you left us by writing what you saw and did during the war. I have seen many movies and read books and magazine articles about combat, and World War II in particular, but your accounts had a special quality that can only be achieved by being, as they say, "up close and personal". From reading your letters I have a new perspective on the life of an infantryman and the effects of war on soldiers, civilians, and property. To have this record in our family for the future Leitman offspring is a priceless treasure. You will never be forgotten!

Your accounts were especially valuable because of the way you presented them. It is very clear to me that you were just attempting to provide some information to a worried wife back in the States about what was happening to her husband, and in doing so presented a personal view of the realities of war and army life. Your letters contain no glorification of battles, no pleading calls for sympathy, no concentration on death and the destruction of cities, no berating of the enemy and no cheering for the good guys. They do contain, however, an eye witness account of a soldier who was lonely for his wife and baby back home. Tired, cold, and utterly uncomfortable, you wrote the story of a brave young soldier who was fearful of what the next day would bring to him, always hoping the Russians in the east and the American Air Force and soldiers in the west would hurry up and bring this conflict to a close so he could return home to his family.

Dear Roz,

I hope Richard has been behaving himself properly. Somehow, I can't get the feeling that I … know him at all. It seems to me that I just took one look at him and I had to leave. It didn't even leave the impression with me that I'm a father even though I know that I am. In a way, you are more fortunate than I am having Richard with you. Perhaps there will be some features about him as he grows older that will remind you of me. I know that I won't be able to recognize him unless you send me pictures but I can never forget the sweetest person I ever met. I can't forget your face, body or your swell companionship and friendship which you have shared with me. Darling, take care of Richard and yourself. Don't change anything. I want to return and find you exactly as when I left.

England   *September 6, 1944*

Dad, on a personal note, I am sorry that I never took the time or gave you the respect and honor you deserved for enduring and playing out, so heroically, this chapter of your life. I admit to you that I was caught up in finding my own way in life, and angry at you for bullying people, especially Mom. I resolved to punish you by ignoring or minimizing your war stories and your war experiences. This was an immature way for me to react. Instead of calling you on your improper behavior and honoring you where you deserved it, I just blocked you out, accomplishing nothing and missing the opportunity of learning who you were and establishing a loving relationship with you.

I have tremendous sympathy for Vietnam veterans and our young boys now fighting in Iraq and Afghanistan, and the challenges they face upon returning to civilian life. I can understand the stress disorders that flow from their experiences during these horrible times in our history. I can feel the unresolved turmoil a soldier goes through by killing another human being in battle and the fear that next time he could be the one whose life was cut short. I feel some shame for not having served alongside my friends due to my student deferments, followed by job deferments, which allowed me to do that. I know that I would do the same again and seek the easiest way to continue living my life as normally as possible, avoiding the army at all costs. Although difficult for me to admit, I don't think I could have endured the hardships you suffered in the armed forces; I was too soft, too afraid, and too self centered to be of significance to our country as a soldier. So Dad, since I can have all these emotions for strangers, why could I not muster just a little understanding for you?

This is my attempt to correct some of that wrong and, I admit, to clear the negativity in my conscience. Yet I know that this can never make up for the disrespect I showed you while you were alive.

The author, Rich Leitman writing to his father.

I'm sad that you did not get to know me before you had to leave to fight in a war. I was born in July and one month later you were on a ship heading into the frightful unknown. Perhaps this was an omen of what things would be like between us later on. Reading your letters to Mom now makes me realize that I too, never knew you very well. I ask myself, "Who was this man who writes so tenderly about the lover and companion he left behind?" I don't remember knowing this man who professed his love so poetically in letters written every day, no matter how tenuous the conditions. Did I meet this person?

What I would have given to have heard you tell me, when I was older, things you wrote to Mom, about how you missed your infant son when you were gone and how you longed for information about him in every letter. I can't remember ever hearing those magical words which seem to flow so naturally in your letters, "I love you." I strain to remember if you ever called Mom darling, or if you were as tender with her when you returned as the words in your letters suggest.

How well does any son know his father when he is alive? For that matter, how well does any son know himself? Dad, I am on a quest to answer both these questions, for in knowing more about your core and soul I will uncover some of mine, which stubbornly chooses to remain well hidden by my shadows, of which I am more familiar. I undertake this journey of discovery with much fear of the pain that will greet me along the way.   I am also feeling anger and sadness over lost opportunities and what might have been between us. But the sweet excitement of learning more about who I am through you is reason enough for me to embark along this quest.

So, Dad, I commit to you that I will undertake this journey, that I shall succeed and that your son will be a better and happier man for it. I promise to leave the evidence of my search for my offspring and later generations so they will know where they came from and who they are. They will learn your story, of how you left home at the tender age of 25 to fight in a brutal war under treacherous conditions. They will learn to see that you were an admiral man with integrity, love for other human beings, and a brave soldier and leader. They will also see that you were a man with human frailties which were exposed and hardened by fear, conflict, and exhaustion.

And now I begin this journey Dad, by saying the words we both found so hard to give voice to when you were here, "Dad, I love you."

Rich

3.

The Letters - War And The Life Of An Infantryman

○○○

SHORTAGES HIT WAR; *Top Brass is concerned – had to switch battle plans*

August 11, 1944   Somewhere in USA

Dear Roz,

I don't know exactly how to begin this letter. Everything is censored now and I can't disclose my location. Things are working out just as I expected and it looks as if I will get some time off Sunday or Monday. I couldn't call as we are kept busy every minute of the day now and I don't even know where the nearest phone is. I know you are waiting to hear from me and I'm sorry I let you down but I couldn't give you any new address until I get my APO number.

In a way I'm glad you'll be busy with Richard as it will help to occupy your mind. My APO number will be changed when I hit a new unit but you can write to this number I give you until I notify you of a new address. Be sure you write it exactly as it's on the envelope.

Honey, I'm going to be looking for your letters from here on so even if I can't write I still would like to hear from you about *yourself and Richard. Honey, I want you to keep your chin up all the while I'm away. I know you can do it. I want you to remember that I'll be careful and take good care of myself for you both. Be good darling, I love you both with all my heart.*

PS. I hope Richard goes to sleep at night now and doesn't cry. I have my name at the bottom of this letter as I censored it myself.

◆　　◆　　◆

Allies have Germans nearly encircled in Normandy; Allies land in the south of France.

August 15, 1944   *Somewhere in USA*

Dear Roz,

I can't get over the way you looked when I left you the other night. We read about it happening to others and yet it doesn't bother us too much until it hits our own happy little home. When the real time to part comes one just doesn't know what to do or say. It's one thing that I consider the most difficult situation I've ever been in. If Richard was older and he could understand what is going on parting would have been twice as hard for me. He is happy and content in his own little world and won't know about what has been going on for many years now.

I really was surprised when you told me that you were going on 23 years of age. I can only picture you as the skinny 17 year old kid I met, fell in love with, and married. Now even though the years go by I can't picture you getting any older. Yet I know it's true. The years are running by too fast and we've not had a chance to really live these past years as we would have liked to. Fortunately, we were given a little boy and now we really have the one thing that will bind us even more.

How many times you've told me that I've changed but even though it looked that way to you darling I loved you more each time we met. I will always love you. I have but one will now, to help win the war and hurry home to you both.

I was told to make out a "will" which I did and it should be sent to you. It's a formality which everyone must go through.

My cold doesn't seem to be getting any better. But you know how hard it is for me to get rid of a cold. I try and picture what Richard looks like and I can't even picture that yet. I'll always remember you though, and I still say you look much prettier since you changed your hair style. Honey, you cheated me on my last leave. I should have seen you at your best all the time. Darling I want you and Richard to buy whatever you need and don't worry too much about saving. Well darling, once again I find it difficult to say good-by. If God is good to us it won't be long before we three are together again.

All my love, Dave.

Grandpa Sam (Mom's dad) with his soldier boys, Dad (left), Milton, and Bob.

FROM BABY DICK

Dear Daddy,

We received a letter today and I knew it was from you because Mommy became very upset and cried for a long time. This scared me and I just wanted her to hold me and stop crying, but all she did was sit on the bed rocking back and forth saying, "Oh Davie, Oh Davie." She misses you a lot. I miss you too even though I don't really know you.

Mommy reads me some of your letters and I can tell you love her a lot. You also ask a lot of questions about me in your letters and I think you will be a good daddy to me. Mostly I need a

Dear Roz,

How I wish I could play with little Richard now. I'd love to be on the couch with you with my head in your lap and have Dick crawling all over my chest, the radio playing to our favorite station and a couple of highballs on the coffee table. Oh yes, that wouldn't be complete unless I was in my pajamas. Oh, another thing, I just had taken a clean shave, showered and washed my teeth. What do you think of that little domestic scene I just described? I can't think of anything that I desire more.

Darling, to say that I miss you is an under rated statement. If it weren't for the fact that I'm kept real busy I'd go nuts here yearning to hold you close to me again and kiss you again and again. It's been a long time since I had any loving and it's really rough on your old man.

Luxemburg   *January 1, 1944*

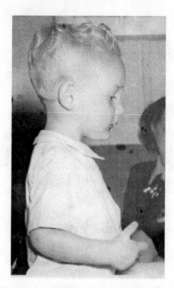

Dick misses his dad.

daddy who will give me a lot of love and hold me when I'm scared, which is a lot. Daddy, you must be very scared too where you are now. I wouldn't want to be there, although I do want to be with you so that you can hold me now.

I liked your idea of lying on the couch with you and Mommy, crawling on your chest. That sounds like a lot of fun. That way I can get close to you both at the same time. I really need a daddy to love and protect me. I hope you come back soon and I worry that maybe you won't. Promise me that you will come soon.

Daddy, sometimes I think that I won't know who you are when you come home. I don't remember what you look like because I was just born when you left home. I hope I don't get scared and cry because maybe then you will leave home again or not love me. I will try to be good so you will stay with us because I really need you.

When I get older I hope you teach me to be strong and brave like you. I also would like it if you told me about what you did when you went away. Come home soon. We need you.

I really love you,   Dick.

The Letters - (Cont.)

Somewhere at Sea - 1

Dear Roz,

Well I'm off to a new adventure. I'll know now whether I could have been a seaman. This is an English boat and they serve fish with every meal. The meals are delicious though and we only eat twice a day. So far I've weathered the trip very well. We keep fairly busy between lounging on the sun deck and batting the breeze all day. The sun deck is reserved for officers and that is the one closest to the heavens. If you stand on deck and watch the waves it's very easy to get sick. It is also best not to eat much but with eating twice a day we are starved at each meal sitting. There are regular PX's aboard ship and cigarettes are very cheap.

Dad with his father, Hyman.

Of course card playing is still the best time killer but I haven't indulged in that form of recreation as yet. I know if I do I'll probably win a lot or go broke. I never could quit when I was losing. You would have gotten a big laugh if you saw me with all my equipment and lugging my cadet bag full of clothes. I really made 3 trails..my two legs and the third a trail of sweat. One good thing about being on the sea is that it's cool.

Honey, I wish I could have seen you once more before leaving. I was so close and yet so far away. Someday I'll be able to tell you about the boat and my crossing. I'm sure you'll find it very interesting. I'd like to see as much of the world as I can now. It's too bad that you don't enjoy riding on water. You see, you can't appreciate what a swell ride this is.

◆ ◆ ◆

Somewhere at Sea – 2

Dear Roz,

Well now I'm drawing the 10% (overseas pay) and I'll be a wealthier man on payday. We are still getting our fish at every meal and I don't like it. Imagine eating filet for breakfast. I tried washing my clothes in salt water but could not get any lather. It's almost impossible to wash anything.

So far I've weathered this trip fine. I still haven't had my sea sickness and our boat has rolled on a few occasions when we hit rough water.

Bing Crosby is on our boat with us and he has a USO show going overseas with him. He is showing his show to the men on the boat.

We have a group of officers in a stateroom with a latrine of our own. It's very nice except for the salt water showers. It's necessary to conserve fresh water so all showers are salt water. We are allowed on deck during the day but not at night. Blackout conditions prevail during darkness.

I guess you're still busy trying to put Dick to sleep. I just haven't got the patience to keep rocking him for hours. I know Richard is going to be spoiled but I guess you can't help it. I haven't received any mail from you as yet and I'm going to be looking forward to receiving a few letters at one time.

◆　　　◆　　　◆

Somewhere at Sea – 3 V-mail

Dear Roz,

The boat trip is beginning to get monotonous. I'm sitting up on the sun deck writing to you now. I can see water as far as I can see. I saw a USO show last night which was pretty good. I still haven't seen Bing Crosby's show.

It's very hot in our stateroom at night and I would dare say that the beds are just too short. Say has Richard decided to go to sleep peacefully or does he still cry? I bet that if I saw him now I wouldn't even recognize him. I will admit that I like traveling but not without you. I like to see you enjoy yourself and get all my pleasure from that.

◆　　　◆　　　◆

Somewhere at Sea – 4 V-mail

Dear Roz,

The weather can sure change quickly. It wasn't long when we were sweating and now we must wear overcoats. I hope we are near our destination as we don't get any exercise and are getting soft. I sleep about 20 hours around the clock. Imagine if Richard would behave himself so well. I don't believe the trip will last much longer and we should reach our destination shortly. This morning some of the boys were seasick. I still don't see how I got away with it because it's not like my stomach to be so peaceful.

I never told you what our stateroom was like. We have 20 officers sleeping in a small stateroom. We sleep two high, or there are two beds in a column. We really are crowded but still more comfortable than the enlisted men. You know a boat is a wonderful place to spend a honeymoon. Lock the door and spoon away the time. I never thought of that myself. Instead I found myself driving eight and ten hours a day on ours.

So honey, you're going to get a pile of letters very shortly. I'll bet it takes you close to an hour to read them all. How you will distinguish between the various sections of the V letters I don't know. But I can't number or date letters due to censorship.

◆　　◆　　◆

Somewhere at Sea – 5

Dear Roz,

My watch stopped running for a couple of days but now it seems to be alright. I guess the salt water really affects the delicate mechanism.

◆　　◆　　◆

Somewhere at Sea – 6

The ocean is getting rough today and the boat seems to be rolling continuously. I finally bought another wrist watch on the boat. My other one stopped completely. It suddenly got cold and today I wore my overcoat on deck. The boat keeps rocking and I can just about write. I feel like an old sailor now. Honey, if you were on this boat today I'm sure you would fly back to the States. I'm sure we are fairly close to land now.

Love, Dave

◆   ◆   ◆

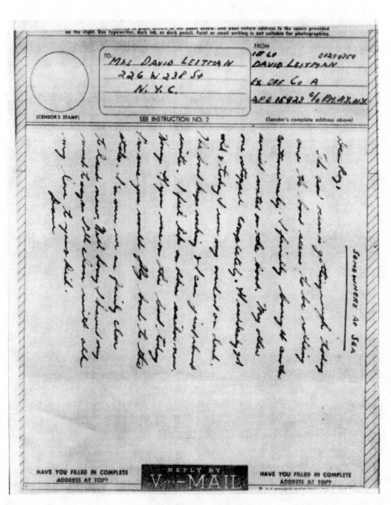

V Mail letter, actual size.

Original letter was censored, photographed and put on microfilm to be
shipped. When it reached recipient's area it was printed on light weight photo
paper at one fourth size, 4x5, and delivered. V-Mail saved space for essential
materials to be shipped.

Rules To Live By

Dear Dad,

This paragraph you wrote to Mom is short but has a tall message. The words, "he'll never hear any swearing from us and we'll always be an example he'll follow (I hope)," is exactly how

> *Dear Roz,*
>
> *That was an interesting and amusing sight you witnessed with the children. However, I didn't think the kids today have learned how to swear as thoroughly at such an early age. I wonder if Dick will be much different when he gets older. However, he'll never hear any swearing from us and we'll always be an example he'll follow (I hope).*
>
> *England*   *September 11, 1944*

I remember it. You set some pretty heavy rules for the way life should be lived as moral individuals in the home, the community and in the world. The rules were hard and fast, black and white. Gray didn't exist. They weren't written out but were repeated enough times that they were known and understood by everyone.

These rules usually began with the words "never" or "always" and "never" meant just what it said, "never." Your rules were designed to assure success, happiness, respect, and safety for us. Breaking a rule meant one of these states of living was destined to evaporate. They were a code for us to live by and you didn't excuse yourself from them. There was nothing hypocritical about you. As you often said, "What's good for the goose is good for the gander."

So what were these rules that guided our lives? I list some of them here, realizing it is the first time any have been put on a page, and I do it for my own edification. I want to see what they look like in print, to feel their impact on me as I write them, analyze how well I followed them when I was younger, and I want to determine what they bring up for me now. I have broken them down into generalized categories although you never presented them to us as anything but stand alone statements, a rule to follow.

The Way to Live

- Never go into a bar to drink. If you want a drink have it at home.
- Never cheat anyone.
- Never owe any money except for a mortgage.
- Never pay interest for any purchase.
- Be the best at what you do.
- Don't gamble more than entertainment money because you will always loose.
- Never smoke.
- Never take drugs.
- Never ask for a handout or welfare.
- Never get into trouble in school or with the police.

Family Life

- Never send your wife a birthday or holiday card or get a gift. It's a waste of money.
- Women should be home at night and not driving around.
- Never go anywhere without your wife. Going alone with your kids is an exception.
- Your wife should be your only friend.
- Never go to a meeting alone at night unless it's for the kids.
- Eat every dinner together as a family.
- Never change a diaper.
- Don't go on vacations without the kids.

- Wives should not have friends in the house when the husband is home and vice versa.
- Pick a profession based on how much you will make, not whether you like it.
- A man has to do whatever it takes to provide for his family.
- Women should stay at home and not work.
- Always set an example for kids to follow.
- Jobs are clearly divided in a house; men never cook, or clean. Women never fix things.
- Never use foul language.

Special Rules for Kids

- Don't send kids out of town to college or you'll lose them.
- Go to a college where you will be at the top. The school name is less important.
- Stay out of the army.
- A student's job is to get good grades. Help your kids with money so they don't have to work.
- Never leave your kids with a college debt. Start them off debt free.
- Choose your child's college and course of study for them. Kids can't make these important decisions themselves.

On Girls and Dating

- The apple doesn't fall far from the tree.
- Never put in writing to a girl that you love her but you can tell her anything.
- Never live with a girl until your married.
- Always treat a girl with respect.

On Being Jewish

- Never let religion run your life.
- Keep your religion secret because people hate Jews.
- Never buy a foreign car, especially German.
- Don't vacation in Europe; spend your money in the States because people in Europe are anti-Semitic.
- Always support Israel because it's the only place where you're always accepted.
- Learn a profession that will make you welcome in another country in case Jews are persecuted here.

Patriotism

- Always support the United States; it's been good to us.
- Always support our fighting men.
- Don't trust any politician. They're hypocrites, don't live by the rules they pass, and are only in it for the money.

I took in whatever you taught me, as any good young boy trying to please and look up to his father would do. I couldn't distinguish between edicts such as *"never cheat anyone"* and *"women should stay at home and not work."* Everything you said had the same validity. If it came from your mouth it was as things should be. I looked up to you as being the wisest man I knew and this was supported by Mom who told us how lucky we were to have a good and wise father. Mom never challenged you on any rules and went along with them as if there was no other way. I wonder what she really felt about the restrictions placed on her.

Dad in his FBI look-alike outfit.

You were a very heavy smoker choosing the extra strong brand Camels as your favorite. Your letters show your strong addiction to smoking in the army. But I have to say, Dad, that I was impressed with you when you quit smoking. Even though I had no idea of how addictive tobacco was at the time, I knew you enjoyed it and smoked Camels all the time. Then one day, when I was in junior high school you announced that you were quitting and setting an example for us to not smoke ourselves. That was it—just like that you stopped and I never saw you do it again. Maybe you cheated outside the house until the urges for nicotine passed. This I don't know, but I never saw you smoke again. I remember you complaining that you were putting on extra weight but that wasn't an excuse for you to pick up a Camel and light it. You quit so you could tell us not to smoke and you didn't want that message to be weakened in any way. Now I understand how strong willed you were to be able to do this cold turkey. I never forgot this lesson and never smoked.

Many of your lessons served me well. I didn't pay for anything on credit, another one of your "nevers." I always paid off my credit card charges when they were due. I knew it wasn't logical but it bothered me to pay a five cent daily overdue charge on late library books and would go out of my way to make sure they were returned before the end of the due day. It obviously wasn't about the money involved. I was breaking one of your rules. Dad, are you surprised to learn how strongly you influenced me, even as a grown man? I am thankful that most of your indoctrinations were beneficial and not destructive.

I waited to buy my first car until I had enough cash to pay for it, and passed on the air conditioning option because that would have meant waiting another six months to save up the additional funds. I made sure my family ate dinner together whenever I wasn't away on a business trip and I tried to live my life setting an example for my children to follow. I never got into trouble in school, and certainly not with the police.

Dad, observing your patriotism was beautiful. You loved our country and no matter how you criticized some of the things that happened here you never let that cloud the love you felt for the nation. You may have had harsh words for the military and disagreed with a war they were fighting but your complete support for our troops was never in doubt. You knew how hard a job it was to fight on the front lines. That's why you didn't want your boys to be in the military. I think you knew you were asking other men's sons to stand in for your own to do a dirty job, and you knew it was dirty. On more than one occasion I've seen tears in your eyes when the deaths of some of our soldiers were reported on the news, and your heart was always with your grandson Frank when he served in Iraq as the yellow ribbon on your front door attested. A large American flag always flew on your house. You marched in a Memorial Day parade when the day before you were too unsteady to go down a flight of stairs without support. Patriotism was very alive in your heart.

Yes Dad, in so many ways, you gave me a solid foundation for constructing my life, and no matter how hard to follow, many of your principles served me well.

I'm going to take a break now and end this letter. I need some time to take in what I have written and to think about some of the other rules you taught us. Many of them are disturbing to me, some have caused pain to me and my family as I tried to follow them, and others still leave me with some confusion. I will get back to you with my feelings about them when my thoughts become clearer. I must continue this conversation with you to further my own healing. So long for now Dad.

Love, Rich

◆   ◆   ◆

Dear Dad,

It's time for me to talk about some of the things you taught me that caused damage to my relationship with my wife, Marlene. When we were first married I stopped sending her birthday cards and our anniversaries and holidays went by with only a verbal acknowledgement from me. I had learned the lesson that it was not important to give cards or gifts on these occasions to a spouse. These were customs started by Hallmark to increase sales and were a waste of money. Marlene was very hurt by this and I slowly responded to her disappointment. I might send a birthday card but nothing on Valentine's Day, a present on our anniversary but nothing on her birthday. I was torn between my teachings guiding me one way, and the response to my actions telling me something was amiss. Eventually, I responded more to what Marlene wanted and less to what you taught but I admit that even today, I wonder what the fuss is all about over a card.

I tried to adhere to the no nighttime meetings rule but this became very difficult. I successfully ran in a school board election to affect some change in our school district. Then reality hit during a teacher strike, which increased my commitment dramatically, and I became uneasy about being out at night. I thought it was all right to devote whatever was required since it was for my children's benefit but my guilt about being at meetings only worsened. As soon as the strike was over I resigned from the Board to be at home again.

Things really were complicated for me at my job. I worked as a chemical engineer for Mobil Chemical Company as a research engineer and then as a manager. My work often required that I travel out of town for plant visits, meetings, and conferences. I had no choice about traveling, it was a job requirement but occasionally the lines between work and pleasure became fuzzy. Sometimes our Division would invite the engineers to a resort site for workshops and review meetings. I was fine during the meetings but when we broke out for some fun activities my conscience became uneasy and I found myself feeling guilty about having fun without Marlene. I began to dread the announcements of the work getaways and greatly preferred to remain in the lab working.

This all came to a head when I told a therapist I was seeing that I was going on a business trip to our plant in Australia for a meeting. He asked how long I was going for and was surprised at my answer. I was going to be away one day for traveling, two days for the meeting and I was returning home the fourth day. I had scheduled no time for sightseeing, taking pictures or recovering from the 24 hour travel, all because I felt guilty for having fun in Australia without my wife. I realized how foolish all this was and she was very supportive of my taking a couple extra days to enjoy the experience and have some fun taking photographs. I gave myself permission to try out this new experience and I found it to be very liberating. That began a change in the way I looked at all business trips and I was actually able to have fun on them, as well as work, and with a clear conscience.

Now I had been seeing this therapist because of the damage caused by some of your other rules. Our children were grown and leaving the nest for school. They no longer needed so much of our time so Marlene started to explore what she wanted to do with her life and I did the same. I was happy to use the free time to do things with Marlene and to relax together at home, imitating you and Mom. Marlene had completely different ideas. She wanted to find new interests and studied massage therapy and Reiki. She spent a lot of time going to meetings on spiritual healing, mostly at night, and even wanted to spend a weekend away with her spiritual friends whom she said she loved. This looked to me like the end of my world as I knew it. My foundation was crashing down.

29

How many rules did she want to break and why did she want to break them? I thought I was the one she was supposed to love, not some women friends. If she loved them where did I fit in? Maybe she should live with them instead of me? Why did she have to drive at night? Didn't she know it was too dangerous for women? How could she want to do massage and touch other people? Didn't she see it was all too sexual, especially touching other men? How could my wife believe in Reiki, healing with her hands? The rigidity towards life that I learned from you was not serving me at all and yet it was all I knew.

I sought out a therapist and with his help I came to see that without some flexibility in my life I could lose my wife and she was the most important thing to me. I had to trust that if I let the bird fly from the cage it could come home on its own. At the same time I needed to explore my own interests, something I had never given myself permission for. Each of us would become separate individuals exploring our passions by ourselves where they are different, together where they matched up, and always come together for love. Oh, I learned more about love too. I learned it was not reserved for some people with exclusion of others. I learned that love for a wife is different than love for children or a parent, and I learned to understand what she meant by loving her friends.

I began an earnest quest for self-development to learn who I was. Along the way I joined the Mankind Project, an international men's group designed for men to help other men, supporting each other in whatever life brings to us. Through MKP I've continued my self-growth, and yes, I've learned to deal with my father/son issues in a healthy way. I've learned that it is never too late to tell your father what you respect about him and what is troubling, even if it has to be done by writing to him after he's gone. I also learned that there are men that I met along this journey of self-discovery and healing, unrelated to me, that I am proud to say I love.

Dad, I never told you about my involvement with MKP because I thought you would laugh at me for being crazy and so soft. So while I thank you for the teachings that have served me, I am unhappy about the ones that didn't work, and that I truthfully don't understand at this stage in my life. Perhaps if they had come to me with a little less rigidity I could have avoided some of the pain in my life, but you were a man from a generation that did not understand self-development. Rigidity and strict rules worked for you and that was all you knew. I can't fault you but I can express some sorrow, and even some anger at how you handled this phase of fathering.

Dad with Richard and brother Mark.

There was another category in which your rules negatively affected me. These concerned our Jewish religion and how we were viewed in the world as Jews. I examine this topic knowing full well that your opinions were formed in the shadow of the holocaust and your time on the front line fighting the Nazis. I do not deny that the holocaust would not have happened if anti-Semitism had not been rampant in Europe and elsewhere in the world, and thriving, if not rampant, in the United States. There is no question that having been a witness to the concentration camp survivors and hearing their stories first hand, you would have been horrified at what happened to our Jewish people and vowed to keep your family safe from it in the future. I can understand this. I can also understand if you harbored bad feelings towards the Europeans at the time because you were risking your life to free them and yet they had turned a blind eye to the plight of the Jews.

It was natural that you would want to protect us by teaching what happened and warning about the potential for it to occur to us again. Not buying a German car and not traveling for vacations to Europe were understandable positions for you to take, although I could argue with you the benefits of some forgiveness for your own well being as time went by. Keeping the hatred you had in your heart all those years did nothing to hurt the perpetrators, most of whom were no longer living, and only caused bitterness and harm to you. I don't fault you for those points of view, but what does cause me distress is the fear you instilled in me about anti-Semitism in this country. I worked for a subsidiary of a major oil company and you cautioned me that all oil companies had a history of anti-Semitism because they had to cozy up to the Arabs. My career would never amount to anything if they knew I was Jewish. Dad, I believe I was treated fairly without regard for my religion by Mobil. It's possible that there was someone who penalized me along the way for my religion but I don't know it as a fact.

So how did your preaching have its effect on me? I was always alert for signs of prejudice at work and did my best to keep my religion to myself. Much of my work was done in our plant in Beaumont, Texas which is the heart of the oil and petrochemical business in this country. My first few years of traveling there were filled with anxiety over religion, especially when working in the plant control rooms with blue collar operators. The only reason for my fear was what you told me. I never saw any sign of hostility towards me as a Jew, yet I continued to fear. When I took my family on a car trip through the deep south you warned me not to go. We did go, in spite of your negativity and the trip was uneventful but less than comfortable for me.

The thing that drove this fear into me so strongly was the advice you gave me when I was young. You said, "America is a wonderful country but you never could tell when anti-Semites will take over here and Jews will have to run away again." You advised us to seek out a profession that would be valued elsewhere in the world to give us the greatest chance of being accepted as refugees.

This message of impending danger was burned into my cellular structure; it was no wonder I was always fearful and on the lookout for signs of prejudice. I have always been an overly anxious person. I don't know where it takes it roots but I know it didn't help to start off on my own in the world thinking everyone that wasn't Jewish hated me.

I say again that I don't blame you, Dad, because I know you were only trying to protect me and my siblings from danger and keep us safe. It's only that I trusted you so much and needed your approval so badly that my mind was ripe for poisoning. Is poison too strong a word? I don't think so. I think a less dramatic message, less black and white, more cautionary than absolute would have served me better.

This had been another exhausting exercise writing this letter to you. In doing it though, I can see where many of my shadows took shape and after all has been said, I find that I understand you more, am less angry and miss you. And yes, I still love you Dad,

Love, Rich

The Letters - (Cont.)

SOVIETS MAKING HUGE GAINS; Capture a town near oilfields; Take 18,000 Nazi prisoners;

August 28, 1944   *England*

A funny thing happened on the train ride. We were sitting six officers in a train compartment. These compartments are just like the foreign trains you see in the movies. All the compartments have doors so that you can walk right out on the platform. On our trains you only have two entrances, one on either side of the train. Well getting back to the funny story. We were riding through Scotland and all the kids would run along side the train asking for chewing gum or cigarettes whenever it slowed down. Well to continue, one of our officers was a confirmed rebel from Texas. These foreign people refer to us all as Yanks. Well he and I were waving to people looking out the window when some kids ran up to us and said, "Hey Yank, any cigarettes or gum?" Well this Texan said, "Hell, I ain't no damn Yankee." It struck me as being so funny right then that I couldn't stop laughing.

I went to Bath and it's really tough to get a good meal. I still can't figure out the two pence shilling, etc. and I have one hell of a time figuring out my finances. Soap is rationed here. We only get one cake every two weeks but don't send any yet until I can find out the score. You have no idea how beautiful this country is. I don't know any country sight where they take such good care of their land. Today three of us took a long walk up on a mountain overlooking our camp. We were able to see for miles in any direction. We are supposed to be in quarantine now but you know how those things are. There is always a way of getting out. I still haven't seen too much of any bombed areas and nothing happens where I'm located so don't worry.

As of August 31 the war bond will stop and I'll arrange to have it sent home from here. The weather is beautiful, not too hot and not too cold. So far I haven't seen anything of the British fog. I had some beer in the Officers Club. They sell a pint for

20 shillings or about 20 cents each. It doesn't taste a bit like our beer and I don't believe anyone can drink too much of that.

I really am sweating out receiving your mail. So far I haven't received any news from you since I last saw you. Darling I don't want to get started right now on how I miss you as I won't be able to go to sleep. I love you a lot honey and I'll live as clean a life away as I did before. Joe K. was the one who said a man has so many charges and if he uses them up when he is young he loses out when he's older. I don't mind waiting till I'm with you again.

I know you are having your trouble with Richard and I'll bet he cries continuously. Say, did you ever try putting him to sleep with whiskey and tea again. Speaking of whiskey, that's just a word here and you can't get any.

Not only do the cars ride on the wrong side of the street but the trains operate in the same manner. The people are full of spunk though and even though they haven't much for themselves they still manage to smile.

Well darling, it's getting late now so I'll close with all my love to my two loved ones.

◆   ◆   ◆

Avignon liberated; City cheers allied soldiers and gives them gifts.

August 28, 1944   *England*

Dear Roz,

We had a little rain this morning but it seems to have cleared up now. This is my second day here and we were told that we would start a training program shortly to keep us busy. I met Lt. Meadows here. Back in the States, they said he was killed by a robot bomb. He is just about the only one left of the officers before me. The remainder are in France. We live in brick buildings here in a beautiful location. What it really amounts to is this. We are replacements and can be called at any time and be sent to France. In the meantime I'm here and resting and living very well.

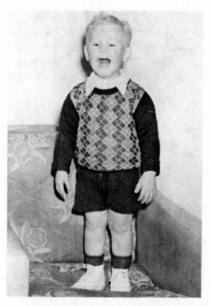

Richard has something to say.

I don't know when I will go but when I do I'll write to you and let you know how everything is going whenever I can write. I don't get the news of the various fronts here and actually I don't know what happened since Paris was taken. You people in the States are well up on your news. I bought a Scotch newspaper and of course they write how well the Yanks are doing. We are all Yanks here. Just about the time I learn how to use English money I'll have to use a franc. We are going to have classes in French and German to pass the time away. I would like to go to London some time and look around but as yet I can't get a pass. Don't worry though honey, I'll stay out of trouble there. Besides I have to wait two weeks before getting a pass.

I have a fireplace in my room and right now I have a swell fire going. I washed all my dirty clothes and I'm all set. My foot locker and bedding roll haven't arrived yet and some say that we (will) never see them again. I have enough clothes on my person to live with and after marching a few miles the other day with all my full field equipment I decided that I'll have to cut down still more. I was really tired going up and down hills loaded down. Funny thing, but when you are near to combat things get real G.I. On this post here we have to wear a tie with leggings all the time. We were told that the mail would reach here today.

Believe me honey; I'm really sweating out your mail. I can't wait till I see something of yours, even a letter. Darling, things can be fine and I can have everything I want but if I haven't got you to share it with I feel lost and don't enjoy anything. I write you this because I miss you very much. Now I even try and remember Richard's face but the way it changes now I know I won't be able to recognize him when I see him again. You'll have to let me know how he looks and whom he looks like. Darling I'll close this letter to you with all my love.

◆　　　◆　　　◆

Some miners ending strike, returning to pits; Nearly 3,500 miners returned to work in central and western Pennsylvania but more than 4,200 still out demanding recognition of mine supervisors union.

August 29, 1944   England

Dear Roz,

Being here we feel that every day will be our last chance to have some fun so we go out at night. Transportation isn't too good and we go to Bath. It's a large city and there are plenty of pubs. I've drank every type of ale, stout, (?) so called beer and spirits -whiskey. I can't feel a damn thing so you see getting drunk here is really mental. Of course the local people can get drunk. I wonder what they would act like if they drank a quart of Mount Vernon Fire Ball whiskey.

The streets are blackened out and I mean black out. I could just about keep from running into sides of buildings. Most of the streets are narrow and winding. I didn't see any restaurants so I gathered that food is rationed too closely for that. There are moving pictures and tea houses. These people are class conscious and the famous English cockney is considered one of the lowest classes. I met some people yesterday that were from London and they told me that they didn't sleep day or night for weeks at a time. I keep on praising these people in my letters to you but they really deserve it. I don't understand people that come from (Wales). They're English has a decided accent which I haven't been able to decipher as yet.

Yesterday evening cost me a pound or about $4. It's funny how every one can figure out our money but we can't decipher theirs so well. A funny thing happened yesterday. Some of the boys started a crap game. Well before each roll every one had to calculate the sums of the various coins and take time out for that. This slowed up the game. Finally they got disgusted trying to figure out this English money and the shooter would throw down a coin and say put the same coin in the pot whoever (fades?) me. Everything is just a novelty to us; so far it's interesting.

When we go to France we have to exchange our money for French currency. A franc is worth two cents so if we have $50 worth we should need a wheelbarrow to carry it around with.

We are finally getting the damp, rainy English weather and getting accustomed to it. Honey, none of your letters have arrived as yet and I'm expecting a stack big enough to fill a suitcase. I wonder if you received any of my letters as yet. They asked for volunteers into the parachute troop. Rowe joined up. Here in England things move much quicker. For example, at Fort Benning a parachutist must get three months training before he can qualify. Here in England he gets one week of physical conditioning and the next week he makes five jumps and he joins a unit. Short and sweet, isn't it? You see honey, the army can really move when it wants to.

Today I finally took my last shot so now I should be able to eat out of a dirty mess kit without any illness. We have a fireplace *in which we keep coal burning continuously to take the chill out of the room in damp weather.*

Well honey, I have to leave you now so I'll close this letter with all my love.

◆   ◆   ◆

Women charge that Germans tortured internees; inhumane treatment common place.

August 29, 1944   *England*

Dear Roz,

I received four of your letters and I'm going to answer them now even though I have already written one letter to you now. I told you that you weren't straining Richard's milk properly. Twenty minutes is fast enough and you shouldn't get too impatient now. Say, I lose my head at times too so don't think you can depend on me too much. Some of my mail will be censored but I don't think all of it will. I didn't put the strip on the envelope. Was any of my mail cut out yet? Let me know if the censor cuts out any part of my letters. Don't be afraid to ask any questions. I can answer certain questions.

I'm glad to read that Dick has my dimples but as I said before I hope he has your looks and features and not mine. Say I'll be looking forward to his pictures. I'd like to carry one of his around and also one of yours. See if you can take a picture of both of you. Honey, I have plenty of faith and I know you'll raise Richard right. I still have my cold although it isn't as bad as it was back in the States.

Darling, the card with my APO address was sent out from Fort Meade and they didn't know when I would leave. Besides, you knew my APO address before receiving the card. In regards to mail, the fastest is air mail as it is flown instead of coming over in a convoy which can take two weeks to reach here. I guess you were looking forward to my mail as much as I was waiting for yours. I know I left you without any definite information but besides not being able to write I didn't have any idea where I was going myself. I'll bet that when Richard lies on our bed naked the mattress really gets a fine spraying frequently. Say, eight to twelve ounces is quite an improvement over what he weighed last so you must be doing a good job, keep up the good work. Tell me, how does it feel to be a mother?

Now you don't have to listen to too many people's advice, you do what you think is right. Richard is our baby and I'll approve of anything you want to do. Well I seem to have answered all your questions so I'll close this letter now with all my love.

Love, Dave

A REAL MAN HAS INTEGRITY

Dear Dad,

I always knew you had the highest moral standards of any man I knew and it doesn't surprise me to read any of these statements in your letters. I know that Mom never had to give a second thought to whether you were cheating on her or going astray while you were in the war. I absolutely know that streetwalkers and prostitutes would never tempt you.

Dear Roz,

The other officers go gallivanting around but I have no desire for any social entertainment. Perhaps you can't see my point but no one else can ever take your place or even make a poor substitute. I'll admit it's a lonely life I lead, especially when I have no idea how long I'll be away from you. Darling, when a man loves a woman as much as I love you that isn't even considered a sacrifice. It's the only way to be. I can't help it if I love you so much that I can't even think of anyone but you. All this may not make sense to you but that's the code I go by and the way I've always been.

When I first met you before we were married I liked you so much that I never took out another girl again. Darling, I'm not putting a halo around my head. What I'm trying to do is tell you in another way that I love you more than anything else.

Belgium   November 15, 1944

Growing up, I never saw even so much as a Playboy magazine, no less more hard core pornography in our home. That was until Uncle Bob got me a subscription to Playboy when I was a young teen. I'm sure it was without your permission, and needless to say, the subscription was allowed to run out and not renewed.

In spite of your hot temper and tendency towards outbursts of anger, I can't recall that you used very bad language, or as you

41

called it, swearing. You had no use or need for it and were quite effective at using other means of getting your message across. The few friends you allowed yourself to have were chosen very carefully and had similar moral standards as you. You didn't go to wild parties with Mom and the conversation between the two of you was never off-color.

Dear Roz,

I know you are probably wondering about my activities with the French and Belgium girls. You can stop as it's not as good as what you've heard back in the States. There are plenty of street walkers for G.I.'s but they aren't too clean. As for myself, I have nothing to do with them. I talk to these girls but that's as far as it goes.

Belgium   *November 10, 1944*

I never saw you and Mom ever cheat or steal from anyone. In fact, I witnessed many examples where you went out of your way to correct errors which were made in your favor. When a duplicate check for some damage to our car was sent to our home by the insurance company, you returned one of them rather than cash them both. Your customers in your provisions business trusted you, and as a result stayed with you until you retired. Receipts for income tax records were impeccably kept and I'll bet that if a lifetime audit were done on your returns the net balance owed or overpaid would be zero. When I would ask your advice on how to respond to some situation you always gave me the high moral ground to follow. Without a doubt, you set very high standards for us to follow.

But I'm sure, Dad, there were times that you were not in complete integrity with your principles. When were those times? What were the temptations that caused you to stray? I wish I knew some of them because they would help me to define who you were. I can only envision you one way, purely ethical, and I know that no one fits that description. I realize that my picture of you is more like a child's vision of his perfect father. This tells me that I have more work to do on my journey of self-discovery. Perhaps in time something will jog my memory and I'll remember some incident that will bring me closer to your truth.

As for me, I have tried hard to live up to your standards and for the most part I have been successful, however I wish I could tell you that I have been more diligent at following the example you set. When I was young it was hard to live up to your standards with the fear of being found out enough to set me off in a panic. For the most part, I didn't stray too much from your teachings. I continue to live my life striving for a high level of integrity and I continue to hold you up as the example to follow.

Love, Rich

The Letters - (Cont.)

Berlin acknowledges US troops have crossed into Germany near Aachen; British in Belgium near capital; Nazis seen fleeing from Belgium.

September 4, 1944   England   V Mail

Dear Roz,

It's getting so that it rains on and off every 10 minutes. Last night I went to the PX and bought up my week's rations. All that I can buy in one week amounts to 6 shillings or $1.20. I had powdered eggs this morning and they didn't taste too bad. Last night I went to the show here on the post and saw the picture Gaslight which was an excellent picture. The little news I heard yesterday was very favorable. Perhaps it won't be too long before Germany throws in the towel. This General Patton must be an excellent tactician especially the way his armed columns are cutting through France.

Darling, I missed you very much last night and longed to see Richard. I wonder how long it will be before I'm holding you in my arms again and loving you. The first thing I do everyday is to look at your picture and refresh myself with my loved ones.

Life here can be very lonely and occasionally I go into Bath. One of the boys went into London yesterday and said the city is really bombed to hell although he didn't see any robot bombs. There are still plenty of people living there. I heard there is a burlesque show in Bath and I think I'll take a ride in one night and take it in. Darling, once again I miss you much and your swell letters about Richard and yourself are doing wonders for my morale. Keep it up darling and I hope you receive a stack of letters one time from me.

◆   ◆   ◆

Axis appears to be falling apart; Finland, Rumania, and Bulgaria seen turning on Germany.

September 4, 1944   England   V Mail

Dear Roz,

I'm sitting in a French and German class now and I can't even hear the instructor so I'm writing a letter again. I hope it isn't too long before you hear from me. I could have sent a telegram but I didn't want you to be frightened by a Western Union boy at your door. No news is still good news until you receive my letters. Those letters of mine must be piling up somewhere and I've written faithfully every day except when I couldn't while traveling.

My foot locker has not arrived yet. Most of the officers received theirs and there is an unofficial rumor that some of them were dropped into the ocean while unloading here. I have most of my clothes in them including my blouse and pinks but I guess I'll be able to manage and get by just with what I have with me. That's what a war is like honey. I understand that about 70 of us are going to train men here like we did at Fort Pickett. Honestly honey, I feel further from the war here than I did in the States. Occasionally I can hear the instructor speaking in German but I don't particularly care about learning that language anyway.

I understand that there are only about 700 miles between us and the Russian troops now. Things must be pretty bad now for Fritz. Well darling, this is the second letter I've written to you today and the sixth V Mail form. Let me know whether I write too small as it is reduced in size. You could get a magnifying glass you know.

◆   ◆   ◆

> **Roosevelt issues Executive Order for government seizure of many coal mines; Secretary Ickes to take action.**

September 5, 1944   England   *V Mail*

Dear Roz,

As I wrote you in a past letter we were told that our mail would not leave here until two weeks after we arrive. Well it's two weeks this Saturday darling. I'm hoping you get enough mail at one time to keep you busy for at least eight hours of steady reading. Last night I went into (censored) and saw an English vaudeville show. It was pretty good except for the fact that the English comedians speak too fast and it's difficult to understand them at times.

Dad (left) and his friends at Fort Bragg.

Transportation here in England is very bad and the only way to get back and forth is by army truck. If I miss a truck or if there are no trucks leaving for Bath I have to take a taxi which are so few in number that they can be very high in price. It *cost me 3 pounds to get in last night – that's about $12 in our money. I'm learning how to use their money at last but it's a costly experience.*

My foot locker finally arrived and I have plenty of washing to do. It still keeps raining on and off every day and if a soldier ever needed overshoes it's here in England. We have wet feet all the time and consequently colds. The mud here is slippery and slimy and we can pick mud off our shoes daily.

The other day I was playing baseball and the next day my legs were sore as hell. They don't seem to heal up too fast and I find walking very tiresome. I was playing baseball this afternoon and that didn't hurt me so much. Of course this continued damp weather doesn't help much and everyone has a cold. I still carry with me the one I carried over from the States.

Today the newspapers had some of our forces in Belgium. Perhaps things are moving faster than even I realized. I wonder whether the German army will collapse before the end of this year. I don't do any hard work and most of my day is spent in complete relaxation.

Here we are standing by from day to day and of course reading about the government having to take over striking coal mines. It rubs against the grain of everyone. I really don't understand why the civilians never did realize that there is a war on. These people here work long hours and they devote their nights to fire watch or the same as air raid warden. I've seen the results of bombing and it isn't a pretty sight. What saves these people is that their homes are mostly concrete. Even so, London has entire blocks of building blasted out by these robot bombs. No one thinks of striking here. It's beginning to get cooler now and the nights are cold. I bet the boys in France are plenty uncomfortable with the limited equipment which they carry on their back.

◆　　　◆　　　◆

Supply chain is taxed as 3rd Army rapidly advances towards Reich; Germans seem to be retreating as few are seen.

September 6, 1944   England

Dear Roz,

The news has been very good and we seem to be moving by leaps and bounds across Europe. Our newspaper, the Stars and Stripes, had an article that the demobilization plan may be published in tomorrow's newspaper. I'm very anxious to read about the priorities for leaving the army. However, not having any combat, I probably won't be on the first list for leaving the army even though I have many years service. Honey, I wonder what is going to happen to us. It doesn't look as if we will be in any combat here but I'm sweating out the army of occupation. However, I won't voice too much of my opinion as I'm not on the general staff and have no idea as to what can possible take place.

◆   ◆   ◆

Peace riots starting to spring up in Reich. Sweden and Switzerland report foreign labor unrest; Nazis working to quiet protests.

September 7, 1944   England

Dear Roz,

Rain again and to top it off I have the GI runs. I don't know what I ate but last night in my sleep I felt as If I was having a baby and that's bad. I can't be more than a 30 second sprint from a latrine at any time. I'm not the only one who has this nuisance so I guess we had some food improperly prepared. Perhaps a cake of GI soap fell into the mashed potatoes.

I can't get a chance to get a haircut here. There is only one barber here on the entire post that I know of and he demands that his *customers bring our own towels. There is a large Officers Club here on the post but we aren't permitted the use of its facilities. It's only for the officers permanently stationed here. That's a fair example of how we casual officers are treated. We have to form a line to go to mess and march at attention. What gets us is that the Officers Club gets a ration of whiskey from the States to include us but we aren't permitted in there. The post commander here was a general who goofed off in combat and is now a colonel in command here. He had a little trouble getting a drink at the Officers Club. It seems as if the replacement officers crowded the bar and wouldn't give way for him...so, he issues an order placing the Officers Club off limits. Nice person isn't he?*

◆ ◆ ◆

A *"substantial segment of eastern France"* is now controlled by American and French forces; Nazi columns retreating from area between the Saone River and Switzerland.

September 8, 1944   *England*

Dear Roz,

Officers seem to be leaving here every day.   There are only a few of us left. We aren't rifle platoon leaders. We have specialized jobs so perhaps we won't be called for awhile yet. Our being called depends on the casualties in the European theatre. Evidently officers holding our jobs are very good at protecting themselves.

We play baseball in the afternoon now to get exercise. My German has improved a bit since attending the classes here however I don't believe I'll be able to remember much of it in a week or so. In regards to demobilization, officers will be discharged according to their essential needs for the war effort. Well I only hope that when I get out there are still a few jobs available. Its funny but I was one of the first ones in the army and I'll probably be among the last to leave.

◆　　　◆　　　◆

Yesterday saw one of heaviest bombings of Nazi targets as 5,000 bombers from Britain and Italy attacked sites throughout the continent.

September 11, 1944   *England*

Dear Roz,

Well its raining like hell today and our tent is a four man haven from the elements. I didn't write Saturday or Sunday as I went to Bristol for the weekend. Transportation is the big problem and although some cities aren't too far away the train and bus connections are very bad. If I would have had more money I would have taken the trip to London. Bristol is one of the larger cities in England and has many pubs and theaters. I didn't find it difficult to get a hotel room to spend the night and then at least I had a place to sleep. The pubs had more liquor than Bath did and I had a good time Saturday night, took in a movie Sunday, had dinner and went back to camp.

There are plenty of sluts (prostitutes) running around if a soldier wants them and they all try to pick up Americans because even a private has a large income compared to English standards. Also, American soldiers populate all the pubs which sell their liquor at high prices and of course, being free spenders, many people take advantage of them. As for myself, I'm down to my last 4 pounds ($16).

Today I bought my weekly ration of seven packs of cigarettes, one bar of soap (two weeks), four candy bars, lighter fluid, razor blades, one can of grapefruit juice and a can of Nescafe coffee. That lasts me for one week. Of course I can buy other toilet items but those items I mentioned are rationed. Also, everything must be bought once for the entire week.

◆　　　◆　　　◆

Very heavy fighting in the Rhine area. Germany considers this battle as decisive.

September 16, 1944   England

Dear Roz,

I remember the girl 'bout 17 years old,
Fresh out of school acted so bold,
The first time I saw her I thought she was fair,
The first time I kissed her I was caught in her lair,
Our friendship then blossomed and continued to thrive,
When we found that we both loved to drive,
But then a dark cloud shadowed the sun,
This happened early in '41,
A message from Congress and off to the wars,
Went the one who loved you, to help do his chores,
The letters we wrote dear helped bind us together,
Then sweet, we knew we were meant for each other,
I remember our marriage you were a bit shaky,
We left our wedding to go for a walk,
Alone together only to talk,
Just as yesterday as clear to remember,
The date, sure it was 16th of September,
Now after three years of love and pleasure,
I know that I want you for ever and ever.

Congratulations on our three year anniversary

As for myself, we have just started a training and perhaps we may move to a new camp soon. We are so far from combat here that actually this camp is not much different from one in the States outside of conveniences. From here we go to a replacement center in France and as the front moves ahead it's necessary to go from one replacement center to another. However, we have six weeks training before us now so by the time we complete it the war with Germany should just about be over. Don't worry honey, I'm okay, and except for my cold I'm fine.

51

◆   ◆   ◆

> *Germany reported it has a new secret weapon — radio controlled explosion boats; They claimed to have sunk 36 Allied ships in the Channel recently. Fifteen other ships said to be damaged.*

September 21, 1944   England

Dear Roz,

One of the officers in our company was in London on pass and he was caught in a robot bomb air raid. However, he was at Piccadilly and the bomb landed miles away. London is a bigger city than New York. He got back today and of course we can all take passes now and if I had the money I would go too.

Love, Dave

HIS ROUGHER SIDE

Dear Dad,

While I certainly credit you with having high standards of honesty and trustworthiness, there are some things you did that I must call you on. I wish I had had the courage to do it when you were with us, but I always seemed to revert to a little boy in your presence and I feared your anger. In any event, I want you to know now how you have hurt me and others with some of your actions in the past.

> *Dear Roz,*
>
> *I can see you complaining that I fall asleep in the soft armchair. Darling, I haven't sat in one of those for months so I will appreciate it. As a matter of fact, I'll appreciate home and all that goes with it. I'd even take the baby out for a walk in his carriage. You see honey, I should be very easy for you to handle when I get home. No arguments, no trouble, just one happy family?*
>
> *Belgium*   *November 14, 1944*

I still don't understand how a man with your high ethical standards and generous heart could have shown so much disrespect toward others. It was as if you got enjoyment from putting other people down. This remains one of the hardest things for me to come to terms with when I think about our past. It was as if you were two different people living inside one human entity.

Dad in front of the grocery store Mom's father owned in the Bronx.

My earliest recollections of this behavior occurred when I was sitting on our front stoop with you and my friends. You teased them with statements such as, "Why doesn't your father take you camping with the Boy Scouts like I do?", and "I bought my kids the first air conditioner on the block," or "the first television set." I also remember you ridiculing the work their fathers did. You even teased a kid about his name by asking him, "How could your father name you Jack when your last name is Kass?" These are the kind of things that stick in the minds of children and can cause pain and damage.

I took on the responsibility at a young age of trying to cover up the comments you made to my friends to make them feel better. That was a huge burden for me and it's been difficult for me to get over it. I recently asked my childhood friend, Ronnie, if he remembered these incidents. I was surprised when he said he didn't. Is it possible that I exaggerated these statements in my childish mind due to being overly sensitive? Or did Ronnie and my other friends just manage to deal with your comments and move on? I often asked myself why my friends kept coming back, electing to sit on our porch rather than some other safer place, knowing what they would hear from you.

I was pleasantly surprised to see Ronnie and his wife visit you during your last year, even though he hadn't seen you in 45 years. Perhaps the generosity you showed to him outweighed the hurt you dealt.

Dad, I was also upset at the way you would speak about girls, especially since you had two daughters. You always said that kids should go to colleges near their homes. I could understand your argument that they are more likely to settle down near their parents if they don't go away, and this was desirable to you. However, you went further and said girls should never go away to school or even sleep in a local dormitory because they would surely become promiscuous.

One of your more common expressions was that "girls are dumb as shit" because they let boys take advantage of them and dressed provocatively. It was one of the few times that you used an off-colored word so I understand how strongly you felt about it. But Dad, how do you think your wife and daughters felt about this comment? You liked to say that all girls had on their minds were boys and talking on the telephone. It was unfair of you to judge the behavior of girls as being worse than that of boys, who were, after all, the ones "taking advantage" and certainly had girls on their minds pretty much all the time too. I cringed every time you made these remarks.

While I'm letting out my pent up frustrations with your behavior let me mention another one. You were very opinionated and berated anyone who did not agree with you in a loud, aggressive voice. If someone said they worked for the government you suggested that they must be "lazy." A grandson that played hockey was "stupid" because he would get hurt and should be spending his time in the Boy Scouts. We all learned to stay away from politics because you were full of venom for Liberals and their agenda. It wasn't that you just disagreed, but you tended to put the other person down in doing it, as if they were dumb and crazy and didn't know what they were talking about.

It was most painful to see you treat Mom the same way. She was not allowed to have an opinion that was different than yours, and if she did you said she was betraying you. What happened to that beautiful man in the letters who hung on every word his new bride said? The one who wrote "no arguments, no trouble from me."

You thought it was funny to tease minorities with comments like "Watch your wallet, here comes Willie," or to ask someone who had a history of drinking, "Still going to the saloon?" Sometimes I wondered why you weren't physically accosted for your crude behavior. You usually said these things to people who worked for you or those whom you were helping out in some other way. Once again, I wonder if those who you offended also knew your generous side and let the crudeness pass by. I have to admit they all seemed to like you.

I ask myself again why I didn't muster the courage to challenge you on your behavior. For that matter, there weren't many others who did. It was easier to let the episodes pass without blowing up further. It certainly wasn't a pleasant way to live and took away from the enjoyment we could have had together. Fortunately for me, I found my voice when confronting other people and vowed early on not to let anyone else intimidate me as you did. I got better at this as I got older and I am much happier for it.

I've searched through your letters to find evidence that this behavior was part of who you were when you were a young man. If it was there, it was not readily evident and I am puzzled that the letters don't reveal more of this rougher side of your personality. I hope when I have completed this journey of discovery I will understand when the apparent transformation took place.

Love, Rich

The Letters - (Cont.)

September 23, 1944   England   V Mail

Dear Roz,

This pay day the four of us in the tent are going to go to some city, get a hotel room near a pub, and have a good time. We keep busy with the company during the day and at night we go to a movie or USO show. At least our time is occupied.

Getting up in the morning is getting to be quite a problem now. My bed is nothing more than a wooden frame with metal straps across it acting as a so called spring. There are boards across the bed in two different places. We have no mattress or ticks so in addition to not having too much comfort we have stripes across our back. My stomach has a surplus of softness so I find it better to sleep on it. In the morning it's damp and cold as the dickens and I hate to get out from under my blankets. Oh how I miss my bed. Don't ever tell me I'm sleeping too much in it when I'm home.

◆   ◆   ◆

September 25, 1944   England   V Mail

Dear Roz,

We bought an electric heater today for over 18 shillings which is almost $4 and it doesn't seem to work too well. However, at least we can warm some water on the hot coils to make a hot drink.

◆　　　◆　　　◆

Pacific War seen stretching up to 2 years after the defeat of Germany.

September 28, 1944   England

Dear Roz,

I have some lice or something in my blankets as I'm still getting bitten up. Anything that bites in the line of insects is sure to get me. I'm lucky that way. Don't laugh but I have a can of insecticide powder for body crawling insects which I am going to spray on my body after this letter. I haven't had a drink in weeks and of course I don't miss it as much as I like to drink a bit just for a change. It's one way to feel good and have some fun provided that you're with the right people.

◆　　　◆　　　◆

Eisenhower tells the Reich and allies that he will not allow oppression of German people.

September 29, 1944   England

Dear Roz,

Today I received the letter you wrote on August 27 at 10 pm. That ought to give you some idea of how the mail comes through here.

◆　　　◆　　　◆

Famine is feared by Germany during the winter months; More reports of worsening conditions in Reich come through Sweden.

October 1, 1944   England

Dear Roz,

Today I received three letters from you which raised my morale considerably. I just finished washing some clothes in my helmet and now I'm going to write a long letter to you. Yesterday was payday here in the ETO and we all were paid off in pounds again.   I have close to $100 out of which I'll have to pay for my rations. We don't have any bonds anymore as all bonds were cancelled as of September. If we want to buy a bond now we have to apply through our finance office here in the ETO and they send the bonds home. However, I'm not so sure I'll have enough money so I'll stand by this month and see how my finances work out. Next weekend I'm going to London and see what is cooking there.

In your letter of September 5 you said you received my first letter. Darling, I was glad to read that news because I knew how anxious I was to receive your mail. You didn't have to worry so much about the trip over as I'm sure that the submarine menace was almost over. In fact as I wrote you we had a very quiet voyage.

Funny, I used to ask you to sing and you never would for me. Now you write that you sing to Richard all the time. Is that the only way you can get him to go to sleep. The snapshots you sent were swell and I'm collecting a small library of your photos in my album now. Keep sending them to me honey as I look forward to them. You're a good wife my sweet. You finally did smile in a snapshot and it looked good. Also, your hair was done up the way I like it. Richard still looks the same to me but of course the photos aren't too clear of him. You looked very pretty and I could have leaned over and kissed you both, that's how near to me your pictures brought you both.

My sweet, you never told me if you receive a letter every day or whether they arrive in groups. I'm hoping that they arrive singly so that you can hear from me at least once a day. Sept. 16's letter arrived too and I too am happy over the fact that we didn't listen to anyone and married. Perhaps you never noticed it my sweet but I always thought my letters were warm and close. I shouldn't think that just the word darling would affect you so much. If by chance previous letters were cold I'm sorry then as I didn't intend them to be that way.

I know our luck won't change because all the bad luck I've ever had was before we were married. I know that whatever God has looked over us in the past will continue to favor us in the future. Both of us are lonely and miss each other. This war can't last forever and when it finally does end and we are all in our happy little home together we certainly will have plenty to look forward to and much to talk over.

I love you both very much and being apart doesn't help matters any. However, we aren't the only ones in that boat and others feel the same way we do. There is nothing to do but sweat it out now and make up for it in the future. Darling, be good and take care of yourself. Keep as busy as you can with Dick and perhaps time will pass quickly. I think of you both all the time. P.S. I'll take your tip on how to write a V letter.

◆　　　◆　　　◆

Allied drive into Italy stalled by Germans; Americans hold high ground near Bologna-Rimini highway but fierce fighting reported.

October 3, 1944   *England*

Dear Roz,

Today I received your cablegram and I interpreted it as a wedding anniversary telegram. I was surprised to get it honey, and I should have sent you one too. It took longer for the cablegram to arrive than a regular letter. I bought some air mail envelopes so I'll send some of my letters to you air mail. Well I can't sit in anymore so I think I'll go to Bath and get a few scotches under my belt. It's been almost 4 weeks since I last had a drink.

It sure is cold getting up in the morning and if it wasn't for the Captain living in our tent I don't think we would make the 5:45 reveille formation every day. Our company now gets a truck to take our men to nearby cities. We got it three times a week so perhaps I'll go along with it on a few more occasions. This weekend I'm definitely going to London. I can get leave for three days and there isn't a place in England that can't be reached in that time (for the censor).

I know that Piccadilly is a hot place to go to and being ready to take a chance on anything I guess I'll have a good time. Darling all this amounts to is just being lonely and having nothing much to do. I'd rather be sitting on our couch with you with my head on your lap and have a few drinks while listening to the radio program. However, when I get home I'll be able to tell you all about the places I've been to and what I did there.

Darling, each day that goes by I miss you more and more and I look forward to that happy day again when I can hold you in my arms and know that you're really there. I want you to wear your hair the way I like it and put on your best clothes. Darling when I get back, our first night we will park Richard with someone and pitch a real party to celebrate. Well my love, I'll close this letter now so until tomorrow all my love to my wife and son.

◆　　　◆　　　◆

Himmler and Goebbels say a fanatical population will fight Allies until the end. Guerrilla war ordered against Allies.

October 5, 1944   England

Dear Roz,

I didn't write yesterday as I wasn't feeling too well. During the day I took a ride on a new tank which was being tested and I hurt my hip bone going over a ditch. Last night I couldn't walk and I went to sleep early. This morning I went to the hospital, took an x-ray which showed no broken bones. I feel much better now that I know I had only injured my tush muscle (right cheek). It's still sore but I can get around okay. However, it's so damp here that it takes a long time for a sore muscle to heal. I received two letters from you today. One was a victory letter, 11 Sept. 44, in which you told me that you didn't receive any mail that day. I don't like victory letters because they are too short. That is I don't like to receive any from you. I write V mail to every one else but you.

You mentioned having three more children which amused me. If it takes as long to have the other three as it did to connect on Dick I'll really have grey hair and perhaps my days of reproduction will have already terminated. It's a very touchy subject with me right now and the less I think of it the better off I am. I enjoy reading about Richard especially the way you write about him. He must be a little angel. I wish I could only hold him again and play with him a little. He probably is growing fast now and I'm sure he must know his mother very well. You certainly can tell now if his formula is correct. You see honey, if you do what you think is correct you'll always be right as no one else can tell a mother how to take care of her baby. You know all his reactions and can tell immediately if anything is wrong with him. You're doing a swell job mom, keep it up.

So we finally have a new linoleum (floor), well that must be a tremendous improvement on our kitchen. However, now I can see you on bended knees washing it after every meal. So Milton bought the baby a high chair. I guess he really likes Dick too. I should think that by this time you ought to be able to tell the direction of fire of Dick's birdie. Why don't you approach him using a diaper as a shield such as the crusaders used. You should get some protection that way. Does he really laugh all the time? Does he giggle at you when you scold him too? Imagine all the trouble you will have when we are both home together and you'll want to know who flicked cigarette ashes on the new rug. We probably will have you going wild most of the time.

Darling, the news of the European front may be good but it isn't completely over yet. There still is plenty of hard fighting ahead and its cold weather to be fighting in now. I was willing to bet that you would buy me the bracelet and not the fountain pen. However, I'll wear the bracelet faithfully and I'm sorry that I didn't send you any gift other than the little poem which I wrote on our Anniversary Day and sent to you. Believe me darling, that had all my feelings about you in it.

One hundred fourteen pounds of fighting woman, that's what you are. You didn't gain an ounce through child birth. I wish I was the same way. I weighed myself today and I weighed 189 pounds which was a loss of a few pounds. Do you think that you're a woman now because your physique has changed a little? Darling, do you think that I can even picture you as being other than the way you looked when we first met. You're just a skinny, pretty kid with a hot temper, always looking for little things that I do wrong. I'll always see you looking that way to me even when you're 70 years old. However, as long as I can get my arms around you and hold you close to me I'll always love you. Don't even get too fat so that I can't encircle you completely. That's an order. I believe I wrote you that I'm living in a tent now shivering at night. There are four officers and no one wants to get up in the morning, it's too cold.

Darling, I believe I've covered everything up to date now. Tomorrow I'm going on pass to London so I'll be able to tell you all about it when I return. Good night my sweet and keep up the good work with Richard. I love you both and think of you all the time.

Love, Dave

Does He Look Like Me

Dear Dad,

In so many of your letters you asked the same question to Mom, "Does he look like me?" I wondered why this was so important to you. In my journey of discovering who you were I read your letters carefully, and at times, found myself reading between the lines. I assumed there was always another clue to find that would reveal something new about my father that I had yet to discover.

Dear Roz,

I'm glad to read that Richard resembles me and happier yet to find that he is more handsome. I'm not handsome at all and I hope he turns out to be a handsome young man. What color is his hair or hasn't it grown yet? So he is turning out to be a fatso. Honey, don't let him get too fat. I know that Pop plays with him a lot and probably loves his little grandson.

Germany   *March 9, 1945*

Richard enjoying a day at the beach.

I thought long and hard about this question which occupied so much of your written words. I have concluded that your response was completely normal and if I were in your position I would ask the same question and never be certain that the answer was correct or the one I wanted to hear. A father separated from his son while he is growing up, a first born infant child, would of course be fascinated with what he looked like. The possibility that his son would have some of his features or behaviors would be amazing to think about. I thought to when my own children were born. Marlene and I examined each one so carefully to see if they had my blue eyes or were they hazel like hers, my course and curly hair or the finer texture of hers. We looked for signs of whether our children would exhibit my poor ability in sports or her superior coordination. This is part of the fun of being a new parent. It is natural and I suspect all new parents do this. Why then would I think it would be unusual for you to be somewhat preoccupied with this question?

Dear Roz,

Honey, the picture of Dick crying was really very cute. Say, he has big cheeks. He looks like a big boy to me. I can just about recognize him as having some of my own features. I wonder why you compare Richard to me when he is crying. This is the second time you have done that.

Luxemburg   *January 2, 1945*

After all, you had not really seen me very much. I was born in July while you were stationed away from home. You saw me occasionally before you were shipped to England in August. That wasn't very much time to get to know me, or to learn to recognize my features, which in any event, were changing rapidly. What did you have to grasp onto, to support what you knew in your head but did not feel yet in your body? Were you indeed a father? You didn't hear me cry at night for a feeding, or be there when my diapers were changed. I learned to roll over and crawl while you were digging foxholes in Germany, and you weren't able to hold me and feel the warmth of my soft body or the smell of talcum powder permeating from my pajamas. You had nothing but the knowledge, that maybe, I had some of your features and therefore validated the concept that you were a father and that thousands of miles away there was another little person that carried your genes and some of your behaviors.

Dear Roz,

You say that Richard has changed a lot since he was born. I wonder whether I'll be able to pick him out as my son when I see you both. Does he look like me and have any of my characteristics. You say he smiles and has dimples. I hope he can always smile and enjoy the life he has before him.

Luxemburg   *December 21, 1944*

Well Dad, when you returned home, I'm sure you were surprised and delighted that I did indeed have characteristics which could only have come from you. Even as a baby, I'm sure you knew my wide thumbs and the two toes on my right foot that are partially joined, were an unmistaken match for yours. I believe I have your ears but Mom's nose, your eyes and skin and Mom's face shape. As I grew older I discovered I have your large boned body but more of Mom's personality, although I pick up many character traits from you also.

It was unfortunate that you missed out on this joy of fatherhood, discovering the child you had created and watching him grow. God, however, was good to you and you came home safely to have three other children and got to see them mature right from the beginning.

I wonder though, Dad, why you became upset when Mom wrote that I looked like you when I was crying. It's clear from your letters you didn't want her to know about your softer side, that you were capable of tears when sadness overcame you. What were you afraid of? Did you always have to come across as strong and macho? I find it sad that you could not be free with your emotions, expressing them with unlimited boundaries.

Finally, I'm wondering, when you did come home, how did I greet you? Did I cry at the stranger trying to pick me up or did I smile and what was your reaction? I hope I treated you well.

Love, Rich

The Letters – (Cont.)

Two miles gained in fight towards Bologna. Germans stripping area in retreat as Americans reach within 12 miles of Po valley.

October 8, 1944   England

Dear Roz,

I just returned from my London visit. I told you in my last letter that I intended to visit London and see what it was like there. Now I have. We arrived there and finally found a place to stay in. Of course we looked for a place to eat and I'll bet that the people in liberated and occupied France eat better than we did. There is only one place to get a good meal and that is in an army mess. Well we went to Piccadilly Circus which is supposed to be like Broadway in New York. Everything cost plenty and we had some scotch in one hotel all day and then when they ran out we bought a bottle of scotch for 4 pounds ($16).

Someone told us about a night club we could go to so Kellmurray and I took a taxi and were riding toward the club when the air raid siren began. We didn't know what to do when suddenly a bomb (V2) came through the air and landed a few blocks ahead of us. Well by that time my knees were shaking and the entire sky was one red flash. After that the all clear was sounded, and we finished our bottle at this private club. It was an experience, my first bombing, and I'm glad it is over.

Well, we finally got back to our hotel and I found that I had spent 14 pounds. We still hadn't seen any of the historic places so we decided to spend the next day on an excursion trip of the city. We visited the Palace, Westminster Abbey, St. James Church, Downing Street where the Prime Minister lives and many other places. The Underground (subway) is like ours except that the trains are much deeper below ground level than ours are. It's necessary to take escalators down to the subway level. The Parliament Building is beat up from bombing but Big Ben is still sounding off the chimes in the tower. Wherever you go you can see evidence of the bombings however, London is so large a city it isn't as noticeable as I thought it would be. However, they clean up the rubbish quickly.

The streets are crowded in Piccadilly Circus but the district was so spread out that you don't know where all the theaters are. It isn't like Broadway where all the theaters are close to each other. I stopped into a department store and bought some of their picture story books. They said it would be mailed to you in about 2 weeks. Well now that I visited London I'll say that I don't particularly care to go back again. I know what people feel like when they visit New York from some hick town. It's all a matter of knowing where to go which we didn't.

◆　　◆　　◆

The American penetration into the heart of Germany continues with an eye on the industrial center. Despite being hindered by supply problems and bitter weather the Allied armies have been pushing back the Nazis beyond the Sigfried Line. Hitler's innermost citadel is being encircled from all sides. Very tough fighting is predicted ahead.

October 9, 1944   England

Dear Roz,

I just finished my laundry and I have a private line strung up between two tents. It started to get dark just about when I finished. I normally save my laundry for Sunday but because I left this weekend I didn't want to let it go as it doesn't take long before it accumulates into a lot of work. Honey, here I was with my helmet and one pail, each with water and I wash in that manner. I don't think I can get the three shades whiter effect but at least it helps immensely. Sleeping between GI blankets gets my clothes dirty twice as fast. My helmet and canteen cup are excellent for shaving and washing. I can do a complete face wash and shave with two canteens of water which is really conserving the liquid and it really is precious here.

◆　　　◆　　　◆

> **The U.S. has plans ready for occupied Germany. Agreement reached on policy by Federal agencies.**

October 13, 1944   *England*

Dear Roz,

The weather is miserable. It's been raining on and off for three days now and the ground is a pool of mud and water. All my shoes are wet and of course when my feet are wet my body is always chilly. It's fairly cold now and although I'd like to write longer I'm beginning to get chilly. I'm not going anywhere this weekend and I'll stick around and get plenty of bunk (rest). We do a lot of walking during the day and a little at night. There are not words to explain the feeling I get if I suddenly get the urge to defecate at night. It means grab a searchlight and overcoat, hop into cold GI shoes, and go for a walk of a couple of blocks to where the honey buckets are located. Of course it's all out in the open, fresh air style, so my bed feels twice as good when I'm back in it again. We try to regulate our movements so those unfortunate incidents are reduced to odd occasions.

◆　　　◆　　　◆

Latvian port of Riga taken by Red army. Tito and his forces have reached Belgrade. The Soviets continue to score victories on push for Berlin.

October 14, 1944   England

Dear Roz,

I've typed one letter to you today so far but I had to leave to go out with the company. This letter will be sent air mail so you probably will receive it first. In regards to haircuts, I just took one today so I'm a little cool around the ears now. My shoes are soaking wet from wallowing around in mud. Do you remember seeing the movie-time news of the mud in Italy? Well the mud here isn't that bad where you sink in to the knees but it is ankle deep in many places. The sun shines for a minute and then suddenly there is a downpour of rain. This happens about 20 times a day. Each time the sun comes out somebody figures it's going to be dry so they leave their raincoat back in the tent. The result is being caught in the rain.

We read in the paper where Hitler said he had a special bomb which could reach America. I don't think you should be too worried about that as if he had that they wouldn't need Henkel 111 planes to fly them piggyback as far as the channel before they are launched against London.

Today is Saturday and I have nothing to do. I could go to some town but we have no transportation today and I don't relish hitchhiking in this weather. Kellmurray went to Liverpool to see some nurse he knew at Pickett, Va. That's a hell of a trip from here and it's about a 14 hour ride one way in these English trains. I wish you could have seen what the English locomotives look like. They resemble our civil war engines more or less and are very small. I like the passenger trains here as they all have compartments and 6 people can sit comfortably in a compartment. The English officers are very odd, the way we look at them. They of course represent the elite of England and it's against their principles to act too friendly with everyone. It isn't exactly that but they are always quiet and dignified. They never *show any emotion in public and I've seen English officers sit in pubs with young ladies and never smile once. They probably have more discipline in their army which is more than I can say for our own.*

The family is growing; Richard, Roz, Mark, Dave, and Susan

The war is moving farther away from England now and it wouldn't surprise me if we all evacuated and left England for France. We haven't got any winter quarters here and we have also heard rumors that we may move to Nissling huts (corrugated metal buildings) on another post.

I haven't received any mail today but I've received so many letters in the past few days that I don't expect to receive any for a few days. I do hope that you have been receiving my mail regularly now. You did write in some of your past letters that the mail was slow in arriving.

Darling I wish I could find the right words to tell you how much I miss you and Dick. I envy you because at least you have Richard to be close to you. I have only your pictures, your mail, and my memories. Of course my feelings and emotions are very strong where you and Dick are concerned and I try to comfort myself in knowing that you're home waiting for me. It's a poor substitute for actually being with you but it's the closest I can get to you. Darling, I really miss you more than you can possibly imagine. Having my evening free I spend a lot of my time just thinking about you and Dick. I know that you feel worse than I do and more because you're more sensitive than I am. I can only hope that we aren't apart too long and that we can finally be united and be happy together.

I'm in the orderly room now and am writing on onion skin paper used for typing. I'm running short on my own writing paper and now I pick up a few pages here and there. Darling, I'll bet your letters are beginning to collect and mount up again. Where can you possibly keep them all? I remember when I left the drawers were full of letters.

Well darling I'll close this letter now and hope that it rushes through the mail until you receive it in short order. Give our son a big hug for me.

Love, Dave

THE MANDOLIN

Dear Dad,

You did not lose your ear for music in the war. I was always amazed at how well you could pick up your mandolin and play any song at all, and sing along to your own music. You never had to practice and you knew all the words too. It just came naturally to you. I always wished I could play like you. You loved playing the old Yiddish songs. Even though more than forty years had passed since you learned those melodies you never forgot them. At family gatherings you would pick up the mandolin, tune it up by ear (which I also found amazing) and begin serenading everyone with songs out of Czarist Russia followed by those sung by the Andrews Sisters recorded here in the States. People from your generation loved to listen and sing along and you never disappointed them. What a gift you had! It didn't take any coaxing either to get you to take your mandolin down from the shelf and have it perform its magic on the crowd.

Dear Roz,

Tonight Yehudi Menuhin will give a violin solo concerto here and I'm going to see him. I enjoy listening to good music and I never really had a chance to hear him before...

Back again honey. I have a pen to continue this letter with. Well the concert was excellent; however, I don't believe that I can get too enthused over classical music anymore. Perhaps I lost my good musical ear. Well that's what the war does for you.

England   *September 6, 1944*

Most of the young kids didn't appreciate what you were playing and it was usually our signal to disperse to the basement for some games. As for me, I couldn't stand it. This had nothing to do with the music or the way you played it. As I said, I envied you and wished I could play as well as you. I just couldn't stand the sound of the mandolin and what it represented.

I really wanted to be able to play an instrument. When I was in third grade you chose the accordion for me to learn. I rented a small 12 button instrument and did pretty well with the lessons I got at school. I can still remember proudly playing *Bull Frog* and *Chordi's Dance,* both one note songs. Before long I was playing in the school orchestra. This signaled my arrival as a musician and I just had to get my own accordion. You took me out and you bought me a brand new, full sized instrument. The guy in the store told me to try it out by playing something but he didn't give me any music to read. All I could do was play *Bull Frog.* It sounded good to me so we took it home.

My private lessons with Mr. Davis were a lot harder than those I got in school. I was very nervous when I had to play for him. That's because I knew I did a terrible job during the week when I was practicing. Handling that huge, heavy instrument was difficult for me. He smoked a pipe and I can still hear the sound of his breath whistling through the pipe as he dated the songs in the book for the current week's assignment. We concentrated on reading notes and playing them correctly. I never understood that every song had a rhythm and a musician should feel the music he was playing. I played like I was typing this letter to you. There were notes but it was all played in mono-rhythm.

I dreaded practicing when you were home. I would try to get it over with before you came home from work because I knew you would grab your mandolin and play along with me. I'd be sitting in a chair with the accordion straps over my shoulder and you would be standing right by my side twanging that darn instrument in my ear. Every few moments I would hear your voice crying above the music, MISTAKE. Of course that meant I played something wrong. Sometimes I heard MISTAKE, MISTAKE, MISTAKE in rapid succession. Of course I made a mistake, I knew it, and didn't need you to rub it in. You never made a mistake, did you? You could read the notes, pluck the strings and yell out MISTAKE all at the same time perfectly. Sometimes I couldn't hold in my frustration and I'd break down crying. This didn't help because it was only an excuse for your anger to boil up and that made my practicing even harder. It didn't help either that you kept reminding me how you just spent so much money on the new accordion and I didn't even want to play it.

Dave playing the mandolin as a youth.

My musical talent never progressed very much beyond that level (maybe for my fear of making a mistake). I never learned to play with feeling, never learned to play chords, which every kid, even the least intelligent ones seemed to know, and I continued to make mistakes.

Eventually we all realized that it was a waste of money and I never saw Mr. Davis and his pipe with the apple tobacco again. I don't remember if you sold my accordion or gave it away but I know it disappeared from the house. Every once in awhile you would remind me how I pleaded to have my own instrument and how I squandered the opportunity. It became a good story for telling at family gatherings, and according to my memory, you rarely missed a chance to tell it.

Years later when I got married, I bought another accordion and gave my musical career another attempt although I did not take formal lessons. I did okay but never really mastered the technique. Eventually that accordion found its way to the basement storage too, where it sits today, almost in brand new condition. For some reason I just can't get myself to get rid of it.

Dave's mandolin on Richard's mantle.

When my kids wanted to play instruments I never pushed them too hard to practice. My memories were too painful along that route. Jennifer was the only one who showed any promise when she took up the violin in second grade. She played all the way through her teenage years and took part in the high school orchestra. She even went to violin camp several summers for 2 weeks. I was very happy she liked to play, even though she and her girlfriend only qualified for the last two seats in the violin section every year, those reserved for the two worst players. She recently confessed that she didn't always play the notes during the concerts and just faked it. Also, the local football and wrestling teams shared the school when the violin summer camp was in session. I guess she had some other things on her mind and a different incentive for sticking with the orchestra than love of the violin.

As for me, I think I have finally found the beat. I learned to hear the rhythm in music and appreciate songs from all eras. I still can't play anything by ear and can't read the notes too well but I am great with a drum and I even think I can carry a tune when I sing.

77

Oh, and your mandolin is sitting on a shelf in my home where I can see it all the time. Of all the things you owned it's the one item that brings your memory closest to me. I smile when it calls out to me, MISTAKE.

Love, Rich

The Letters – (Cont.)

> *Strategy to defeat Japan is taking shape as war in the Pacific moves to the eastern section.*

October 15, 1944   England

Dear Roz,

I just finished censoring some mail and usually after I finish I've no desire to write however today I feel like writing now and writing my daily letter to you.

I slept until 11 this morning, washed and went to dinner. Our dinner today had chicken as its main dish and it was good too. I returned back to my tent, washed my clothes, and took a shower and shave. Today is the first day it hasn't rained although the weather isn't too good as it may rain any minute. After I finish this letter I have some sewing to do, a little thing such as shortening my sleeves on a field jacket. A man can get along without a woman up to a certain extent. By that I mean he can do his own washing and cleaning, even sewing, but there isn't any substitute for loving. I think that's where the women know they have us at a disadvantage. We're always around to take more punishment.

The Captain took off for London on Friday and some officer at Battalion Headquarters has been looking for him ever since. I'm acting Company commander now with Kellmurray at Liverpool and I was told to tell the Captain to report up to Bn. Hq. as soon as he returns. He really is AWOL as his absence isn't authorized. That's the only way to go though, as they require all kinds of paper work and requests in order to get a 24 hour pass.

I hope you don't find this paper too hard to read off as it's onion skin and all I have at present. I should get my ration coupon tomorrow and I'll buy some writing paper if there is any available.

This post is run with favoritism. There is a definite priority on everything. First come the officers who are stationed complement, then come the enlisted men. They are called the cadre here. All casuals and replacements come last. It's just like two separate armies. The cadre officers and enlisted men live in brick buildings and the replacements live in tents. The cadre can buy articles like pens, cigarette lighters and other little novelties and the replacements can't. The officers have their own Officers Club and count the number of replacement officers in their requisition for whiskey, but we can't get into their club and our share of whiskey which we should get according to the rules, goes to the cadre officers. We can't complain about anything here. One officer, a captain, in our training Bn. here had an argument with one of the cadre officers. He was placed in a package and left for France yesterday. That's the way they operate here. All politics and plenty of hand-shaking. They take good care of themselves and stick together like glue. None of them are too anxious to see combat either.

At present all casual officers are restricted and we all have to stick around in case any changes are made in the roster. None of us are leaving though and our company officers are among the few in which new officers were pulled out. It may be a bit difficult for you to understand but I guess it's still the same luck which we've had since we've been married.

Just because I've been doing my own washing darling doesn't mean that I'm so used to it that I'll do it when I'm home. I don't want to do anything that will remind me of the army after I'm out. I guess you were right darling; I'm just about fed up now. It's almost four years now that I've been in the army and by the time I'm discharged I should have had my fill. Darling, all I want when I get out is a little money so I can stay home, and plenty of loving to make up for lost time. I think I'll have all my meals in bed and woe and behold to anyone who annoys me while I'm between the sheets. I'll keep all the fresh air out, as I've enough of it now and more at night when it really gets cold.

I still have my cold and the sniffles but everyone here has a cold except the cadre. As you can see I'm in love with them but all the replacement officers feel the same way because of the screwing we are taking here. Say honey, I keep telling you time and time again what I'd give just to be near you. I hope you aren't getting annoyed reading it so often. I miss you more than words can possible explain. I don't even enjoy going anywhere anymore and I get the blues a bit more often now. Being in love the way I feel has hit me hard especially since I have no idea as to how long it will be before I'm home with you again. I wish to see Richard and note how he's grown since I last saw him. I want to hold him and play with him but even that's impossible. I'm relying on you to let him know about his father and when I'm home again there's nothing that would tickle me more than if he called me daddy the first time he saw me. However, perhaps that's asking for too much so I'll do my best to make him love me on his own by being a good daddy to him.

No darling, there isn't any substitute for loving and don't we all know it. My sex life has been shot to hell since I've been here and of course I don't see any immediate solution for it either. Of course, there is an easy way out but you know me, and I don't go in for it and I never did before either. I guess everything will taste better when I'm home again. I hope you have been controlling your feeling as I have and of course I know that it isn't too easy on you either.

Honey, this is certainly an upset world we are living in at present and I hope that Dick hasn't any such experiences during his life as we have at present. I've just about covered all that I can think of to write at present to I'll close this letter to you with all my love.

◆　　　◆　　　◆

Wilhelmshaven burning after bombing by RAF despite bad weather. Hamburg, Duisberg, and Cologne also bombed heavily.

October 17, 1944   England

Dear Roz,

Last night I went to see a movie here on the post. It was a mystery picture, Murder in Times Square. I returned back to my tent after the picture was over and found Kellmurray back from his pass in Liverpool. He went up to see a nurse he knew back in the States and he had a good time while there. The Captain is back too and he is waiting till the Colonel returns from his leave to be punished for being AWOL over the weekend. I wonder if you can follow all I have written but things are so SNAFUED here I doubt whether any one on this post can honestly say that he knows what is going on. As for myself, I just listen to all the rumors floating around and disregard them all. The only thing official is that which one reads on orders.

The only rumor which holds some water is that we will move to winter quarters on another post here in England. That would be good news as it's cold as hell here at night. The only place to keep warm is at the mess hall but that is so far away now that it's almost a small hike just going to eat.

It rained like hell last night for a change so the mud situation hasn't improved any. I wear one pair of dry shoes and always have three pair of shoes drying. Whenever one pair dries up I immediately rub some water repellent on it and try and waterproof the shoes however there isn't any substitute for overshoes or rubber boots and it isn't very long before those get wet again.

Darling, whenever I begin writing about my feelings for you I just don't know how or where to start. I want to write how much I miss you and Richard and how much I love you both but it seems as if I have exhausted all the ways of saying this in past letters. Someone shows me pictures of their family and immediately out come my own private photos of you and Richard and darling, I am very proud of my collection. I noticed that in your letters you are beginning to get that lost feeling as you can't go on any more the way things are now. I got that same feeling just about the same time as you did and believe me honey, it's a tough feeling to combat. It sort of leaves you with an empty feeling. In thinking about it I decided that there must be some thing to ease the pain and there is. First we must believe that God is watching over us, protecting us, just as he has done in the past. We have our baby to love and when I think of everything that I would like to do for him I know that I can take anything until I can be with him again. Then there is you and I. I can't think of anything more beautiful than our love for each other. I know that I could wait indefinitely as long as I knew you would be there when I returned. I love you enough to take any hardship we may have to contend with now. Darling, try and look at things in the same way as I do and I'm sure things will look a little brighter. Darling, I've just exhausted my supply of words and besides my two fingers are getting sore now so I'll close this letter with all my love.

◆　　◆　　◆

Soviet army eyeing attack on Warsaw as 1,000 tanks are reported along the Vistula by Berlin. Red army140 miles from Adriatic Sea.

October 17, 1944　　　　　　　　　　England

Dear Roz,

I feel like bitching now and I'm going to do it. It's been raining so long now that the raindrops on my tent even keep me from taking an afternoon nap. Rain and mud all day long, that's all we have to look forward to each day. On top of that, we are located in a valley and all the rainwater from the surrounding hills help to add discomfort to our misery. All my shoes are wet and nothing ever dries here. Now I feel better. It's off my mind.

Richard Leitman with Michael Hollander

◆　　　◆　　　◆

RAF bombs Essen once again.

October 24, 1944   England

Dear Roz,

Today our men had stoves installed in their tents. They haven't furnished any coal so everyone is burning anything they can get their hands on. We still haven't any stove in our tent. It seems as if we have to get special permission to have a (stove) put in our place. So far we have had one fire already. Some stupid son of a b---- threw a bottle of lighter fluid in the stove and the entire tent went up in flames. Now we will have an investigation and someone will decide that all the stoves should be removed as they constitute a fire hazard. That's the way things run in the army. Sometimes it's better to just laugh at everything and let it go by. Anyone who tries to figure out why things are done in the army will wind up with a Section 8 discharge, especially at this replacement depot.

Something new has been added. Today and tomorrow no passes or furloughs will be issued. Anyone caught anywhere in England will be apprehended. That's the way they round up all the AWOL's. Interesting isn't it? That's done now and then to find out how they stand in general. I can't figure out why anyone would want to go AWOL in this country. Yes I can.... some of these men live with some of these English commandos (one who offers her body for a price...10 shillings and up). I'll bet you didn't think that went on here. It does and more openly than back home.

◆　　　◆　　　◆

Truman campaigns for Roosevelt, attacks Gov. Dewey in Madison, Wis.

October 25,   England

Dear Roz,

Last night I slept in the Orderly tent. The stove was warm and the CQ brought a cot and seven blankets in for me. He had to be there to answer the telephone and we both slept there. This morning the guard woke us up at 5:25 am.

It's been two months since I've slept in a warm bed, in between sheets and with a soft pillow under my head. Believe me honey, every time you go to bed just thank God that the war is so far away from you that you can have those luxuries and can go to sleep without having to worry about bombs falling. That's one reason we are here, to keep the war away from our loved ones. We must be willing to make certain sacrifices for that.

Darling, my training schedule is complete this week. I didn't know whether to tell you or not but I promised to keep on the level with you and I know your man enough to take the good with the bad. I think that after we complete our training we may be here a few days more and then leave for France. This is only my opinion after seeing how things are running here now. They seem to be sending everyone out to close up these camps in England. I don't know whether we go into another two week restriction on our mail again. I was really very lucky to be here this long and get around to see the country here. Darling, I could go through anything as long as I know you love me and will be waiting for me when this is all over.

Honey, I was just listening to the news and the Russians are in Norway already. I don't believe this war will last too long now and the pressure is on from all sides and, with the winter approaching, it's going to be rough on one said country.

Love, Dave

I KILLED MY FIRST MAN.

Dear Roz,

Darling, would you change your feelings towards me if you knew that I killed a man. It's something which I never knew how it would affect me. I don't think I'll ever forget that short episode as long as I live. It happened in my first attack and that's why I mention it. I walked right into a well concealed machine gun position and without even thinking, fired. I was scared to death then but after that I pulled myself together. No one ever gets accustomed to fighting and the longer a soldier is in combat the more nervous he gets. They call it combat fatigue.

Germany   *December 2, 1944*

Dear Dad,

Your letter contains a few simple, isolated sentences that say so much and, at the same time, leaves so many unanswered questions. Oh yeah, Roz, a.) I killed my first man, and b.) Do you think differently about me knowing this? Is that it! Sure you were scared in your first attack but what about killing that man. It's just the way you told her about the incessant rain making the roads muddy or what you ate for breakfast that morning. It's no wonder that I have so many questions about who you were.

Dad playing baseball.

To me this is one of those life changing events that would have shaken my very core until it became fully accepted and digested by my soul. I can see at this very moment how all sides of my darkest shadows would be competing for dominance with my rational brain for control of my emotions and thought-- thrill, guilt, fear, joy, revenge, omnipotence, sadness, the desire for more blood. I could never envision myself sweeping it off to a recess of my mind with a simple sentence or two and go on with business as usual.

Dad, why didn't you write about what you were feeling? What were your emotions? Were you upset? Or proud? Did you have feelings of guilt? Were you even in touch with your emotions or were you totally isolated from your feelings? Was your fear of the situation so intense that it blocked anything else from your mind?

I can remember you expressing some of your emotions so I know they were there inside you. I am most familiar with your anger. It would not take much to set you off, although I will confess that you got over upsets very quickly most of the time. However, there aren't many people who knew you that didn't witness your sharp outbursts. Mom taking too long in the shower, a grandchild that didn't say thank you, or one of us disagreeing with you on a political viewpoint, were all reasons for your anger to come out. Yet killing a man couldn't shake even a hint of feeling from you, or did it?

It took a serious family crisis for your sadness to show, such as a divorce or death, though anger usually overtook the sorrow and you eventually found someone to be angry with. It was as if you needed anger to feel good. Anger was your most familiar and loyal friend. Even the genuine sadness you displayed if Mom got sick eventually turned into anger towards someone, and ironically it would often be Mom. I don't think you knew how much I feared, and became angry with you, when you'd burst out in one of those tantrums. I was always on edge around you fearing something someone did or said would set you off. I especially couldn't stand it when you were shouting at Mom. No one was off limits and no action was too small to warrant your comments. I wonder if killing that first German soldier and some unresolved processing of what you went through in the war had something to do with this.

Joy was another emotion you were in touch with. You had a beautiful smile and we could always tell when you were happy. I saw that smile when Marlene and I would visit. It was very evident when we brought one of our grandsons with us and you talked to them about their lives. It was evident that you loved them, although you never told them that. You smiled when we sat with you at the Port Washington dock on a nice day, looking out at the shimmering water in the bay.

Dad in a rowboat with Mom.

You were happy when you bragged about your granddaughters Julie and Randy, or my brother Mark. You were thrilled when Mom sat in a chair next to you and held your hand. After our visits with you I would try to remember the joy and burn it into my mind, because I wanted to see you as a happy, pleasant man, but I admit that the memories of your anger were often stronger.

I think that feelings of rejection played a huge role in your life, and mine, but you had a way of framing rejection to look like something else. Relatives didn't visit you because they were "no-good" and selfish. Your brother-in-law moved his family, with Mom's sister and our cousins, away from your town when we were younger because he thought he was "too good" for the old neighborhood. A grandson didn't visit or say thank you enough times for special gifts you gave him because he was a "lost cause." The "lost battalion" was another way you described a family who didn't visit often enough. You never admitted that this was really about rejection and what you needed was to feel loved. Would things have looked and been different if you told them you missed their company because you loved them? I think so.

Dad, maybe it was your generation of men that found it so hard to be in touch with love and knowing what they were feeling. I am sad because you did not know it was possible and okay to work on the issues that were troubling you. You just lived with them and covered them up however you could. Enter anger.

Is that what you did with your emotions when you killed the German soldier? Is that why it was so difficult for you to work out your anger issues later on in a more mature way? How I wish I had asked you these questions years ago when I had the chance.

Love, Rich

The Letters – (Cont.)

> *General de Gaulle said the Allies are not providing weapons to the French army and the French are being excluded from talks concerning the occupation of Germany.*

October 26, 1944   England

Dear Roz,

Today we were given a class on German weapons. We all fired them and learned how to use them. Although some of them are good I don't believe any are better than our own. We had steak for dinner today. I'm telling you we have the best mess hall I've ever eaten in since I've been in the army. There aren't many officers here and yet we seem to get more food than is good to eat. I believe I'm putting on weight. I do a lot of walking during the day and that's the only form of exercise I have.

Today the orders came out organizing our company into a package for shipment. We lost five of our officers and they will leave with another group. Kellmurray and I are still in this package.

My tush is okay. I wrote you that I had an X-ray taken the next day following the accident and the results were negative. I healed up all right. My left shoulder has been sore for weeks and this damp weather here in our little (camp) really prevents our muscles from healing properly. I did have lots of fun riding the tank but I didn't think it was worth it after I was hurt. I know that you would certainly have enjoyed being with me on some of the rides I have taken.

Darling, it won't be long before I'm writing you about France. I'll try and describe everything to you and I hope you'll get a good picture of what it's like there. I ask you not to worry while I'm there. I promise to dig the deepest foxhole in France. Besides, it won't be dangerous where I'm going anyway. No matter where I go Darling, I'll always have you first in my heart.

◆   ◆   ◆

The Germans are digging in at Bologna but the Americans are waging a bitter battle against them. The 8th army is pushing into Italy.

October 27, 1944   England

Dear Roz,

This will be the last letter I will write to you from England. Now that I'm leaving here I don't feel any different than when I left the States. I'm writing this to you with the hope that by writing to you it will keep you from worrying before you receive my next letter. I don't know how long it takes for a letter to arrive from France but if there aren't any restrictions on it you should receive it in the same length of time.

I exchanged my money for francs and I originally had 2 pounds ($4) which is 200 francs. A franc is worth 2 cents. It looks something like the size of a dollar bill. I won't take my footlocker with me when I leave. That will remain in England so from here on in all I have is my pack, bedding roll and one piece of luggage – my cadet bag. I guess I'll get by all right. Others have done it before me.

When we leave here we probably go to another replacement center and spend more time there. I'd rather you know what's taking place than to keep you in the dark and you'd probably worry twice as much. I know it's no use telling you not to worry about me but I'll write as soon as I get there and let you in on what's cooking. Perhaps there won't even be any delay in the mail as it didn't seem to move too quickly from here.

I haven't received any packages from you yet so I'll have to sweat them out again. I know it will be weeks before I receive any mail again.

◆   ◆   ◆

October 30, 1944   France

Dear Roz,

Well here I am sitting on a box in France writing to you. So far things are pretty rough. I thought the mud in England was bad but it's worse here in France. I slept in a pup tent last night and I guess that's going to be good from here on in. For breakfast this morning we had spam, hard tacks and cold tomato juice. Kellmurray and I slept in the same tent. All the equipment we had was that which we had carried on our back and believe me it was heavy. We walked about four miles in mud up to our ankles.

There isn't too much evidence of fighting except for all the shell casings lying around. We are bivouacked here for the time being and we still haven't hit any replacement center. I had two blankets last night and believe me honey, I near froze. Our baggage finally did catch up to us and tonight I will sleep in my bedding roll. I'm still using my old A.P.O. as we are a group of bastards wandering around with no organization. There is a fire burning about 20 feet away from here and there are soldiers and officers around it.

We are burning shell containers lying around and they provide good heat. It's very chilly but my platoon sergeant managed to get some coffee somewhere and we had black coffee to warm us up. We are safe here and I don't know how long we will remain here or where we will move to when we do.

I'm on French soil now but I don't feel any different than in England. Darling, if I could only impress you with the fact that I'm safe here and there isn't any immediate danger. Last night I told Jim that we should cover ourselves with the same two blankets and sleep on two but he is too sanitary and said we should use our own. During the night he woke me up and told me to move a little closer.

It's chilly as hell out here now so I'm going to call this letter short and get around the fire. I was standing so close to the fire before that I thought my whosis was on fire and one of my whatsis was toasted. Now I can (get) close to it again and warm up a bit.

◆　　　◆　　　◆

Mexico is restricting immigration with tighter law.

October 31, 1944　　　　　　　　　　　　　　　　　　France

Dear Roz,

I'm still in the same place as I was. Last night it was windy as hell and we had occasional showers. I'm telling you it sure is rough living the way we are now. So far we haven't had one hot meal or coffee. Our meals consist of spam, biscuits and tomato juice or grapefruit juice. They don't seem to be able to get any rations here. There is a fire burning continually near my tent and that is the only way to keep warm.

All my possessions are here in my tent with me and I'm a bit crowded. I wonder what I'll use when my sleeping bag doesn't reach me. I'm writing lying down in my tent now and its cold as hell but I'll finish this letter to you.

The first thing I saw when I hit France was one of the beachheads that was invaded on D-Day. It must have been rough going up that final hill off the beach, as we walked up it, and (we) had to take a break at the top. It was so muddy we took two steps and slid back one. There isn't too much water around and that which is to be had is mostly for cooking and washing cooking utensils. I haven't received any mail as yet and only God knows when it will reach us. I haven't seen a post office as yet and we aren't allowed to wander around the areas because of booby traps still being present. I think we will leave this place and go to a regular depot soon where there are barracks. Last *night I found an earthworm on my face and woke up quickly enough.*

Today is supposed to be pay day but yesterday was Sunday and nobody even knew it. Every day is the same here. My morale is good and of course I look at the pictures of you and the baby and I know why I'm here. All the boys are in good spirits now and we make the most of everything. Darling, I want you to keep thinking of me but please don't worry. I really could be much worse off than I am.

I'm wearing my long johns and it's been ages since I last wore them. Honey what I wouldn't give to kiss you now. I wouldn't want to hold you in my arms unless I could bathe and get some clean clothes. I don't want you to tell me that I have B.O. I'm only kidding though, I'm not really that bad.

Honey, please try and take this right. Hold Dick in your arms and tell him that his father is a long way off thinking about him and his mother always. Tell him that when I return we will play lots of games and the three of us will have many good times together.

I have nothing to do other than censor mail so I can be an active member of the fire detail. I certainly am catching up on my sleep as I go to sleep when it gets dark at 7:00 pm and wake up in time for breakfast at 7:00 am. I haven't had a fresh egg in ages and the only eggs we had in England were powdered. They don't usually taste like eggs though.

Well darling, I'm in good health and I intend to stay that way. Keep your chin up and don't worry as I'll come through all right.

◆　　　◆　　　◆

Mail to US prisoners should arrive quicker as Red Cross plan is enacted to speeding letters to Germany.

October 31, 1944   France

Dear Roz,

I'm in the office of the replacement company in charge of our company. They have tables and lights so I'll stay in here unless I'm kicked out. Everything is dirty here including the paper but you'll have to excuse that. I just returned from supper. They had jam sandwiches, real bread for the first time and hot coffee. Up to this time all we had were those biscuits in the C rations which we have in the radio cabinet back home. I can't see how fellows with bum teeth eat it. One of the boys was soaking them in cold water so he could bite into it with his false choppers.

Dad patrolled the NJ beaches before going overseas.

I fixed my gasoline lantern this afternoon and then I took a nap. One of the officers went down to the beach, borrowed a truck, went to the navy and bought an entire carton of packages of cigarettes for 30,000 francs and sold them to our men. We were beginning to run short and there isn't a PX in miles. He also picked up 6 cases of C rations and distributed them to the men. We do all right by ourselves.

The beach is loaded with equipment. There are British, German and American vehicles bogged down in the mud on the beach. It is possible to buy wine from the Frenchmen but so far I haven't been able to get any. I'm telling you that it's rough living. At least I was broken in gradually by living in a tent in England. England is a haven compared to this place I'm in now. Say honey, I sure would like to sleep in our bed with you just to feel like a white man again. I think I'll shave tomorrow to keep from going to native. Darling, if I complain about anything back in the States, why you just go ahead and kick me right in the pants.

I've been constipated since I hit France and when I expose my buttocks to the elements the cold wind cuts any desire I had short. When I get home I'll spend hours in our bathroom. I haven't been paid yet and don't know when I'll be paid. Every truck that goes by is buried up to the axle in mud. Our trucks really have to be sturdy to stand up under the treatment they are getting. It's been raining on and off all day today so no one is dry at all.

◆ ◆ ◆

The Reich admits that Russian troops are gaining on Budapest.

October 31, 1944   Belgium

Dear Roz,

Tonight when I go to sleep I'm going to dream about you and Richard. I wonder what Dick looks like now. I bet he is a big boy and can really wake up all the neighbors when he screams. Does he still look like me or is he changing? He should have some of your characteristics as I know you're the mother. That's a sure thing.

Love, Dave

GENEROSITY

Dear Dad,

I have always honored your generosity and loyalty. A man is judged by his actions and there is a great chorus of those whose lives you have touched and whose heart's sing in grateful thanks to you. If you knew of someone in need you didn't ask any questions; you were there for them in a way that was meaningful and timely. You sprang into action before you had to be asked, often to the surprise of the recipients. I believe it was because of your open heart and extremely generous nature that people were willing to overlook the ridicule of your humor and harsh criticisms you were apt to deal out. The roaring bull was known to have a lamb's heart.

> *Dear Roz,*
>
> *One surprising thing happened to me. I received my first whiskey ration. Of course someone cheated on us down the line. We are supposed to receive 1 bottle of scotch and 1 of gin but there was a shortage of gin. The officers tossed and I won. I'm doling it out to my men in degrees. Now that I have it I have no particular desire to drink it but when you live as close as I do to the men, and also go through the same ordeals, the bottle always passes around. There isn't too much distinction between officers and enlisted men, that is outside of orders which have to be followed*
>
> *Luxemburg*   *December 15, 1944*

The most generous form of charity is said to be given when someone is offered a way to earn a living and provide for themselves. That was exactly what you did for several people when you were an owner of a delicatessen-restaurant in Flushing, NY. Counterman, waiter, there was always a spot if someone needed a position. These were not just any jobs, but employment that provided very good income in exchange for hard work. You were willing to take a chance and offer an opportunity to those you loved. I think that if you could have had your way all the employees in your restaurant would have been family and loved ones.

Dear Roz,

Darling, don't hesitate to buy you a spring outfit. I'll be sending you money again as soon as I'm paid. I want you to have everything your heart desires.

France   March 21, 1945

When we were youngsters you were a provision salesman selling kosher meats to delicatessens on your truck route. You got up at 5:00 am and often didn't get home until 6:00 pm. You lugged barrels of corned beefs, tongues, pastrami, and bundles of frankfurters into store basements to be weighed in. It was hard work but you never complained. I remember numerous times the Boy Scouts or our Synagogue had a charity event and you would donate a full bundle of frankfurters to them. When a neighbor was sick or couldn't work you brought them packages of meat or frozen chickens. You never thought about the cost to you, only the benefit to the recipient.

When I graduated from the Polytechnic Institute of Brooklyn I began a job search because I wanted to get married. Graduate school seemed out of the question. After paying for my entire undergraduate education you told me to apply to study for my Master's Degree and marry Marlene. You would help us and we shouldn't worry about it. I'll never forget how we would travel from my Brooklyn campus to your home in Laurelton, Queens every weekend to pick up our "Care packages" of steaks, cold cuts, lamb chops, chickens, and whatever else we could carry home on the Long Island Railroad. You did this for us for four years until I finally graduated with my Ph.D. in Chemical Engineering. You never complained, never put us

99

down about taking so much from you, and indeed, made it possible for me to get my graduate education, get married, and have our first child, Norman. You said that if I did my part and got good grades, you would do your part and make it possible for me to be schooled. I heard many parents say that their children would have to earn their way through school or take out loans. You saw it differently; a student's work was his studying and no one should start off in life owing money. How fortunate I was.

Dear Roz,

I gave the people here a box of cocoa and we are getting a chicken tonight. Actually honey, I can take what I want but I was brought up to treat people like people and although I have a hate for these German people I still am not taking too much advantage of them. All we did was move in and took over everything in their house except their chickens, cows, and daughters. Yes my love, one 18 years old and the other 26 years old. Some of the men are licking their chops sexually but so far no attempt of rape has been made. Did you even know that an officer gets first choice? I may be tempted but I know my will power will suffice satisfactory.

Germany   *February 16, 1945*

There was one weekend we forgot something at your house after visiting. I don't remember what that item was but I do recall that you drove out to us late at night to deliver it. Nothing was too hard for you. It was as if you considered your free time valueless and gave it away to whomever needed it. Boy Scouts leader, taking the scouts away for weekend overnight hikes, giving people rides if their car broke down – what didn't you do? These acts never seemed like a burden to you, you were just being who you were.

Dad at a Memorial Day celebration.

When your friend Jim had to go into a nursing home, you drove his wife Ronnie to see him every day and picked her up when her visiting was through to take her home. You did this for months until Jim finally passed away. What greater way is there to tell someone, "I care for you." Your home was always open to visitors, and in spite of knowing they would be subjected to your rougher side, they came in droves. Beautiful meals were served and everyone was made welcome.

You were as generous to us at home as you were to others. Mom had complete control of the finances in the house and you trusted her. You never asked why she bought herself a new dress, which she rarely did, or why we had new sneakers. Whatever we needed you got us. Our family didn't have a lot of money but whatever you did have was spent ungrudgingly on us. You didn't need expensive clothing or cars for yourself. You were happiest when you saw us with something new. The first air conditioner in our house did not go into your bedroom but into the room I shared with my brother Mark. I can remember the whole family sleeping across our beds when it got especially hot.

My first car was a new Chevy convertible with air conditioning you bought for me and Mark. I am truly amazed at how generous you were with your minimal income and negligent savings.

Dad, while I was giving the eulogy in the cemetery at your funeral I looked into the large crowd of people in attendance and I couldn't see one family you had not touched with your generosity. I hope, when my final breathes have been taken, people will be able to say with regards to my generosity, "like father, like son."

Love, Rich

The Letters – (Cont.)

Russian paper, Izvestia, claims the US troops are in Iran illegally, without a pact, in play for oil.

November 5, 1944   France

Dear Roz,

I have a few minutes before I leave again for a new depot. I'm standing by with all my equipment. Pack and unpack. Last night we had steak and it was the first good meal since I hit France.

◆   ◆   ◆

Roosevelt wins but his vote margin is the smallest of all 4 elections.

November 9, 1944   Belgium

Dear Roz,

I haven't written in the past few days because I couldn't get the chance to write. We are moving around and now I'm in Belgium. This is just the nicest country I've hit as yet and the people here are very friendly. France is all shot up and there is plenty of evidence of a war going on there. Riding around in box cars is really rough and of course, with no toilet facilities, it didn't help any. Now we are living in a building with a roof over our heads which is much more than I expected. You still have no cause to worry as I still have a few more stops before I'm in the front lines.

The Germans cleaned out France and Belgium and the people here are really down but not out. When we arrived they brought us out some coffee and cake and there are soldiers living in civilian homes all over town.

103

◆   ◆   ◆

Russians cross Tisza River; win 45 mile bridgehead near important rail hub with Slovakia.

November 10, 1944   *Belgium*

Dear Roz,

We are in what is called a rest camp. Units which have been at the front are taken here for a rest period. I still am a replacement with this package and haven't received any news as yet. So we are sitting tight.

I meant to write more about France in my previous letters. They have outdoor urinals on the streets. All it amounts to is stepping inside a tin enclosure with about two feet of your body concealed. Women can stand and see you and talk to you while you're taking a pee. I'm telling you it's really comical but that's the custom here.

Some places I've seen were really bombed to the ground and if it weren't for that, I'd feel exactly like a sightseer and not a soldier.

There is a place across the street from us where I can go and wash up and get some clothes washed. For a piece of soap or cigarettes you can get anything you want. The women of Paris can really dress and some of the coats and hats I saw there were beautiful. Their hats seem to be very large and some of them do their hair up straight up in the air. I guess it's held together by combs. They also have silk and nylon stockings and I'll be damned if I know where they get them. They were cleaned out on food though and they have a definite shortage of soap and cigarettes.

I sleep on the floor here in a sleeping bag and it's the best luxury I have. Someday I'll be back in a bed again.

Darling, I miss you terribly. It's a lonely time for both of us and of course I want to get a look at you and the baby again. I always wanted to watch my baby grow up but I lost the opportunity on this one. However, if I wind up this war without having my NUTS shot off we will have more children. (The) next one will be a girl that looks and acts exactly like you. I show the picture of you and the baby to everyone who is willing to look at it.

◆　　◆　　◆

Armistice Day celebrated by Allies in Rome.

November 12, 1944   Belgium

Dear Roz,

Of Course some GI's have already located the local house of ill repute and the price varies from a cake of soap up to about 100 francs. My social life here has been confined to a little drinking and some sleep. It's so dark due to blackout restrictions that I can't see where I'm going and I'm glad I bought the searchlight in England.

I don't know what to write about this place. Men go every day and there is no telling when my turn will come. However, with my number of special duty it may be some time yet.

I don't worry about that. It was too hard for me before we were married. I know that we both can do without certain things but when I get back home I intend to make up for some of the lost time. I'm getting the urge lately but I did it before and I can do it again. Don't worry about me honey, I'll stay clean.

◆　　◆　　◆

A book written in a German prison camp writes of gas chambers; 3 million Jews executed.

November 13, 1944   Belgium

Dear Roz,

Some of the men are having difficulty with their wives back home. They suspect them going out every night. A soldier never can fight well knowing that his wife is untrue to him.

◆   ◆   ◆

Russian army closing in on Budapest.

November 14, 1944   Belgium

Dear Roz,

I have a bad case of the runs and I have all I can do to hold out until I hit a latrine. I'm taking pills and everything else for it but it hasn't gotten any better yet. The water here is very bad and we can't drink it unless it has been purified with tablets, iodine, or chlorine first. I could use a couple bananas and that should do the trick.

I quit drinking too much as the stuff is expensive and doesn't pack any wallop. I have one or two beers at night and that's all.

◆   ◆   ◆

Germans put up a heavy fight at Metz but Americans tightening their grip as they crush the Nazi counter-attacks. British and French continue to advance.

November 16, 1944   Germany

Dear Roz,

Well, here I am in Germany. I wonder if this country will be the end of my wanderings. I'm in another replacement depot here. It's damn cold in this country and I finally decided to get myself the GI long overcoat. I don't know why I was told to bring my blouse and pinks as the only time I wore them was to go to London. So far the little I've seen of Germany (it) is the same as any other country here in Europe. Honey, did you think I would even be in Germany? Of course here there is plenty evidence of a war going on and I'm getting accustomed to various sounds. I passed the anti-tank dragon teeth of the Siegfried Line and they didn't look very impressive.

Believe it or not darling, here we live in tents on army cots. The officers have a tent here with a stove and tables for writing letters and that's exactly where I am now thawing out. I sure am hoping that I stay here a little longer; it's a good setup.

Honey I will admit I'm getting closer to where the activity is. I finally got a good idea of our air corps and you probably will read about it in the papers back home. As far as going into combat goes I'll admit that I'm just as scared as any other replacement however I understand that it doesn't take too long to become accustomed to it and then it turns out to be a job just like any other job. I know that in a situation like this one always tends to imagine that the worst is ahead. Why people look at things that way is because of their own particular problems. Those misfortunes are always in the extreme minority so you see it isn't really as bad as it looks off hand. Darling I know I'll be all right as I have so much to come home to.

◆   ◆   ◆

Germans evacuating 7,000 troops from Pointe de Grave northeast of Bordeaux, according to French military sources.

November 17, 1944   Germany

Dear Roz,

This morning I gained a little information about myself. I'm in what is called a forward replacement depot. From here we go to a division. That's the straight dope darling so we have to face facts here. This place is strictly business. I can hear plenty of artillery action where I am now and it took me quite some time before I went to sleep. I will admit that I didn't sleep so well last night.

It's cold as hell in Germany and I'm being issued a set of overshoes. I understand that jerry sent some artillery over last night but believe it or not I was asleep and didn't hear it.

◆   ◆   ◆

Churchill may stop aid to Zionists unless they oust the gangs from Palestine, accused of committing terrorist acts..

November 18, 1944   Germany

Dear Roz,

Another day gone by and I'm still here. I didn't sleep so well – too much artillery noise. Had pancakes and oatmeal for breakfast, hot coffee and washed. This brings me up to what I'm doing now, writing to you again.

I don't get too much news about what is going on in this sector but I can tell we are advancing by the sounds of artillery moving further away. I guess we must be gaining on all fronts but it's only a guess.

Love, Dave

SPEAKING THE NATIVE TONGUE

Dear Dad,

You always loved playing around with foreign languages. I know you were fluent in Yiddish and spoke it when you were a young boy at home. You were also pretty good with German, having learned it in school and the army, and you knew some French which I think you learned overseas.

Dear Roz,

I stopped in some department store and inquired whether I could send anything to America and I couldn't. I might add that I have a hell of a job trying to explain myself. I can't talk French but the most important thing is "we, we" which means yes. However, some people speak German and I get by with that language. It's a lot of fun with many arm and hand motions thrown in.

Belgium   *November 10, 1944*

This is one of the joys I share with you. I loved studying and learning French and German in school. I can still read French pretty well, all based on my two years of study in junior high school but I can't understand a word of it when it's spoken. My college German is very weak but I guess I could get by if I had to. I learned Hebrew studying in an Ulpan, a school for immigrants, in Israel when I spent a summer there in 1962. I knew it very well then and I bet I could be good again if I concentrated on it.

But back to you now. You certainly threw the phrases around when you had a chance. One of your favorite was, *Es darf sein a besserer weg,* meaning, "There has to be a better way (to live)." You would say this whenever things got difficult. When we went to a restaurant, all the customers were sure to hear you call out *garcon* for the waiter, or *mademoiselle.* You tested every language you knew on the server hoping they would respond to something. You joked with your barber in Russian and I'll never know where you learned anything about that tongue. When it was time to get up from our chairs you'd say *levez-vous* and if you needed a knife at dinner you'd ask for a *messer*. When you wanted someone's attention you would shout out *achtung*. We all knew exactly what you meant.

Dear Roz,

Darling, German is the language spoken here. I'm the only one in my platoon who can speak it a little and it helps us a lot. Yesterday, one of my sergeants requested the local house of ill repute so I asked a young fellow who lives in our building. I had a lot of fun as I never did learn how to request those things in German. He finally gave me the name of some girl and her house number and this sergeant took off. In an hour he was back complaining that the line in waiting was too long to sweat out. We had lots of fun anyway. Whenever any of the men want something they ask me how to say it in German.

Luxemburg   *December 27, 1944*

Yiddish was your favorite though. You had your health aides trained so that when you said *oy*, they would respond with *vey*. Once they caught on you drove them nuts calling out *oy* every five minutes waiting for the response.

Everyone who made a mistake was a *klutz* or a *schlemiel*. You even taught us the difference between *schlemiel* and *schlemazel*. As you loved to say, a *schlemiel* spills the soup and it lands on the *schlemazel*, the one with the bad luck. You used to say that Yiddish had more words to describe a clumsy person than any other language and you would proceed to recite as many as you could. Besides the ones I already mentioned there were *schmenuff*, *schmendrick*, and *kooney lemel*. I wish I could remember the rest of them.

If you got a waitress who knew a little German you would sing a German song to her and try out some bawdy language in German. Of course it was at the top of your lungs so the entire restaurant would hear. At this point Mom and the rest of us would look at each other with a "here we go again" look and sort of giggle but we really wanted to hide under the table. It's a good thing you wore your veteran's cap all the time so people gave you some slack and played along with you. I recall one time I heard you say to a waitress, *"Voulez-vous coucher?"* which means, "will you go to bed with me?" You never used language like that in English but somehow the foreign words allowed you to let down your mask of propriety a little.

Dad, looking back I'm glad you could have some fun with simple things like language. I'm sorry I lost patience with you when you began your repertoire in public and I regret feeling ashamed at your behavior. In some respects I wish I could muster up the courage and have some fun and play with people the way you did. You really did no harm and I'll bet those waitresses are still wondering what ever happened to that sweet man who used to sing to them in German.

Love, Rich

The Letters – (Cont.)

Germans have evacuated Faenza area; British and Indian troops find them gone.

November 18, 1944   *Germany*

Dear Roz,

We had another movie tonight, Casablanca. I saw it once before in the States.

◆   ◆   ◆

American air force pounds German rail lines and infantry position after a quiet day yesterday. American 1st army makes small gains.

November 19, 1944   *Germany*

Dear Roz,

This morning I had a little censoring to do. It seems that the only duty of the Officer of the Day is to censor mail. I suppose it could have been a larger assignment of work but I breezed through the mail and now I'm devoting my time to you.

You probably read in the newspapers of big things going on the western front. I know there is plenty of activity but I'll be damned if I know how they are making out. I guess we must be pushing ahead slowly. The damn artillery makes a hell of a racket and at night it seems they do their best to keep us awake. I'm still in the same replacement depot. If I move out I'll be in the 1st Army. You probably are reading about them in the newspaper now.

I wear size 10 shoes and when I went to the supply tent to get overshoes and an overcoat all I could get was size 14 shoes and a large overcoat. My feet are like Charlie Chaplin plopping around the mud. My overcoat is only about (?) inches off the ground. However, with all the mud around here overshoes make a world of difference.

◆   ◆   ◆

Estimates released by OWI show Japanese war dead 13 times American; 277,000 to 21,000. Japan has not depleted is manpower.

December 1, 1944   Germany

Dear Roz,

This is the first chance I've had to write to you. I scribbled a note earlier today but I didn't sign my name on the bottom of the letter and it may not go through.

You'd laugh if you could see me now. I have a two weeks growth of red beard. I haven't had a chance to shave yet.

Yesterday we came off the front and we had showers and a complete new change of clothes. I'm in the 4th Division, 1st Army and you probably are reading what we are doing in the home newspapers.

I know you are worried about me after not hearing from me for so long but darling I couldn't write. After seeing what combat is like I'm still smiling honey. This episode of my life is not going to change me in the least. It's rough and some people do get hurt but not too many. I'm in a good outfit and we get along fine. Most of the men got German pistols and other equipment off German prisoners we captured but I'm not interested in any of that crap.

◆   ◆   ◆

Japanese Navy is no longer a major threat to U.S. forces after taken heavy losses. Any point in the Japanese Empire can be attacked by our planes, either from aircraft carriers or land bases.

December 2, 1944   Germany

Dear Roz,

Darling, your ever loving husband doesn't take his clothes off when he retires in his luxurious foxhole at night either. I have a roof over my hole with three layers of bags and nothing can penetrate it. I have dug so many holes I hate to look at a damned shovel. All our digging is done with a shovel the size that children use to play in the sand with. We get hot meals here whenever we can get food up, and by God, it certainly is a relief to get away from K rations.

Darling I'd rather work 12 hours a day and never complain rather than be here. I wonder why everyone is striking back home. They should send those strikers over here.

◆   ◆   ◆

Germans are seen withdrawing from Italy; British threat in Bologna-Faenza a factor.

December 2, 1944   Germany

Dear Roz,

I can't write much about what we did but you probably read in the papers where the 1st army has begun to move. I read today's Stars and Stripes and it seems as if all the armies are moving forward. I would say that if any of these strikers back home were on the front line a few days or even a few minutes they'd go back to work immediately.

Speaking of 4F's, you should see some of the prisoners we have captured. They look like 6Z. One good thing about moving forward is that the jerries leave us good dugouts. However, I'm always unfortunate enough to have to dig one of my own. And how I can dig.

It was raining continually and it finally stopped so now we have a chance to thaw out and dry our stuff. I heard of (a) delousing station but there aren't any lice. What we do is go to a certain point, take showers and get all new clothes. My shawl certainly comes in handy and I've been wearing it since. I can't tell you how long I think this war will last as I don't know myself. The fighting hasn't been too easy of what I've seen, however I'm hoping for the best. I miss you very much and after the war is over I'd like to erase this episode from my mind.

◆   ◆   ◆

Less than a month after Athens was liberated the city now seems to be facing a civil war. Other countries in Europe watching to see whether free elections will be replaced by conflict after the war in other countries.

December 6, 1944   Germany

Dear Roz,

Surprisingly enough, no one seems to get sick even though we live under adverse conditions. I still have my nose cold but I don't think that will ever go away in cold weather. It has been raining every day and yesterday we had some hail drop for a few minutes. Sometimes we get a little snow but we've always got mud and that is our worst enemy as far as the infantry soldier in concerned.

I miss you terribly. I wish I could hold you in my arms and kiss you and crush you to me. Along more humorous lines the birdy hasn't let out a peep in weeks. I guess he is scared to death.

I hope you aren't too lonely sitting in without any recreation but honey, we will make up for all that when I'm home again. I'll never leave you again and I can't think of anything which I appreciate more than just being with you.

◆   ◆   ◆

Russians continue to make huge gains south of Budapest. Capital is threatened.

December 9, 1944   Germany

Dear Roz,

Well I have good news for you now. I last wrote you that we may move and we did. For the first time since I've been on the continent we are living in buildings and have heat and lights. My command post is the best location I've seen yet in Germany. Our mission here is different too. It's a sort of a real period with a holding defense. The last place we were in up in the woods near Aachen, you probably heard of that place, all we did was attack every day.

◆   ◆   ◆

Budapest is nearly encircled as two Russian forces meet. The Hungarian cabinet escapes to Vienna.

December 10, 1944   Germany

Dear Roz,

Well another day gone by and all is well. It's dark now and I'm writing from my office. I developed a hell of an appetite and I can't stop eating. My stomach feels as if it will burst right now. I had 4 pork chops for supper.

I have an entire farm house for myself here with every conceivable luxury so I'm not hurting. Why I even hear that we are getting our regular PX rations tomorrow...Cigarettes, chocolate bars... real living honey.

◆　　◆　　◆

The Japanese report that fires have broken out in Tokyo for the second time. Enemy radio reported 'small formations of B-29's dropped some bombs that started fires in the city'.

December 11, 1944   Germany

Dear Roz,

Today was a busy day for me. I was pay officer and I had to go from one outpost to another. In one platoon area I had fried chicken, in another they had killed a young cow and I had veal cutlets, and in another I had steak and coffee. I can just about move after eating so much today. It took me from 0800 to 1900 to finish and now I'm back in my CP. It snowed today and was cold and miserable.

Dave's father, Hyman; his mother, Fannie; Dave; and his sister, Ruth.

Now to answer some of your letters. In your first letter you're very angry at me because I didn't use air mail stamps. Darling, it's difficult to get them; that's why I asked you to send me them. You have to understand that there are no post offices on the Siegfried Line. I also can't help it if the mail takes long to reach you. I'm trying to write as often as I can under adverse conditions. And don't accuse me of being tight for a cent. Really, I had to laugh when I read your letter after what I've been through. Of course you still thought I was in England when you wrote it so I'll take the blame on myself. I promise to send air mail whenever I can.

Love, Dave

AN INFORMED CITIZEN

Dear Roz,

Back home people spend lots of money at resorts as this one here in Bavaria to vacation. I get the same for free. Wonderful isn't it? Now that all hostilities have ended I can think back to all the countries I have been in and it's really amazing. I have practically seen most of the continent already. What I have seen of Europe only convinces me that our country has more to offer than any here. The things I have seen in Europe also convince me that all of the so called European civilization is only a mask for what all these people really are. Life means nothing here. They talk about how wonderful family life in the home is. They all hate war, and yet they do nothing to prevent wars, and in their mad jealousy to outdo each other they forget all that very quickly and can only think of the barbaric method of doing things.

People may talk about the terrible communists and their way of doing things. Although I am not communistic in any way I can appreciate their way of doing things now.

We had a special school back in the States to learn our special officer's military government. Look how they goofed off in Italy. Suddenly those people we had been fighting for months became our buddies. The black market is prospering there and all political factions are fighting each other for control. Look what happened in Greece. Did they learn anything from all the errors they made? The answer is so far, no.

There is no set policy here in regards to refugee Germans and displaced personnel from other countries. They tell us to pick up all people on the roads and hold them. We pick them up as ordered and wind up at the end of each day with over a thousand stragglers who want to go back to their homes. At 9 o'clock all civilians are to be off the streets. What are we to do with all these people? What are we to feed them? Where is the military government officer? No answers to any of these questions. I can guess that they are all sitting in the large cities living in a luxurious style and issuing their muddled orders to our unit through channels. I am certain that this same situation is now taking place in Russian occupied Germany.

Although our policy is not to bring communism to Europe, Stalin just sits back and lets us make a fool of ourselves after we have so disorganized our area it will be ripe and easy plucking for communism. Stalin is really very clever in predicting our failures. It has happened in France, Greece, is occurring in Poland now and is certain to take place in Germany. I am willing to bet my bottom dollar that within ten years all of greater Europe is communistic.

I have never written or discussed politics with you before and you must be very surprised to receive a letter like this from me. It's only that I have some leisure time to think now and after going through what I have I'm not too keen about my son going through the same thing twenty years from now.

I even wonder whether the conference in San Francisco is of any great importance as the newspapers write it up. We definitely lack a good foreign policy and what we lack even more is some good intelligent diplomats.

Well darling, I believe I have said more than I should have now. Perhaps I am writing about something out of my limits and bounds but if I am, then that's exactly how the world problems strike the person of average intelligence. So that completes my letter for today. Darling, I hope you don't find my letters too uninteresting as I haven't too much to write about now.

Germany   May 13, 1945

Dear Dad,

I loved reading this letter. It shows a part of your personality that was so open to me. I will always remember how aware of worldly events you were. You listened to the news regularly, read newspapers and books, and you were always ready to debate the latest topics with anyone who would give you a chance. Your wealth of knowledge was truly amazing. I don't think there was any subject you did not know about and did not have an opinion on.

Your favorite books were war stories, either fiction or non-fiction. When you were reading you would share the storyline with us and include your opinion of whether the author was accurate or all wet. It didn't matter if you liked the book, once you read it you had its major points burned into your memory, available for instant recall. You knew what events a historical novel may have omitted to tell and you were eager to point out exaggerations.

Your opinions on books and authors were usually black or white, as were most things in your life. I remember you commented that a James Michener book on Poland never mentioned the millions of Jews that lived there and so you labeled it garbage. A biography of Eisenhower never mentioned that he was partying as D-Day began and so, it too, was crap. Most books, however, you were tolerant of and liked.

Dad and Mom on their engagement.

You liked to debate about the need for drilling for oil in Alaska, cracking down on illegal immigration, the merits of the Truman presidency, and the failure of George W. Bush's. You were a loyal fan of Bill O'Reilly on Fox Cable network news and rarely disagreed with him. You enjoyed bashing the social agenda of Liberals, but reserved some harsh words for Conservatives as well. You loved John McCain because he was a war hero and hated John Kerry because he had photographers filming him during the Vietnam War. You said you never saw a photographer on the front lines so Kerry must have paid to have them film him, to push his political future.

No one escaped being judged, everyone was vulnerable. Once you formed an opinion it rarely ever changed. From my perspective, debating with you was futile. I could not win a debate on your "facts" no matter how undocumented or wild they seemed to me. You just screamed your points out louder and shouted me down with a few personal insults thrown in for good measure, but this does not take away from your broad interest and knowledge of so many subjects.

It's unfortunate that you did not have a chance to go for some college classes when you were younger. You would have loved the opportunity to delve into many more cultural areas. Dad, in my opinion, you were the type of person who the great founders of the advanced learning institutions had in mind when they set up the original programs of learning for knowledge's sake. You would not agree with me, I'm sure, because you thought a college education had to lead directly to a good job or it was a waste of time. This is one area where I knew you better than you knew yourself and I say you would have loved plunging into history, literature, languages, and science, without a clear notion of where it would all lead. That's the beauty of the way your mind worked and you would have found a way to turn all that knowledge into a living for your family. And Dad, I get the last word on this.

Love, Rich

The Letters – (Cont.)

Tokyo radio reported the Palace Grounds hit by bombs.

December 13, 1944   Luxemburg

Dear Roz,

I'm writing from my new home. I made a slight change, nothing much to speak of. I guess in reading the newspapers you can see where big gains are being made all along the front. I'm hoping that General Patton really goes to town and breaks loose in his sector. I was reading where all those congressmen are visiting the continent now. I hope they find out what they want. I know I'll never see them as I never see the high ranking officers of my own unit. It's really much different than in the States. Back in the States our colonel would be around every day to find something wrong with us while here I've only seen him once and that was when we first met him in the rear. That's the way it is in the army. When General (McNain?) was here he visited the front and was killed here. It was an accident and I'll tell you about it someday.

The weather here is changing to real winter weather. It's cold and it rains almost every day. I hope it is clear each day so the air corps can move but so far the weather hasn't permitted too much activity.

◆   ◆   ◆

> *'The War is Lost'.* **Field Marshal Friedrich von Paulus and General Walther von Seydlitz, along with scores of other high ranking German officers called upon the German people to rise up against Hitler and Himmler for the good of Germany. Their broadcast, from Moscow, said the war for Germany is lost.**

December 15, 1944   *Luxemburg*

Dear Roz,

Before we know it Christmas will be here. One of my men is getting a real good Christmas gift, a 30 day furlough to the States. The only one who left from our company too. The qualification was to be hit or wounded twice and go back to a general hospital. We have men who were hit but never were evacuated. This sergeant was my platoon guide and he needed a rest. Whenever he heard artillery he would sit in the fox hole with me and shake. He couldn't help it. I'd give him a cigarette and talk to him but it didn't help. I finally was glad to see him go. I hope he really enjoys himself and gets some rest. He should, being that he comes from a quiet town in Virginia.

I'm not ashamed that I didn't wash today as that happens many a time. Perhaps I'm changing for the worst but when I get home I know that the temptation of a shower will draw me like a magnet. I hope my teeth don't go bad as I have neglected them terribly. To be truthful darling, I should wash here but the last place I was I couldn't waste the water needed for washing. It was more important for heating a cup of coffee after being in mud and water all night and day.

The enemy fired propaganda leaflets over to us asking us to quit or give ourselves up. We do the same thing and I wonder if these do any good. I know I've captured jerries that waved the safe conduct leaflet at us and said," Kamerad."

◆   ◆   ◆

Fierce battle rages for airfield at Metz.

December 18, 1944   Luxemburg

Dear Roz,

Darling, write me all about yourself. In most of your letters you only write about Dick. Remember you are still my number one girl and I'd like to read about you. I can picture you thinking and acting the part of the mother but to me you're still the 17 year old girl I met years ago and married. I don't know why I picture you that way but in my mind you'll never age. It probably will strike you funny as you read this, as you are thinking that it's no easy job giving birth and raising our son. I realize it's hard but I hope that when we both are old and gray I still feel the same way.

As for Richard, the little I remember of him is just raw meat hanging from his little bones. Perhaps I may sound hard in what I say but darling, I've never really seen him and I probably couldn't pick him out from amongst five kids. It really hurts when a father can't recognize his own offspring but that fault is not mine. Let's blame it on world conditions.

◆   ◆   ◆

Nazis pouring men into offensive against our lines. Situation is serious in several zones. We regain Stavelot and Monschau.

December 21, 1944   Luxemburg

Dear Roz,

I don't see why you should be broken up about Dave (M.) going overseas. I didn't notice any of your relatives breaking out in tears when I left. I'm sorry darling, I didn't mean to offend you. I'm just a bit tired and sleepy now. I'm a little jumpy now. I guess I need a rest. Other than that I'm still all right.

I guess by this time you've read the newspapers about the German counterattack. I don't know what to make of it myself but it may be their last attempt before they poop out.

◆　　　◆　　　◆

The German counter-offensive is fierce in many zones. Liege position dangerous as the enemy closes in. Meanwhile, the RAF bombed Trier and the Americans driving into Nazi positions elsewhere.

◆　　　◆　　　◆

December 22, 1944　　Luxemburg

Dear Roz,

I know you have been reading the papers about the counterattack the Germans launched and you must be worried. I'm still in excellent health and intend to remain that way.

RAF is attacking German positions round the clock. Hitting rail lines, Luftwaffe bases.

December 25 1944　　Luxemburg

Dear Roz,

Darling, things turned out rough here but we didn't give an inch to the German attack. It was really rough.

◆　　　◆　　　◆

> *Germans only 4 miles from Meuse and strengthening troop in area near river. Americans are pounding their flank and driving forward.*

December 27, 1944   Luxemburg

Dear Roz,

Today I had 2 fried eggs. We moved into houses with civilians and they have chickens so.... we had eggs with fried potatoes. They tasted so good that we didn't know whether to eat them quickly, eat them slowly, or just look (at them).

All the papers we read praise our unit for the way we held in the counterattack. I'm hoping that we are given a good long rest as it was hard on us sweating out one attack after another after going without sleep for days. There was an article in the Stars and Stripes about a prisoner who my platoon captured--save it as a souvenir.

◆   ◆   ◆

> *The French are expected to call up 200,000 troops soon to help with the German counter-offensive.*

December 30, 1944   Luxemburg

Dear Roz,

I have some captured jerry paper and I'm writing by candlelight. Incidentally, you can send me some candles. We have no light and we can always use candles. I live in a cellar now and it's cold as hell. I sleep with all my clothes on. I can use a shave as well. My beard doesn't grow quickly since I stopped shaving. I promise to shave often enough when I'm home. You'll never complain of my beard rubbing and hurting your face.

I guess everyone back in the States became worried over this recent counterattack. I myself don't know what to make about it other than we stopped the attack in our sector.

◆   ◆   ◆

In the western sector of Italy, Germans seen increasing movement of troops and supplies.

December 31, 1944   Luxemburg

Dear Roz,

Today is the last day of the year. Happy New Year darling. I hope that it will find us home together. I'm looking forward to this war ending quickly so we all can go home. I'll be damned if I can see what the Germans are fighting for. They don't eat well and it's only their officers who keep them together. We have many who give themselves up.

Today I was on patrol and ran across a few dead jerries. I borrowed a cleaning kit for my rifle off one. I don't go in for any souvenirs as others do. I have only one interest and that is to get home with my family.

I guess the Germans aren't too happy with their attack as they certainly are getting their lumps at present. At least we were able to get them out from behind their Siegfried Line. That was a tough nut to crack at Hurtgen.

Love, Dave

A Visitor

My father, for example,
who was young once
and blue-eyed,
returns
on the darkest of nights
to the porch and knocks
wildly at the door,
and if I answer
I must be prepared
for his waxy face,
for his lower lip
swollen with bitterness.
And so, for a long time,
I did not answer,
but slept fitfully
between his hours of rapping.
But finally there came the night
when I rose out of my sheets
and stumbled down the hall.
The door fell open

and I knew I was saved
and could bear him,
pathetic and hollow,
with even the least of his dreams
frozen inside him,
and the meanness gone.
And I greeted him and asked him
into the house,
and lit the lamp,
and looked into his blank eyes
in which at last
I saw what a child must love,
I saw what love might have done
had we loved in time.

—from Dream Work (1986) by Mary Oliver

THE STRAIN IS SHOWING

Dear Roz,

I'm back with the Company again and I have just finished reading all my mail. I was especially interested in your mail as you are beginning to write with a new slant on things. I can't understand why a woman attempts to read in between the lines of everything I write. I never did attempt to give you the impression that I'm jealous of you having a bath. Darling, what I've been trying to tell you is that everything you have at home is only found in the U.S.A. That's what we are fighting for. I'm sure I said that I'm glad that you had everything at home to add to comfort which the people here have never seen.

Of course you misinterpreted my writing, that with all the luxuries you have you can do very well without me or something like that. No darling, that was not what I intended to write. I don't want you to be so choosey in what you write to me and I wasn't mimicking you or belittling you over the joke you sent me.

Honey, just what is wrong? Your letter doesn't even sound anything like you. I know that at times I may not write too well or may be a bit sarcastic but I didn't mean to and its only when my emotions are swayed by some incident here do I write that way. Darling let's forget all this nonsense and get back on the ball again.

Please don't feel that Dick is the only one you can write about. Darling, please write the same old way and don't think in trying to choose your words. I look forward to reading your mail and I don't care to read a letter different in character than the person writing it.

Darling, I miss you very much. Be careful of your cold. I hope Dick doesn't have too much trouble teething. From your letter I know he's growing to be a big boy. It just dawned on me that Valentine's Day had passed. Thanks for remembering it Darling. As for myself, I'm afraid that I goofed off again. I don't remember dates and had no idea it was Valentine's Day. Darling, please don't feel too badly as you're my Valentine every day of the year.

Oh yes, I remember another choice subject of yours. You wrote that I try to write every day because of habit and that's not true. I write because I want to write to you. I want you to receive mail from me so you don't worry. I want to write all that I can to you.

Darling, that just about covers all I have to say. Please be your old self again in your letters. I think of you and the baby always,

Germany   *February 24, 1945*

Dear Dad,

My heart is crying for you. You must have been terribly surprised and hurt by what Mom wrote. I can feel the pain you were going through when you read her letter and I want to cry out... THAT'S NOT FAIR.

Dad, these two letters have so much in it for me to digest it is taking me quite awhile. I wish I had the letters Mom wrote to you so I could see both sides of the discussion and attempt to see where Mom was coming from. Although you questioned why she read between the lines of your letters, I must do exactly that to try to understand what she was thinking and what she must have been going through at home.

I probably shouldn't be doing this but I must take sides in this lover's dispute between my parents. Dad, I sit solidly on your side. I have read every line in every letter you wrote to Mom for the past several months and I cannot not see one thing you wrote that should have been taken in a negative way by her. You were extremely demonstrative of your love for her and me in every letter. You have tried to keep her informed of what is going on without overly worrying her about the horrific conditions you faced on the battlefield. It was very obvious to me when you were using sarcasm as a mode of humor and I never took any of those passages to mean you were serious, although I didn't always think they were very funny. When you talked about the conditions you saw in Europe and compared them to those in the States I knew exactly what you were getting at. Europe was a very different place than it is today and most people can't imagine it being so poor. The war made conditions even tougher on its citizens.

Dear Roz,

Darling, many a time I want to write about how much I miss you and Dick. I don't know exactly where to start. I find it very hard to keep from getting blue when I think of home and finally wind up my letters. Please bear with me and be patient. Don't try and find too many faults with my letters because I don't always think normally under these adverse conditions. I try darling, but I get choked up in the writing. Be good darling. I love you both with all my heart so write and let me know that all is well again.

Germany   *Feb. 15, 1945*   *(the next day)*

Furthermore, I don't think it was fair for her to write you letters which would clearly be upsetting to you while you were fighting on the front lines. Your conditions were filthy, cold and utterly uncomfortable. You were plagued with body lice, you were tired from lack of sleep, and fearful at all times that you may be breathing your last breath. She knew how much you looked forward to her letters because you reminded her of it daily. How could she consciously make things worse for you?

I can see no rational reason for Mom to be upset by anything you wrote. I chose the word rational very carefully because I think her response to you was totally out of character. I believe she must have had great difficulty struggling with her life and living conditions at that time. I try to picture what it was like for her but everything I come up with can only be a guess. We do not have her letters to you which would have explained things much better.

Mom's greatest fault is that she never thinks she deserves to put herself first, before anyone else. She treats herself as if she deserves constant punishment and the role of heroine is very familiar to her. What turmoil was she going through then, to warrant such a response to your notes?

Maybe it was because she missed you terribly and was wracked by constant fear after listening to the evening news broadcasts of the war on the radio. Was she thinking that she would have to raise me alone as a young widow? Maybe her imagination ran wild after reading some romance book or listening to stories her friends told her and thought you would find someone else in romantic Paris to love as soon as you went on leave there. Perhaps she worried what it would be like living with you after you returned; after all, you hadn't lived together at all since you were married, and in truth, hardly knew each other. I believe she must have been wrestling with some pretty dark demons when she wrote to you.

Despite all this, your response to Mom was beautiful. You gave a clear explanation of what you meant to say and why she misunderstood you, written in soft, clear words. They told her, in the most loving words, that you wanted her to write to you from her heart and to have patience with you. You followed up with a mature request when you wrote, "Darling lets forget all this nonsense and get back on the ball again." I must tell you that I am greatly impressed with the way you handled this situation but I am at the same time greatly puzzled.

Dad and Mom going someplace special.

These letters do not sound like they came from the father I knew. Where was the uncontrolled anger and rage and where were the accusations of crossing you? The father I knew would have no tolerance for a wife that questioned his motives. He would have demanded to be treated better and not questioned. When he was under as much stress as you were on the front lines, my father would have a very short temper and would have no patience for flowery words. I'm missing something here and I have no idea what it is. I can say that I never saw the man who would have said those beautiful words in this situation. If I hadn't seen your signature and recognized your handwriting, I would not have believed it was really written by David Leitman.

When did the transformation take place? There had to be a transformation because my father would never have been able to pretend so well with his words, especially under wartime conditions. Was it the war itself that did it to you, or was it a combination of war and readjustment to a civilian lifestyle?

Whatever it was, I was cheated from knowing my "original" father. Were you aware of the change taking place in yourself? I wonder how my life would have been different if the change hadn't taken place. These are some more of the questions that remain unanswered.

I think I will read these two letters one more time to see what else I can take from them.

Love, Rich

The Letters – (Cont.)   1945

> *The Supreme Headquarters found that the Germans killed 115 prisoners. They lined the Americans up 6 deep to be shot.*

January 1, 1945   Luxemburg

Dear Roz,

Last night was New Years Eve. At 12 midnight the jerries rewarded us with a Roman candle fireworks exhibition. I didn't know they observed these holidays. It's cold as hell now and I still wear the woolen scarf you gave me. As a matter of fact, I'm wearing it continually for two months. I caught a nose cold and I can't get rid of it. It's most annoying. It snowed again last night and the countryside looks real pretty. It's too bad we can't be enjoying it together in peacetime.

Right now I'm sitting next to a stove warming up and trying to get up the ambition to shave a week's growth. I practically forgot what it's like to wash every day. I know I can use a bath however in this cold weather one doesn't get too smelly. I'd bet you'd notice that I have BO in a second. I remember how particular you were about cleanliness. I don't believe you would enjoy living the way I do here.

We received a new officer here and he's taking over my platoon. I move up to exec as I'm the ranking officer next to the CO. I'm staying with him until he is oriented and then I go to company HQ.

Darling, this is the first day I've been able to relax during the day and write a decent letter. I'm usually out trying to improve our position. My platoon is always striking out on an exposed flank and we always have to keep on the ball.

◆   ◆   ◆

American troops cut the German waist above Bastogne. Enemy is fighting fiercely to loosen Allied hold.

January 2, 1945   Luxemburg

Dear Roz,

You probably will wonder how I find so much time to write. I've been relieved of my platoon and although I live with them I have a job more or less of supervisor. It's pretty quiet here now and everyone is going through all the buildings looting. I haven't reached that stage as yet but I did find a picture of one of the towns here.

This morning I took a shave. We are in the 3rd army now and General Patton demands for his soldiers to have their hair trimmed and be cleanly shaven at all times.

◆   ◆   ◆

1,100 American bombers taking their toll on German supplies from the Belgian border to Frankfort. The 8th Air Force striking for 12 straight days. Meanwhile, RAF pounding Ruhr plants.

January 4, 1945   Luxemburg

Dear Roz,

Today I gave our mail orderly enough francs comparable to $100 to get me a postal money order. I'm going to mail it to you when I get it. Also, I did sign the voucher sending you $50 out of last month's pay so within a few weeks you should receive $150. Buy yourself a good outfit honey. I want you to dress well.

◆   ◆   ◆

RAF hits Berlin and Hanover with 1,000 bombers. American fliers hit supply lines.

January 6, 1945   Luxemburg

Dear Roz,

Today was a big day. I received my first package. We had a good headquarters dinner. Tomorrow we will have kippered herring for breakfast. Also I have one bottle of cognac as my ration. I was promised one bottle of gin, one of scotch, and two champagne bottles. I've paid for them already. All I have left is 1500 francs. Also, I was told that we can't get it until we turn in our empty cognac bottle. This is a screwy world, isn't it?

You wrote that the censor cut out a lot of my letter. I'm on the front now and I still do not have any idea as to what's going on. By the way, I'm in General Patton's army now.

◆   ◆   ◆

83 Japanese ships destroyed by U.S. Navy sinking 25. 330 planes hit in Okinawa and Formosa.

January 7, 1945   Luxemburg

Dear Roz,

Today we had a war correspondent with us in my OP. We beat off the first counterattack and he wanted to write up the story of the battle. I heard about these boys but it's the first time I ever saw them. I still have yet to see any rank up here with us.

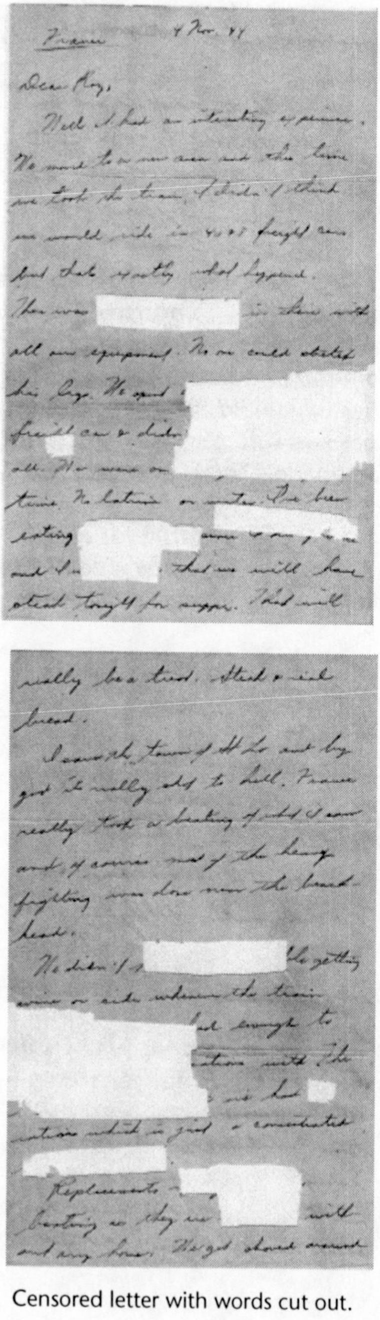

France 4 Nov. 44

Dear Roy,

Well I had an interesting experience. We moved to a new area and this time we took the train. I didn't think we would ride in 40 & 8 freight cars but that's exactly what happened. There was in there with all our equipment. No one could stretch his legs. We spent freight car & didn't all. We were on time. No latrine or water. I've been eating and I that we will have steak tonight for supper. That will really be a treat. Steak & real bread.

I saw the town of St Lo and boy it really shot to hell. France really took a beating of what I saw and, of course most of the heavy fighting was done near the beach head.

We didn't getting water or eats whenever the train enough to ation with the we had ration which is just a concentrated

Replacements bouncing as they are will out any time. We got shoved around

Censored letter with words cut out.

My feet have been bothering me lately. My heels get sore when I walk. I don't think my shoes fit so well.

Darling, how I miss you and Dick. Not a day goes by that I don't spend idle time thinking of you and Dick. Darling, sometimes I can even feel you in my arms, and subconsciously I hold you closer and tighter. I know that it's harder on you physically than on me. You still have your every day life. I don't have any sexual desires. It really surprises me and sometimes I wonder why I never seem to have any desire or feelings. Living the way I am now I can go on indefinitely without feeling so if I'm losing out (?). I think the real reason is that because if I can't have you I have no desires for anyone else. I wonder if all this sounds strange to you.

In one of your letters you tell me that I should go out and have a good time and also let you know of all the women I go out with. Honey, there aren't any women where we are. All civilians we moved from front line areas. Besides, you're my shining light and no woman I ever saw could even give me the same feeling as I get when I see you. You'll always be my No. 1 girl. You'll see darling, I'll be a model husband when I'm home.

◆   ◆   ◆

Reports of new anti-Nazi actions in Germany.

January 10, 1945   *Luxemburg*

Dear Roz,

Well I finally lost my writing paper, stamps, envelopes and everything connected with letters. I'm getting so damn absent minded that I can't locate or remember where I placed various items. We made a move out and I lost it during the move.

By God, its cold as hell and my feet are freezing now. At present I'm executive officer and I have no platoon anymore. So far it's

*just taking care of small things. Things are very quiet here now
and I keep reading the newspapers looking for any worthwhile
news. I keep wondering what you thought when you read
about the German counterattack. You probably knew from my
letters that I was stationed somewhere in the vicinity of it. You
probably were worried and I've been trying to write to you and
let you know that all is well with me.*

*Today I received two bottles of champagne as my whiskey
ration. We get everything except whiskey which only means
that officers to the rear make the best selections first. I don't
particularly care for champagne and I'd settle for one bottle of
rye whiskey. However, I can't complain. I still haven't sent the
money order as I haven't received the money order from our
mail clerk yet. I requested that $50 be sent out of my pay and
you should receive that within a week or two. If things remain
the same way next month and I find no way of spending any
money I'll do the same thing again.*

◆　　　◆　　　◆

Russian army closing in on key German base near Komarno.

January 10, 1945　　　　　　　　　　　　　　　*Luxemburg*

Dear Roz,

*$100 special. Just got the money order so I'm mailing it to you
quickly. The mail clerk is leaving now so I'll make this a short
letter. Buy whatever you want. Consider it my Christmas gift to
you and Dick.*

◆　　　◆　　　◆

MacArthur moving swiftly uniting beachheads in Luzon. Americans are reported 10 miles inland. Expecting a fierce battle soon.

January 11, 1945   Luxemburg

Dear Roz,

I think the reason I'm not receiving mail now is because the jerries captured a hell of a lot of our mail in their attack. However, it should begin coming in again soon. Yesterday I took a shower. It was cold as hell and we undressed in one building and went into a barn next door wearing overcoats over our bare skin. Well it was a good shower and I got a clean change of underwear. It's been 6 weeks since my last shower.

Darling, it's real winter weather now and I can't see how there can be too much fighting.

◆   ◆   ◆

Norway still occupied by Soviets due to lack of allied replacement troops.

January 12, 1945   Luxemburg

Dear Roz,

I'm making it my business to write a letter every day. We were told that with the amount of fighting there must be some men who rate awards of one type or another. Well as executive officer I have my hands full writing them up. This keeps me pretty busy. The Stars and Stripes had an article on one of our companies and I'm sending it to you. Also, a copy of our regimental newspaper with a commendation from the General.

Dad, Mom, and Richard with brother Mark in the carriage.

Darling, don't be alarmed though. We don't fight every day. Now we have it very easy and we relax during the day. I finally was able to buy one of those cigarette lighters that are always advertised as going overseas to the men of the armed service. We got one this month and I snagged it. It cost me 50 francs or a little over a dollar.

You make a very silly remark. Have I found another that I love? Honey, I haven't seen a woman older than 14 in two months. I think the jerries took them all away but if you think I can fall for some 14 year old country kid, you're sadly mistaken. Don't worry, I won't forget you. I still love you darling.

So you took a permanent wave. You must be fixin' to step out with someone. Honey, are you still faithful to your daddy? I know you are.

◆　　◆　　◆

Patton ambushes Germans in surprise ambush. Takes 400 prisoners. Germans caught in squeeze play.

January 12, 1945   Luxemburg

Dear Roz,

I've been writing up awards all day today. I've put men in for bronze stars, silver stars and even the DSC. Darling, you say that every one hears from me except you. I think I can explain that. I've been writing V mail to everyone else and saving my letters for you. I know now that V mail is much faster. Darling would you rather receive short notes or these letters which I can really write how much I love you. Why it takes at least 2 Vmail letters to tell you how much I love (you) honey. Please don't be angry as you know that I'd much rather not write to anyone until your letter is off in the mail.

So Milton is intent on joining up. I'd rather see him in the navy. At least he'll never have to live under the same type of filth as I do. It's clean in the navy and they are always sure of getting a hot meal. I think if he is foolish enough to want to join let him and let him also'v find out for himself.

◆　　◆　　◆

German attack halted in Belgium as counter-offensive falls apart there.

January 13, 1945   Luxemburg

Dear Roz,

Today I received the package with the whiskey, fountain pen, Camels, and pipe. I drank part of the whiskey, smoked a few of

145

the Camels, am now smoking the pipe and I'm writing with the new pen. That is exactly how useful everything was. I didn't notice any wristband. Darling thanks a lot. You needn't send any cigarettes anymore honey, as I have more than I can use now. I hope I receive the bracelet as I'm looking forward to wearing it again soon.

So You Gripe About Weather

IF YOU have any complaints about the weather here, take a look at Pfc. Dominick Del Corso (left) of 406 South 15th St., Newark, and Sgt. Frank Andress of Elkton, Md., on 3d Army front in Luxembourg.

Speaking of the cold, for defecation purposes we have a hole dug and it's very cold while one is indulging in the act. Boy o'boy, I'd like to be sitting in our bathroom reading a paper and relaxing. Oh well, those days are good to look ahead to.

Honey, we're eating hot meals again and I believe I'm getting fat. What do you think of that? Honey, it was good to receive a package from you. It made me very happy and I felt very close to you.

I was awarded the combat infantry badge which is rewarded for meritorious combat service. It's a badge with crossed rifles on a blue field with a wreath around it. Doesn't mean too much honey other than for not going to the rear when trouble starts.

Honey, things are going well with me. Since I had a little snort out of my milk of magnesia bottle my cold is practically better already.

Say honey, I'm in a good mood now and I wish I could just kiss you for your package. I'd love to crush you in my arms until you screamed and then I'd tell you how much I missed you. Darling I promise never to ever think of anyone else so don't even write me that I stopped loving you.

Honey, tell my son that I'm going to take him to wrestling bouts, boxing bouts, baseball and other sports when he gets older. Tell him that I'll play with him when I get back and we'll have great fun together. Oh yes, we'll take mother along too.

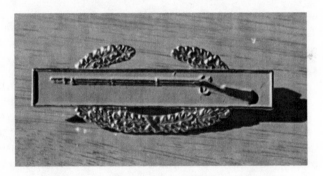

Dad was awarded the Combat Infantry Medal.

◆　　　◆　　　◆

Stern Gang in Palestine resorting to tactics used by the Irish Republican Army to drive the British away.

January 14, 1945   Luxemburg

Dear Roz,

This month I begin my 5th year of soldiering. Remember when I joined for one year.

◆   ◆   ◆

Commander of the U.S, Army Air Force, Gen. Arnold, said much more in store for bombing raids on Japan. Just getting started.

January 14, 1945   Luxemburg

Dear Roz,

I finally got a chance to write a type-written letter to you. I'm going on pass tomorrow and so far I don't feel too enthusiastic about going even though it's my first pass in the ETO. I sent you all my money but my pass is only for about ten hours. It seems that General Patton only approves of passes less than 24 hours. I just noticed that once again I have the wrong year on my date. I can't seem to remember that this is the beginning of a new year. I am getting more absent minded every day, something like Al.

It's been so long since I last attempted to type that I lost my speed and also where most of the keys are located. Besides, I'm writing by candle light now and I'm not even able to read what I'm writing. I am just about able to see the keys.

We captured some records from the jerries and believe it or not the voice (Sinatra) was included in a few of the records. We are also getting to see moving pictures very often. Darling, I'm *getting accustomed to this type of living and I'm sweating out what it will be like getting back to civilian living again.*

Well darling, that's all for today. I hope this letter brings a few smiles to your pretty face. I want you to smile always darling and I'll do the same. Keep doing the good work with Dick and I'll help you later in his future training. So long for now darling and take care of my best girl.

◆　　　◆　　　◆

Confirmation from Germans of order to kill GI prisoners. Food shortages in Reich was given as reason for slaying

January 16, 1945   *Luxemburg*

Dear Roz,

This is the day after the day before. In other words yesterday I was on pass. I don't feel as if I did right going as there wasn't too much to do. Another officer and myself were given a jeep and 12 hours in the city of Luxemburg. There were too many soldiers there. We managed to contact his brother who he hadn't seen for over two years and arranged to drive halfway and meet him. Well we had two quarts of scotch but riding 40 miles in an open jeep in the cold weather soon cleared our minds and the scotch didn't take too much effect. We finally stopped at a place to eat and although I paid in Luxemburg money I received change in French francs. I gathered that we weren't too far from the French border.

Dave as a youth.

Well we drove back at night under strict blackout. The other officer decided that he wanted to get his horn scraped so I went with him. We kept riding around from one house of ill repute to another and the women, about 40 years old, didn't particularly strike our fancy so we left. Now mind you although the thought of what he had in mind tempted me it was only because of liquor I had to drink. Of course you understand. Little Joe has died as far as I'm concerned. I'll be a wolf after this war is over. I hope I don't go sterile in the interval. This is definitely a joke.

Darling, all in all I can still say that I've been faithful. Of course after the war the stories will be spread about the French prostitutes in Paris. I understand they really go in for real orgies but who the hell is in Paris. That's only for rear, rear, echelon personnel.

Well darling, it was my first pass and I told you exactly what took place. I returned about 4 pm. That's all for now honey. Don't worry about me, I'm fine. Take care of yourself.

Love, Dave

I'VE HAD ENOUGH OF WAR

Dear Dad,

This is one of the most difficult letters for me to write to you. Even now, I sense a deep sadness in my heart. I am fortunate to have escaped service on the front lines fighting a dreaded enemy. I never had to endure the horrible conditions that you were subjected to. I don't know the sound of incoming mail, and the fear that it might be addressed to me. I have never seen a friend with his guts hanging out and crying in pain, knowing there was nothing that could be done for him. I have not experienced looking into the terror filled eyes of the enemy, just yards away, trying to shoot me before I end his life first.

Dear Roz,

Darling, I'm getting tired of this war. Many people even here don't know what war is like. It's only here on the front where the enemy is close and we keep alert constantly can we realize what combat is like. Those people back in the States never will realize what their boys are going through here. Perhaps it won't be long before it's all over. As for myself, this is just a job that one gets accustomed to. It's grim and has effects which one never forgets. I'll never forget having to direct artillery fire on my own men who were being surrounded. Darling, don't worry about me changing. I'm still smiling and still enjoy a good joke. War has its amusing points too.

Luxemburg   *December 30, 1944*

War always begins with principles someone believes are worth fighting for. They start with words, resolutions and threats, broken pledges or the collective greed of a nation's people or maybe only its leader. The provocations are sterile, without pain and easy to enflame. Sometimes the underlying cause can't be rationally explained. A chance spark, without much meaning or intent, enacted by an anonymous perpetrator, begins an accelerating downward spiral of events that cannot be stopped, ending in a hell no one envisioned, not even the young men who would be chosen to be the front line players in the second act of a terrible tragedy.

Before the first shots are fired, do we bring the soldiers from the previous engagement, those who have seen the cost in human terms, into the discussion? Do the television correspondents question them about the sacrifice and downsides of a heated battle? Is the debate whether to engage, to negotiate, or to overlook the current incident a fair one, or is it one sided and fanned with patriotic slogans and words of hate? Are we being fair to the innocent civilians on both sides who will be asked to sacrifice so much, and the young boys who will be asked to do the work for the grown-up leaders, changing them forever? A youth is asked to give up his skateboard. A boy not old enough to drink in many states, who probably never voted, and who is too immature to marry, is given a weapon to kill and maybe be killed.

Dear Roz,

Darling, I want to write to you every day but you can understand that there are times when that is impossible. I know you are worried sick over what I've been in and what I'm doing here but as I told you in the past I'll always take good care of myself. I always have been open and honest in what I did but when the time comes to write from here I never know what to write.

As for myself darling, I've seen enough to make me hate war. I don't ever want to discuss or talk about this episode of my life.

Germany   *December 6, 1944*

But you know all this. You were that young boy, recently married with a son you barely knew and your life was changed forever. Dad, how does it affect a young mind when a boy is called to war and taught to kill? How do you turn off the killer switch when your tour of duty is completed and you become a civilian again? How long does it take for the nightmares to end? Of course I understand why you hated war and had had your fill of it.

I know many wars are necessary to fight as were your battles in World War II. The Nazi machine had to be stopped and their brutality put to end. As difficult as this experience was for you I never heard you say that the war was a mistake. You knew what you were fighting for and you accepted your responsibility honorably.

You could see the difference between supporting our fighting men and women while being opposed to the war they were in. Every time the television reporter talked about the Iraq war it was your signal to start blasting President Bush and how he was sacrificing our young kids for nothing. You cried when Marlene's brother, Irwin, was killed in Vietnam at age 18 and blamed that war on President Kennedy, who, you said, chose to take a stand against communism in a country with a large number of Catholics. You hung a yellow ribbon on your front door when your grandson, Frank, went to fight in Iraq, and an American flag hung on the side of your house. Your patriotism could never be questioned and you maintained a tender heart for our fighting children.

The war had a profound effect on you in many ways which were visible. I also continue to wonder about the unseen ways the war changed you. I remember when we all visited Israel in 1987 for my son Steven's Bar Mitzvah. This was before the Intifada and the region was peaceful. One night we decided to drive up to the top of Mount Scopus in Jerusalem to look out over the lights of the city. Mount Scopus is the site of the Hebrew University, but to get there we had to drive through small Arab villages as we wound our way to the top. I didn't realize what was occurring to you at the time, and that a deep fear had set in.

When we got out of the car to take in the beautiful site of an illuminated Jerusalem, you ran right over to some soldiers, who routinely position themselves throughout Israel, and told them we were trapped in enemy territory and needed an escort to get down from the mount, back through the Arab villages. They did escort us and I remember being somewhat annoyed that you had overreacted and cut short our beautiful evening. It never occurred to me that you were thrust into a situation where you were forced to relive your wartime nightmares. I was pretty insensitive, but I wasn't tuned in to your feelings and sensitivities at the time. I realize now I should have checked in with you throughout our trip.

I knew you carried a pistol for protection when you owned the delicatessen. Mom's dad was killed in an armed robbery in his grocery store in The Bronx thirty-five years earlier so I suppose this made you more cautious. I didn't realize how important guns were to you until I read your letters. We were not a gun family. You mocked hunters who spent all day in the woods trying to kill a little squirrel. You advocated gun control, yet I recently found out you had several pistols in your home, all legally registered. This was a secret part of your life, hidden from your children, only discovered after you were gone. How did you keep them hidden from us? If you thought you needed them for protection, why didn't you tell your children to get a firearm when they were older? Weren't we just as unsafe without a pistol? I believe you were caught in a paradox of knowing guns in themselves were unsafe to have around and weren't needed, and the scars you carried from combat, looking for snipers behind every tree.

I know I am a different man because of your war experience. An absent father for the first year of my life, returning home filled with nightmares and a short temper. Fears that would surface in unsuspecting ways at seemingly random times, all resulting from combat. I wonder, how different I would have been if you had not served as an infantryman in Germany. How would my fathering of my own children then have been different? War has its harmful effects on many generations.

My wish is that our leaders will realize the cost of war cannot be measured by statistics and territory occupied. It is far more reaching, affecting generations to come. May they choose wisely between the options available to them before they call up the troops, and then only when the victory is worthy of the sacrifices. Dad, you have my respect for the sacrifice you made for our country and I am proud of you. I only wish I had told you this in person.

Love, Rich

The Letters – (Cont.)

Speed of new German jet plane poses threat to allied armies.

January 16, 1945   *Luxemburg*

Dear Roz,

When I went to the rear on pass and asked a signal corps officer how things are he said, "Mighty rough here. We received some artillery, about 20 rounds, the other day." He was trying to impress me with how dangerous a position they were in. Of course he was dressed in greens and wore tie bars all over him. I don't wear bars on anything but my shirt collar. I never advertise the fact that I'm an officer. Those that have to know it, do.

Perhaps our sex life has dwindled, but what do you mean by the statement that I'll appreciate you more when I get home. I hope you don't feel as if I neglected you in the past.

So you cast your first vote. Perhaps I should be happy but I'm not. I don't want to know that you are getting older. I always like to picture you as a kid about 16 years old.

◆   ◆   ◆

Churchill denies the Germans are holding out and prolonging the war because of unconditional surrender position.

January 17, 1945   *Luxemburg*

Dear Roz,

Today I had an interesting experience. We found a large sled which is towed by a team of horses. We hooked it to a jeep and took off for a ride. The roads are icy as all hell and it wasn't long before we were really tearing along at a fast clip. We came to one sharp curve and then it all happened. The sled turned over and three of us went hurtling into space. I landed on my face and arms. I'm sore as hell now and I probably will feel worse tomorrow. The other officers are sore too but none of us were hurt. I always get bruised but never bad enough to be sent to the rear.

I just heard the good news about Warsaw being taken by the Russians. I hope their offensive will be a deciding factor in the termination of the war. Today I start my fifth year in the army and I will admit that it's a longer period of time than I ever expected to be in service. It won't be long before I'll really be an old timer in this army and my status will be that of an army veteran. I'm only kidding about this honey as I don't want you to get the impression that I really enjoy this type of living.

Oh yes, I got into a little card game yesterday. It was the first time I had played in a long time and as usual I had my unlucky day and went completely for 1500 francs. Money has no value here and I'm sending you an additional allowance of fifty dollars each month. Will you please let me know as soon as you receive the other money I sent?

♦   ♦   ♦

Although France has been liberated it is going through the worst winter of the war due to food shortages and destruction. French people showing bitterness and resentment.

January 17, 1945   Luxemburg

Dear Roz,

I'm in a hell of a reckless mood tonight. Maybe falling off the sled today affected my mind. I feel good tonight because for the first time since I've been in combat I'm listening to Bob Hope's program coming from Atlanta, Ga. All this talk of USO entertainers appearing at the front to entertain is strictly s—t for the birds. That looks good in the papers. Time out. Back again while Jerry Colona is singing.

Say honey, what wouldn't I give to be with you right now? I'm getting the urge for your companionship again and it hurts going on this way. Another few months of this type of living and I'll feel like a virgin again. It will be very interesting to see my own reactions when we are together again. In case I forget a few of the important musts that I learned in my youth I'm sure you will remind me as your memory was always better than mine.

For the censor who may read this letter I might add that in over three years of married life I doubt whether I've seen my wife over 100 days. I also hope my wife enjoys this letter as much as you do.

◆   ◆   ◆

American soldiers are using TNT to break through icy ground to make foxholes. The winter has been a serious hindrance to our forces.

January 18, 1945   *Luxemburg*

Dear Roz,

Today I received one of the packages you sent me. It contained one box of cookies. I immediately opened the box and I can truthfully state that there aren't too many left at present. Every one seemed to enjoy them including myself. Oh well, that's what it is for. By the way, I'm still waiting for the bracelet you were sending me.

One of the men received a letter stating that he just became a father. He has been overseas over a year now so you can easily imagine how low he feels at present. His views on women have hit rock bottom. As for myself I can't think of anything cheaper than a woman who feels that she is sacrificing more than her husband, risking his life daily. Darling, I'm not trying to give you a lecture. I'm only citing one example of things that do happen. I hope you don't misunderstand all I have just written.

Honey, do you really miss me very much? Each day that goes by finds me longing for you more and more. All of my future is entwined in both you and Dick and outside of that I can't see one good thing ahead. Already I'm wondering what our next little one will look like. Am I too far ahead of myself? Honey, does Dick look more like you or myself? Although you write me much about him you never mention this point. I guess curiosity has the best of me. As for yourself, I know that you're not exactly leading too happy a life at present. I realize that the way things are now it's much harder on you for many reasons. I want to help but I can't. There isn't anything I can do outside of writing often. I can only hope that you don't get disgusted and throw caution to the winds. I know you will always stick by no matter how long it takes.

◆   ◆   ◆

British troops northwest of Aachen widened the front attack line to more than 7 miles. Allied fighting making gains.

January 19, 1945   Luxemburg

Dear Roz,

This morning we had a snow blizzard and now it's as clear as a bell but cold. Well it looks as if the Russians are really going to town again. I suppose they will attempt an all out push now. In any event, I'll probably be in the middle of something myself soon. If only this would be the final drive and then home. I think that's about all the American boys have to hear.

I'll tell you something now. The day of the big counterattack I was supposed to go on pass but I refused. I didn't particularly care to go anywhere. Speaking of passes, one of the men who went to Paris was telling me about what he saw. He went into one *of the cafés and there were about six prostitutes sitting naked at the bar trying to get him to buy them a drink. Prostitution in Paris is a big business especially now with all the Americans there looking for some excitement. I suppose they get it too, also with syphilis and gonorrhea at times.*

What you have heard of Paris is true. The people there all have money but there isn't any food or cigarettes so they pay enormous prices for them. At present, many GI's are being tried for selling food to the Frenchmen. They should be too as we never get combat field jackets or shoes. Everyone in the rear areas have them. It's the old army game, every one handling combat equipment in the rear takes what he wants first as it goes down the line. The only thing left is the same equipment as we have now plus some used clothes so we wind up just the same.

Everyone here has been making fox holes by blowing up the ground with TNT. This place sounds like the 4th of July. I'm sweating out the Russians getting to Berlin and finishing this war here. I understand they still are going strong. Of course, we have no radios here and all the printed news we get is at least 2 days old. Darling, how can I keep you from worrying.

Honey, just how long we'll be apart before I am home again is the big question. I'll never feel right until I'm holding you in my arms again kissing you while you are sobbing away. That final moment that I hold you in my arms again is going to be the biggest thrill of my lifetime. Yes darling, I love you very, very much and until I'm with you again I can't get interested in any kind of amusement.

◆   ◆   ◆

> *Fighting has quieted in the Ardennes sector. Our men cleaning up.*

January 24, 1945   Luxemburg

Dear Roz,

It was so cold this morning I was practically frozen. Last night I slept in a sleeping bag, have 2 blankets and my overcoat over me and was still cold. Just about the time I fell asleep a heavy artillery barrage was fixed on the enemy and the ground shaking from the concussion woke me up. Later on during the night I had what is called a lovely dream, the first in a long time, and that woke me up again. The last time I was awoken to be told it was time for chow. That's how I spent last night.

Today I've been sitting around a fire and my chest is warm and my back cold. It's real living. I'm looking forward to seeing the article in Life magazine about the 12th Infantry. I wonder whether our company got any write up at all as we jutted way-out into enemy territory way up in the corner east of Echtenacht. We were the extreme right that held first and started the line around to the north.

Well today I haven't heard any news about the Russian front. I'm hoping that they are still going strong in the east. Anyway I'm sweating it out. I hope it isn't too long before this entire mess is over. I'm tired of it myself. I think I'll quit shaving until I go to a rear area. Sort of a strike for rest area.

◆   ◆   ◆

> **Major non-Communist resistance groups are meeting in Paris to discuss participation of Communists in government.**

January 24, 1945   Luxemburg

Dear Roz,

I haven't been able to write for a couple of days but today it isn't too cold and I can hold a pen in my fingers without freezing them. I'm back to outdoor living again and it's not too comfortable in this weather. It snows every day and all my stuff is always wet and frozen. However, I can't kick too much. I still wear the scarf I received from you last Christmas and it hasn't left my neck since I came overseas. I'm a little crammed here and my writing may not be too good. You'll have to excuse that though.

Darling, I was very happy to read of the confidence you have in me and I hope I justify or at least prove to be half the man you think I am.

◆   ◆   ◆

> **The Advisory Council of Allies has drafted a treaty for war end. Reported that all short term issues have been solved.**

January 26, 1945   Luxemburg

Dear Roz,

It snowed again last night and my overcoat had a few inches of snow on it. The cover over my hole is just a little short so I threw my overcoat over my feet and this morning I was snowed under. However I was very warm and comfortable. I was issued a new type of snow boot. It's almost long enough to reach my knee. However, it's warm and prevents trench foot. I finally got rid of my size 14 overshoes. Those were really clumsy and I couldn't walk very far without getting blisters on my heel.

Today has been a fairly warm day and the fire keeps me very comfortable. I was also issued a new 17 jewel Waltham wrist watch so when I get a chance I'll send yours home for you to use.

Darling the news from the Russian front is still very good and I still hope they continue to advance. I'm hoping that the war ends with a big surprise for us all. I'm very sorry to tell you that I'm back to platoon leader again. In this last objective another company lost a few officers and one of ours was transferred to that company. I'm back to the first platoon again. We all came through fine with hardly a scratch. I wonder whether the newspapers print everything about the 12th Infantry and what it does. It seems as if some brass just sits up at night figuring up attack orders for us.

◆   ◆   ◆

A report has been issued showing the heavy toll the Japanese have suffered five months after the U.S. Third Fleet began sweeping the Pacific under Admiral Halsey. Called a Japanese disaster.

January 31, 1945   Germany

Dear Roz,

First, I was in Germany again and it wasn't too bad getting there. Once again I began itching and suffering from lice so I went to see the doc at our aid station and his diagnosis was exactly the same. After going back through various ambulances I finally wound up at a very rear hospital and they still have no showers here. I really need a shower, some bug powder and clean clothes. Other than that I'm fine. I don't expect to be here more than a day so you can continue to write to my old address.

Oh yes, an advertisement in the Stars and Stripes that my bracelet was found caught my eye and I'm sending it to you. I've already written to them and perhaps it won't be long before I receive it.

I will say that living in a fox hole was rough as hell. I froze at night. Here in the hospital is nice and warm. I have pajamas and a cot with a "pillow". What more can I ask for? I hope they don't send me back too soon as I certainly can use a little rest. Combat is a tough strain on my nerves.

◆   ◆   ◆

U.S. commits to try Nazis for outrages against Jews and others in the Reich. British in agreement.

February 2, 1945   Germany

Dear Roz,

Well today my last day of vacationing terminates. I leave this hospital tomorrow morning. I've had every meal in bed as for three of which has been chicken. Honey, this is real living and it's almost a dream. I had all my clothes taken away so now I received part of them and have to go back through a replacement center. I don't believe it will take more than one day to get back. They also found nits in my hair in addition the lice on my body. Oh yes, I'm really going to hell with myself. I was thinking that you wouldn't even let me enter the door of our house. I hope you don't hold it against me when I get home. I promise to bathe frequently.

Honey, I keep my ears open for news of the Russian front. How much longer this war will last I don't know but I hope the Russian action will bring it to a close very shortly. I'm getting tired of fighting. This is the first real break I've had so far and I spent most of my time sleeping. I've only written to you so far. Now I leave tomorrow to go back to rough living. The other night before we were relieved I sat up in a hole with my sergeant holding each other to keep from freezing. Finally I sent a carrying party of about 10 men back about a mile through snow 2½ feet deep to bring back blankets. I was company commander for two days. Our CO was trapped in a tunnel and couldn't get out so I carried on. *Actually it isn't too bad honey, but I'm tired of living in filth and dirt. I try and make the most of it.*

You probably haven't read about my unit as yet as it hasn't been released for publication but you can always bet we are never left out of anything. Honey, how are you and the baby getting along? I can picture you scanning the Herald-Tribune *every day for news of my unit.*

◆　　　◆　　　◆

Expect allies to engage in a massive attack on western front soon.

February 4, 1945   France

Dear Roz,

I'll admit I'm slightly confused at present. You see when I left the hospital I expected to go back to my unit. Instead I found myself going back to the rear and right now I'm in France. The reason is that after leaving the hospital one must go back through replacement depots which is where I am now. I don't know what excuse I'll be able to give when I get back as I supposedly told them that I was going back for a shower and so far I've been gone four days. I'll probably be considered as being AWOL. However, I know I'm leaving for another depot tomorrow and from there I go to my unit.

It's been a wonderful rest and I've had a good chance to relax. The only thing that bothers me is my conscience. It seems to me as if I left every one that I know holding the bag while I'm back resting. After fighting with my men as long, a certain spirit of fellowship exists. I won't let them down and they are in the same feeling as I am.

The snow has melted quickly and it's been raining continually. I know that we have plenty of mud to look forward to until summer time.

Dave with Richard and younger son, Mark.

What I read in the Stars and Stripes about going to the Southwest Pacific from here has me a little worried. I would like to get back to the States first and spend at least 30 days with you. However, someone is going to remain here and it's hard to say right now who it will be. Of course all this will take place provided the Russians keep moving the way they have been.

I doubt whether our army can defeat the Germans alone. I don't believe the United States has made a total war out of it. There is only a few of us fighting when there should be three times as many armies. It's always the same divisions in every battle and we should have many more.

Being 4F is a lot of noise as the jerries have men 50 years old firing at us. I've captured all kinds of men and the way I look at it, if they can pull a trigger and hit our soldiers they are good enough for the army. Yes darling, our war department goofed off on that deal. Perhaps now they will attempt to correct their errors.

By the way, have the allotments reached you as yet? I hope you received everything I sent you. I'll send you more money when I am paid this month and you can also spend that as you wish. I haven't too much use for any money here myself.

Well darling, how much longer I'll be away from you I don't know. I miss you every minute of the day and I keep thinking of what it will be like holding you close to me. It's even a good feeling thinking about it. Then I remember how fresh and sweet you always strike me and at present I don't believe you would enjoy my presence too much. Is your cold improving any? As for Dick I know he is a big boy now. He probably can crawl around by himself and get into plenty of mischief. Keep trying darling and don't feel too blue. I'll always love you and keep thinking of you always. Nothing more to write about so I'll close with all my love.

Love, Dave

PRAYING TO GOD

Dear Dad,

You didn't seek God when you were in the war and you didn't find Him afterwards. This is another part of you I never understood. One could say that you were the luckiest man on earth. You survived being on the front lines with relatively minor injuries. You had a wonderful wife and four healthy kids who made their way in the world, becoming self-sufficient and contributing to society in their own ways. You always had employment, lived in nice homes, were healthy most of your life and died at the ripe old age of 89. You never owed money to anyone and had visitors that came to see you throughout the years. There are not many people who can claim to be so fortunate. What more could a man ask for?

> *Dear Roz,*
>
> *I don't know why you seem to think that I have you out of my mind. I know you think of me always but at times I can only think of what I have to do. It's hard to explain. I haven't felt the urge to pray to God yet. I think of it at times but that's another thing which I can't explain. It's just that at times things happen so quickly that there isn't any time for thinking about anything but self preservation. I'm not trying to alarm you at all darling but everything here is topsy-turvy and impossible to explain better than I have. Darling, if I write something which doesn't sound right please overlook it as I probably was on edge when I wrote or down in the dumps.*
>
> *Luxemburg*   *December 25, 1944*

Yet you never credited God for smiling down on you during your journey, for always looking out for you, for keeping you safe from the sniper's bullets. How else can one explain your good fortune? I'm not saying your life was easy; it was far from that. But things always turned out well for you. You didn't have much to complain about when the whole record is examined.

Richard Leitman with Michael Hollander

How do you explain this when most other people were not so fortunate?

You said your mother didn't want you to be a shuckler, one who sways back and forth during prayers, as is the custom among many religious Jews. This was her way of saying that she didn't want you to be ultra-religious. She didn't imply that there was no place for God in your life. I believe her advice meant for you to keep religion and everyday living in a balance that works for you.

As children we joined a Reformed Temple, one that was not so strict in preaching all the rules. When I was young, my brother and I studied for, and celebrated our Bar Mitzvahs. We went to Temple on the major holidays, lit Hanukah candles and always had a Passover Seder. Mom lit candles on Friday nights. Our home was not strictly kosher but we never brought pork into our kitchen. When we had breakfast in a diner, however, you loved to have bacon with your eggs. Clams on the half shell were another one of your favorite treats, but eaten only outside the home. Like many Jews, you believed in keeping your home "purer" than your body. My childhood years were indeed a mix of religion and secular living as grandma advocated.

Later on in life you became bitter towards religion and often criticized it. Of course these were the years I remembered best because I was older. It always came down to, "Where was God during the Holocaust?" That was the big discussion ender, the unanswered question that troubles many Jews even today. How could something like that have happened to millions of strict-practicing Jews who followed God's laws as fervently as they could?

It was difficult for me to learn more about your belief in God, being a member of the Jewish nation, and following religious customs, which I see as all separate things. The discussion always came down to the Holocaust and deteriorated from there. I wish you had been more open to exploring this important subject and I wish I hadn't been so intimidated by your raised voice and emphatic statements, and pursued the discussion. Now I will never know the depth of your thoughts.

168

On a family vacation.-Dad, Mom, Richard, Susan and Mark.

I am going through my own religious, or should I say, spiritual search. I have gravitated more towards finding God in less traditional ways, through meditation, by walking in the woods, by photographing flowers. I have difficulty accepting the logic behind obeying hundreds of religious rules that don't have obvious relevance to my life. I don't look down on them or find fault with those who believe in orthodoxy. These rules and traditions just don't have meaning for me. I believe God, the God of all mankind, has been kind to my family and I offer my thanks and blessings for that in my own way.

I am happy to be a member of the Jewish nation and proud of our contributions to the world culture and advancement of society. I also believe that knowledge of our religion is important to pass down to our children and grandchildren so they can make good decisions about how to find spiritual happiness and peace in their own lives.

You must be wearing one of your beautiful smiles as you hear my silent voice speaking to you now about God and religion. I write words from a world based on belief, rationality and feelings. You, on the other hand, are in a place where you are privileged to know the truth. My belief is that you are sitting in God's court with other righteous people looking down on the loved ones you left behind, and putting in a good word for us when we need it the most, to where it will do the most good,... to God himself.

Love, Rich

The Letters – (Cont.)

American army wins race to enter Philippine capital, Manila, 110 miles from beachhead.

February 5, 1945   *Belgium*

Dear Roz,

Still on my way back. I arrived here and still am not on orders to go back. This is sure a funny army. It is necessary for every able man to be at the front and I can't seem to get back. Of course, I can't object to the rest I'm getting. Perhaps good luck is still in my favor as I have no idea what my company is doing.

It's been raining regularly now and all the snow is melting. Also it is getting a little warmer. Tonight I went to see a Belgian movie. They speak in French and have italics written as in silent film days in Flemish. I had an idea of what the picture was about but that's all.

Everyone seems to be pushing on the both fronts and I gather that the increased pressure should bring this war to an end. I don't know how the jerries can take the continual pounding they have been getting. I know they must be having many casualties at present and they are stuck for replacements. The Russians seem to have stopped for a breather. Perhaps they are just massing some equipment for a final drive. I hope that is true.

The hardest thing of all is not receiving any of your mail. I should have a stack waiting for me upon my return. Unless I get back soon I won't be paid for this month. Isn't that tough? Imagine not having any money to spend here. However, if I'm not paid I'll send twice as much the next payday. How is our private bank roll coming along now? I know it's hard for you to save much with all your added expenses. However, don't deny yourself anything you need and whatever is left put away in the bank. I'll try and help you along as much as I can from here as I

171

have no need for any money unless I'm told that I'm getting a pass to Paris.

Honey, since I've been in the rear away from any nervous tension I've returned to normal sexually and I find myself missing you very, very much. It's been a long time for me now and I've been having some weird dreams lately. I know it's harder on you and I know you will wait for me just as I am. We both are only human but our love for each other is great and can only be satisfied with each other. Sometimes I lie and think about what it would be like when I see you and I feel fine until I realize how far away from you I am, and not knowing how long it will be before I hold you close to me again.

◆   ◆   ◆

Russians have upset a new Nazi pogrom by their sudden sweep into Germany. A confidential report from Berlin claims Nazis had planned to exterminate the remaining Jews in Germany.

February 7, 1945   *Belgium*

Dear Roz,

Today three officers walked in at dinner time and they were all dressed up wearing the CTO ribbon with 3 combat stars on them. They wore crossed rifles and I asked them what outfit they were in. The answer I got almost knocked me off my feet. They work in 12 Corps headquarters. I was in the 12 Corps until recently and I know that their HQ was 26 miles behind the lines yet they walk around as if they have been fighting this war personally. There are many people taking the credit that the dough boys are doing. We never even get a chance to get a combat ribbon issued to us. These other people have a job, it's true, but all they sacrifice is being away from home and nothing else. I used to say it's tough on Sonny B. being overseas so long but believe me honey, outside of the infantry and close artillery no one gives a damn how rough it is on the infantry. Of course they all sympathize with us and that's as far as it goes.

Some ordinance officers came in today with footlockers and all types of luggage. All I own is what's on my back. I don't know why I'm complaining like I am, other than it disgusts me the way combat men are treated in replacement centers by these men who are limited service.

Honey, I guess this war can't last much longer with the Germans as they have plenty of trouble now. However, having seen enough of them, I know that they aren't quitting as yet. I lost some good men the other day who were hit, one of which I liked very much. To us on the line, as long as they are shooting at us the war is still on and doesn't end till they lay down their arms and weapons.

Darling, please don't lose hope and keep me posted on how things are at home. I'm always interested in hearing about yourself and Dick. I know he is growing into a big boy now and must be starting to get his teeth.

◆   ◆   ◆

RAF bombing Berlin with huge number of planes.

February 9, 1945   Belgium

Dear Roz,

Pardon this V mail letter but all my stuff is packed up. I'm still at a replacement system and was supposed to go back to my unit today and it was called off at the last minute. Now I wait again until I'm notified. I missed lots of fighting as I've been gone about 8 days now. I hope they haven't got me on the records as being AWOL. This is really turning out to be a vacation.

I keep my ears wide open for news from both fronts and it looks good yet. At present I'm wondering whether the fall of Berlin will terminate the war on this front.

◆   ◆   ◆

Six ships have been sunk off Canadian coast by German U-boats.

February 10, 1945   Belgium

Dear Roz,

Still back at a replacement depot. I still have no way of getting back to my unit. I was put on orders but there isn't any transportation available. It's not bad being here not doing anything but resting. I'm getting so lazy now that I don't have the ambition to even go for a walk.

I follow the news intensively and it seems to me as if most of the news is being censored at present. We moved forward a few miles on the front and I was fortunate to miss a lot of the attack as my unit will always be in the middle of everything. A good angel always seems to look over me. I think it's your daily praying that is guiding my fate.

You know honey, every day (that) goes by while in combat I always thought that this war can't last forever and when I thought about home with you and Dick I felt elated. No matter where I am or what I am doing, what keeps me going is actually you and everything you represent. I try and picture you in your everyday life and I can't do it. The only thing I hope and pray for is to be with you holding you close to me kissing me and loving you. Yes, my life these months since leaving you has been empty from my personal view.

Little Richard, born at such an inopportune war era, doesn't have the slightest knowledge of all that goes on while he gropes for his daily meals. He is a war baby who lacks the daily fondling of his father. I think about him, try and picture what he is like and I can't do it.

◆   ◆   ◆

> *Enemy counter-attacks have been stopped by the Fifth Army.*

February, 12, 1945   Belgium

Dear Roz,

Rain every day now for at least a few hours, after which it clears. I'm, still at the same replacement depot. We call them repple depple as a nickname. My vacation keeps on from day to day and I'm not the least bit sorry. I'm at least 100 miles from my unit and if no one comes to get us I stay here until they do. Honey, lying around all day doing nothing is monotonous. I want to be with my family for a least one short visit. I can't kick though and I hope that whoever is looking over me continues on in the future. Darling, keep praying and keep your own morale bright and gay.

◆   ◆   ◆

> *Attacks by our B-29's have slashed Japanese output of planes. Japan dispersing plants to make targets more difficult to hit. Good results have been reported in a new blow at Iwo.*

February 13, 1945   Germany

Dear Roz,

Well I was shipped back to a service company where I am now and I'm waiting to be sent back to my unit. Since I left many advances were made and we pushed forward a hell of a lot. I was glad to hear that we did not have many casualties. One officer I knew pretty well was killed by stepping on a mine. In my company all is well. Things used to be very quiet in the rear, now once again is the old familiar sound of friendly artillery. I listened to the news last night and tried to get the latest news. All I succeeded in doing was to hear the results of the Big Three Conference. Well it doesn't look as if I will be paid this month and I also missed out on the form to send you money through this new PTS method. (Personal transmittal of accounts). Next month I'll send a money order. I still don't know whether you have received any of the money I sent you in the past. Having not received any mail I'm looking forward to a personnel visit with my mail clerk.

What can I write of here? The normal day on the line is not one which could interest you. You read enough about that in the papers written up by skilled writers and reporters. Even the weather is a poor subject. Mud and rain again everywhere. I'm glad I have these high boots, they are worth their weight in gold.

Notice my handwriting it's getting bad again. I'm writing on my knee and that could be a cause for it. Darling I miss you. What more can I say. These few words carry all the sentiment in my head. Our Bn. Commander just left for the States on a leave. Last month he was in London. It's necessary to be a D-Day man here in order to get the finer jobs and passes. I should be on some pass list to Paris, however. Even that must be a long way off. What I wouldn't give to go back to the States right now.

◆　　　◆　　　◆

The future of Europe is being discussed at conference in Crimea. Continent seen at a crisis point with Russian advances and German issues on the agenda. Poland and Balkans a concern.

February 13, 1945　　　　　　　　　　　　　　　Germany

Dear Roz,

I was just listening to the news over the radio. It still sounds good and the Russians have announced the taking of Budapest. Other Russian units are still moving forward and on the western front the British armies seem to making good progress. The 3rd Army reports the taking of the town of Prum. I don't believe I have to tell you which division took that town.

I suddenly got a sore throat. When I cough it's a dry cough and seems to rasp my throat and it's most annoying. I will take care of it and get back to good health again.

One the humorous side, the jerries seems to be suffering from a case of the GI's. All the prisoners we have taken here have to relieve themselves every few minutes. I guess the German medics must be having plenty of trouble now as loose bowels can develop into making a soldier practically useless.

◆ ◆ ◆

Patton's men pushing Germans back across Sigfried Line. Finding housing acute as Germans are crowding pillboxes.

February 14, 1945   Germany

Dear Roz,

I'm back with the company again and I have just finished reading all my mail. The picture you cut out of the newspaper with the sled is the one I was riding on when we hit the ice and all of us were thrown out. The sled was smashed and I had a sore jaw and shoulder for weeks. My jaw is almost better now. We used to hook it up to a jeep and have it tow us around. Garrison autographed it, he is the jeep driver. The other two are company runners and they were wounded a few days ago. I'm sending the picture back to you.

I'm not exec anymore. One of our officers blew his top and was sent back. I guess I have another platoon again. We never did have an exec before as we were always short on officers. Things are quiet here now and the biggest thing is the mud here. It's the same way it was up at the Hurtgen Forest.

◆ ◆ ◆

> **The Third Army repulsed two counter-attacks; one near Pruem and the other near Lutzkampen.**

February 15, 1945   *Germany*

Dear Roz,

Well I'm back again with the company. I'm living in a house with German civilians. I'm back with my platoon again. Everything is well and quiet. We have a radio here in the house. These German radios are set to receive only one station. We get Radio Luxemburg *and some German programs from N.Y.*

One of the German towns Dad captured. He stayed in the house with the X.

I watched this German man here listen to the German news. I could understand part of it and I watched the German's reaction to the news and he didn't look too well. A little pale around the gills. However, in speaking to him he says he would rather have the Americans as the victors other than the Russians. He lives here with his family. We just moved in and took over. Last night I slept in a bed which was very comfortable. I slept very well last night.

The news is still good. Our air force is blasting Germany with the largest raids since Normandy. The little German I speak is improving every day. This bird here just asked me if he could leave the area. I made it quite clear that if he leaves this building he may get his a-s shot by soldiers around us.

I think by this time you are probably reading about the 4th Division. We must be off the secret list at last. When I returned to my platoon there were some old faces missing. A few of the men were suffering from exposure and caught bad colds. Now I can tell you that the weather was really brutally cold and we would have to dig in the hard ground and scrape the snow off the surface. We all carried TNT with us to blow up our own fox holes. Now the snow has thawed and all these streams are swollen. Everywhere is mud. The sun comes out for a few hours each day but even so one can hear the shells whistling over our little haven to remind us of the war.

I believe that I'm in about the only building with four walls from the front all the way back to Bastogne. The air corps really raised hell here and you'd agree too if you could see the ruined villages and German equipment all around. Yes, they do help considerably. All the livestock in the area was killed by various means. The Germans use a lot of horses and they're lying around dead. It's still cold but we probably will begin clearing up this mess before long. Funny, after being in the hospital I can't look at wounds any more. I've seen too many in too short a time.

My letters are getting too gruesome lately. I don't know what is happening to me but I can't seem to write in any other way. You will notice that I am writing on the stationary you sent in the package. It's a real change for the best. My pen doesn't scratch at all while writing. I wrote to the Stars and Stripes for my bracelet but haven't received it yet. I'll let you know when I receive it. I just ran out of ink and am using Fulhalter Tinte, German green ink.

Love, Dave

Where Were All The Jews

Dear Dad,

I'm surprised that this was the only time you mentioned seeing a Jewish refugee in your letters. With great efficiency the Nazis managed to exterminate nearly the entire Jewish population in Europe in a few years. On your long march through Germany you encountered only one Jew. The concentration camps you passed held other prisoners and these were the refugees you saw streaming by. Where were the remaining Jews?

Dear Roz,

I had a very interesting experience today. We moved into a beer garden and there were about 20 young girls there who came from East Prussia and one skinny young fellow about 20 years old. As soon as they found out I was in command they all wanted to do favors for me and this young fellow slid up to me and told me he was a Jew and was he permitted to stay where he was. I spoke to him and told him to sit down and spoke to him. He was the first Jew I've ever met in Germany. He had just escaped from a concentration camp near us and he told me that some Jews were just shot and he escaped. The damn Nazis are just ruining everything before they sink. I gave this kid some of my food, candy and some coffee. All the krauts looked on in amazement. Well I gave him some extra stuff and said good bye. I only remained in that town about an hour. We are getting closer to the real Nazi's fortress and we get beaucoups of prisoners. The regular soldiers and volkstrom give up very quickly.

Germany   *April 30, 1945*

It seems as if the Germans moved the Jewish population outside their borders for extermination. The German camps were for political prisoners, communists, ordinary criminals and those civilians unfortunate enough to get on the wrong side of an officer in the Gestapo or SS. Did you know about the final solution for the Jewish problem when you were in Europe? If not, you must have wondered why you did not see any Jewish people.

I wish I had asked you these questions when I had the chance. What did you think when you heard that young Jewish boy's story? What else did he tell you? There are so many questions I never asked and I'll never know the answers to. This was one of the greatest tragedies of the Nazi era and on this your letters are silent. To me this is another tragedy. A lost opportunity to get a first hand description of the horrors of the Nazi regime and your letters are mute.

This surprises me because being a member of the Jewish people was always so important to you. You went to a Jewish day school, were active in Jewish social clubs as a child, spoke Yiddish at home, and loved Jewish culture. I remember growing up hearing that you always supported Israel and could separate religion from being Jewish in your mind. Why, then, weren't you more alert for the plight of the European Jews? Surely you knew they were in trouble when you were there. As one who shares your views on being Jewish, I am keenly sensitive to this omission.

Dad, I do not cast blame on you for this lack of information. Perhaps you didn't see or didn't know more about these refugees than you wrote. I put all the responsibility for the unanswered questions on me, for not caring enough to engage you with my curiosity when I was younger and waiting until it was too late to inquire. This is just another example of my missed opportunities.

Love, Rich

The Letters – (Cont.)

> *Two German spies who came here by U-Boat were sentenced to die by hanging. Decision by Military Commission.*

February 15, 1945   Germany   (to his sister-in-law)

Dear Bea,

It's late now but I'll answer your letter tonight. How can I let my ever loving sister-in-law's mail wait? Do you really think that Dick is a combination of Roz and myself? I sure am waiting to see him and see for myself.

You were right in saying that I'm in the thick of things. If I was 100 yards further I probably would be sleeping with some jerries tonight but don't say anything to Roz about that. However, things aren't too bad here. I still don't believe I have the qualifications of a good soldier. Just between you and me, most of the time I'm scared to death. The longer I'm in combat, the worse the feeling. With each attack order the bottom drops out of everything and I wonder if this will be it. However, I've survived so far.

I know that you and Roz spend lots of time together so keep her morale up, won't you?

◆   ◆   ◆

> *French to get an occupation zone in occupied Reich. Invited to sit in Berlin with other Allies. DeGaulle accepts offer.*

February 16, 1945   Germany

Dear Roz,

Honey I hit the jackpot on mail again. I received at least eight letters from you. Our bank account is beginning to rise once again. I know we'll need the money when I'm home. Even Dick has more money now that I had when we were married. I'm beginning to get packages again. Now that you have my correct address your mail will come in quickly. Send me packages with food and anything else you know I need. That bottle of milk of magnesia hit the spot.

Mom (left) and her sister, Beatrice.

Honey, the pictures of you and Dick are swell. I enjoyed looking at them. Everyone is convinced that I'm a proud father. All you wrote about him is true. By the way, thanks for the stamps. I have enough for a while now.

I don't believe that you have grey hairs. I don't believe that you are getting older. I can only picture you the way you looked when I first met you. The pictures of yourself were very good. What do you mean you wish you had married a 4F'er? If you did you would probably be very happy and contented today but of course your son would probably be different in many ways.

The town of Echtennach is ruined. There is no town. All the buildings are destroyed. The beautiful rolling hills contain mines and booby traps. Does that answer your question?

You received the $50 I sent, did you receive the money order for $100 yet? You should have it by now. I gather from your letters that the car is still running. At least it can get to Brooklyn and back. How is your gasoline situation now?

Now that you use the word bitching I guess your virginal days of innocence are really over. In the army our higher commanders always say, "Do as I say, and not as I do." Can I use the same system with you? Hell no. It's getting so that the American women want equal rights with men when it comes to swearing too. I'm only being humorous again so don't get mad and read in-between the lines again.

◆   ◆   ◆

Dresden in ruins and on fire as 500 U.S. planes bomb town, easing way for Soviet troops to enter. RAF tears into Berlin, Mainz, Nuremberg, Duisberg. 6,500 missions flown from Britain.

February 16, 1945   Germany

Dear Roz,

It's about 9 PM now and I'm going to write to you again tonight. I wrote one letter early this morning. No mail for me today. I was hoping that at least one letter would arrive but my mail comes in bunches.

Today I gave the civilians here some cocoa and we had chicken for supper. Tomorrow morning we will have eggs again. I'm very lucky in a way. This house is just about the only one in about 100 miles that isn't demolished. Of course the only reason *why I haven't any brass here is because we are breathing down jerrie's throat. They don't bother us any and last night a few gave up. We scared them by halting them in the darkness and it was all over just like that. I don't think they have too much desire to fight.*

My platoon always seems to stick out ahead of anyone and we have less trouble. The enemy artillery is always going to the rear over our head. Our air corps is really going to town and I've seen a couple of demonstrations recently. I'm the only one with a radio and after I get the news we give it out to the rest of the company by telephone.

I just washed my socks and they are drying. Darling, I don't like to write about the war but other than that I haven't too much subject material. What do you think of my letters? Do they seem gruesome and horrible? I don't mean them to.

The news was very good again today and what keeps them Germans going is beyond me. They have nothing more to fight for, all is lost. They are only causing more destruction to their country and wasting needless lives. Of course, realizing that they are kaput, finished, (they) are just pulling the remainder of Germany down with them.

Right now some jerries are getting a hell of an artillery barrage. I hope it gives them the idea that all is kaput. That's an everyday word to a German.

We finished our scotch today and tonight I was sent down ½ bottle of gin. They take good care of me here.

◆　　　◆　　　◆

Richard Leitman with Michael Hollander

A large naval convoy of supplies for Russia evaded U-Boats and German planes carrying torpedoes.

February 17, 1945   Germany

Dear Roz,

I'm taking your advice and am sending you some of the pictures. It's very hard to take care of so many and I don't want them to be ruined. I'll do my best to take care of those which I keep. Honey, the eggs I had this morning were really delicious. We had cereal, eggs and bread and butter and coffee – a real breakfast. We only eat twice a day now as we don't walk around at all during the day so we don't get much exercise.

◆   ◆   ◆

Bombs continue to fall on the Western Reich to help the Canadian Army. Oil plants are also hit.

February 17 1945   Germany

Dear Roz.

I received a letter from you tonight and also a very cute Valentine's card. What did you think of the terms of the Big Three Conference? I heard all the pros and cons of it argued over the radio already. As for V-Day, I couldn't say how far away it is.

Darling, I'm not in the midst of hell, as you say. I don't want you to worry as I can always take care of myself no matter how bad things look. As far as my being dirty goes I was only kidding. I'd love to get under a shower and linger there for hours.

The picture of the sled you mailed was the same one as the one we had. Yes, I did lose some money gambling but that's all over

186

with now. I know I'm lucky in love so I guess that explains my gambling losses. As for our finances we seem to be getting up amongst the wealthy people now. In two months we'll begin feeling like rich people. Even Dick is off to a flying start. Sure I think that Richard is a good looking kid. Not only because I'm his father but he looks good to me.

I am glad to read that you're gaining weight. Pretty soon you'll weigh as much as Frank Sinatra. This outdoor life really is swell for you and I'll bet you're the picture of health now. If Pop says you're looking better, then you must because he is pretty critical in his opinions and doesn't voice any unless he really believes he is right, especially where his children are concerned. I'm sure he knows you better than I do. Didn't he see you grow from a baby to a woman? I only received you for a short time in the latter stages. As for my own opinion, I never want to see you grow old. I always picture you as this young girl who didn't know too much and found out everything through my expert teaching. "Yeah Man." Sort of cocky, am I not? We have a long period of happiness to look forward to together. I don't believe it will be too long before I hold you close to me again. Yes honey, I still think of you all the time.

Goodnight, darling. I hope my mail reaches you quickly. Please let me know how long it takes. Your mail takes 11 days to reach me.

◆   ◆   ◆

Soviet Army crosses barrier at Dresden as Russian planes bomb Berlin.

February 18, 1945   Germany

Dear Roz,

I lost my good home and now I'm in a large jerry dugout again. We have about two inches of water on the floor at all times and the roof leaks continually. The weather is improving and it's getting a little warmer.

◆　　◆　　◆

Russian Army tightening its grip on Breslau in Polish corridor.

February 20, 1945 Germany

Dear Roz,

I received a letter from the Stars and Stripes telling me that this other private with my name has received my bracelet. I've already written him a letter requesting him to mail it to me. Maybe I'll get the bracelet before the war is over.

It's a little chilly here in my hole and the roof drips water. I'm glad I have the shoe pods but the rubber is cold and the floor is wet all the time. I don't mind as long as we remain here. When I hear the order to attack I get leery. Jerry sends a little artillery at us occasionally but it never hits near us.

Don't tell me that you're getting the itches too. I know very well what it feels like but at least you have a bathtub to cure yourself in. I'm very jealous.

◆　　◆　　◆

Our fleets gunboats have eliminated Japanese from Iwo beaches. We win a foothold on Iwo in hard fighting

February 20, 1945 Germany

Dear Roz,

I also received a letter from Bob telling me how he wanted to ease the pain when you didn't hear from me in weeks and said I was probably captured. Don't mention this to anyone. I'm still in good health and am still in the US Army. I guess the jerries do not particularly care to capture me as yet. There wasn't anything *wrong with me outside of my lice and I had a few days rest in the hospital. I hope you weren't too worried as I did write you what was up.*

Honey, I've only been kidding you when I wrote about you not letting me in the house if I was filthy. I know you're a bug on cleanliness and just thought I'd pull your leg a bit. Don't' get too excited about it.

◆　　　◆　　　◆

Reports of Poles being interned by Russia. Britain backs Polish protesters.

February 21, 1945   Germany

Dear Roz,

Darling, I'm getting a little fed up. I find myself getting more scared every day. It seems to be a normal reaction for older men on the line. Don't worry though. I'll always manage to keep going.

◆　　　◆　　　◆

Worms hit by RAF while out forces blast Nuremberg. Seen as help to Patton's troops. South Reich rail hub is target.

February 22, 1945   Germany

Dear Roz,

Once again I'm sorry about yesterday's letter. I started writing and someone began raising hell in the next sector. It wasn't very much but I couldn't concentrate on writing. It was dark as hell with a poor light and every time an artillery round

would land the concussion put out the light. Today has been a beautiful spring day; a little chilly perhaps but at least the sun is shining.

Two of our machine guns just opened fire on one little German and made mince meat out of him. Of course everyone has to run over to search for souvenirs.

It's getting cooler at night again and we try our best to keep as warm as possible. Clothes are sent up to us quite often and we change clothes and send the dirty ones back.

The news is still pretty good and it doesn't look as if the Germans can hold out much longer. However it's hard to say when this damn war here will be over.

Love, Dave

No More Outdoors For Me

Dear Dad,

I can understand your sentiment when you wrote that you had your fill of outdoor living. As I read your letters from England and from the Continent, your words were so clear about what living conditions were like for you, that I could feel your discomfort and I found myself hoping the weather would dry out quickly and warm up for you. I don't know how you managed to bear with those living conditions for so long.

> Dear Roz,
>
> Sitting here in my dugout it's dark as hell and always damp. The damn water drips through. We have buckets all over the place to catch water. Some day I'll look back to all this and enjoy a hearty laugh. This great outdoor life. Remember when you would want to go out on a picnic? Honey, those days are over with now. I don't think I'll want to go outdoors too much. I'll have to develop this prison pallor.
>
> Germany   February 22, 1945

When I first heard you lived in tents it didn't sound that bad. Many people actually go on vacation tenting, and look forward to it every year. Of course they go for a week or two and pick the choicest seasons to do it. I haven't heard of too many people on camping vacation in the winter.

I cringe when I think of you wet for days on end, and with no way to dry your clothing because of constant rain and cold temperatures. As a gardener I can picture the mud you lived with and I could feel your words in my chest when you said that mud was the enemy of the infantry soldier. I felt your joy at finding a German foxhole, so you wouldn't have to dig your own in the frozen ground, even though you found it was filled with inches of water and your feet were always wet. I shivered when you told of nights needing 9 blankets to stay warm, and then only by sleeping up against your tent mate for body warmth.

I can only guess what it was like waking up on freezing winter nights in a cold tent, putting on damp, chilly rubber shoes to walk through the snow because you were sick and needed to use the latrine. It upset me to learn you needed to use insecticide powder to kill the lice on your body more than a few times. How uncomfortable I would be if I could not shower for a month, wash my face to get the sweat off, brush my teeth every morning, or eat more than minimal meals. Could I get by being cold all the time, depending on chocolate bars for energy?

Yet you endured all of this, and more, knowing that your real purpose was to lead men in pushing the enemy back, in attacks that were exhausting and life threatening. How did you do it in the conditions you were living under?

No one would even think to fault you if you refused to go camping when you returned, and yet, Dad, you volunteered to be a Boy Scout leader for me and my brother, Mark. For years you organized overnight hikes and camped out with us and the other leaders so we could have fun and get the experience. Sure I often heard you say at the time that you had enough roughing it and didn't need to camp out any more. I heard it, and in my excitement over what the overnight adventure would bring, dismissed what you were saying as just some more teasing from my father. I actually thought you really loved that stuff too.

Dad, I had no idea of what you had to endure in your army years. I never realized just what a sacrifice you made for me in being a Boy Scout leader until I recently read your letters. You could have easily elected to sit on the sidelines and let some other fathers shoulder the responsibility of being a Scout leader. You could have been a leader and still chosen not to go on the overnight hikes. I certainly wouldn't have given it another thought, but you chose to jump in fully so that you could be with you sons during their scouting years and share your knowledge with our friends.

The boys in the troop loved to have you on the hikes. We looked forward to the Adventure Trail you would set up by yourself. I remember a team of boys would get a compass and the first set of directions; walk 200 feet into the woods at a compass reading of 125 degrees. We would do that and look for another note, usually sticking out from under a rock or tacked to a tree, giving further instructions on where to go. Sometimes when we reached the location there would be a leader lying on the ground looking hurt. We were to use our first aid tools to find out what was wrong and administer first aid to him. When we got it right he would give us the next set of directions. This would go on for hours until the last set of directions took us back to the camp site. We loved it. We never knew what we would be tested on at each station. It could be knot tying or some other outdoor skill. It was all fun to us, especially if we found the location easily. Most of the time, however, we were far from the target. It was great.

Dave and Richard on a Boy Scout overnight hike. (first two on left)

I remember once we went camping in the winter. We scouts didn't think it would be any different than the fall and springtime camping we did. We were in for a big surprise. We thought we were freezing to death, especially in our tent at night, and we couldn't get our cooking fire to start because the wood was frozen. Of all the leaders, you were the only one who checked up on us regularly to make sure we were okay, that our tent was sealed up enough. You brought us extra blankets to put over our sleeping bags and helped us start a fire for cooking and to keep warm. Looking back on it now, I think you were probably the only man amongst the leaders who lived through winter camping and knew the dangers. Wow, it's just occurring to me as I write this how you must have been reliving your army experiences all over again and took charge as you did for your platoon in the war, making certain that your men would be okay. Eventually, I became an Eagle Scout and I look back on my years in the Scouts as being fun and rewarding. I owe much of this to you.

When my own children were of scouting age they didn't want to follow in my footsteps. I got them involved, instead, in the Indian Guides, another program that was sponsored by the Y organizations. I took them camping and slept with them in tents. I enjoyed reliving my scouting days and spending time with them in a fun setting. I admit, however, when the bugs were too bad, I would sleep in the back of the station wagon, and I didn't enjoy it very much if my tent leaked. One time we set up the tents in my backyard for an overnight experience. Although it was autumn, and the weather was beautiful during the daytime, we got so cold at night that everyone wound up sleeping on the floor in my house. I wonder how I would have done in the army living the way you did. Unfortunately, I think I know.

Dad, you earned my respect for what you went through in the army and how you overlooked those hardships to make sure your son had a full childhood. I wish I could have understood this when I was younger. I love you for what you sacrificed for me.

Love, Rich

The Letters – (Cont.)

Invasion of Iwo seen as vital to our strategy as we need air base within range of Japan. We are paying a heavy price to achieve this objective

February 24, 1945   Germany

Dear Roz,

I received a package and a letter so I'm writing my second letter to you today. First don't send me any more soap. Second, how about the whiskey? I haven't received more than one ration. The package I received today included candles, herring, powdered milk and noodle soup. I can use those but don't send too much powdered milk. Candles can be included in every package. I can always use them. Thanks a lot honey. I'm not complaining but I don't wash enough to use a cake every two months. Don't get frightened.

I never did get the bracelet and I wrote to the private who received it. I don't need any clothes.

We received a ration of Spanish wine that was captured from the Germans. Putrid stuff. I'm sending you a 1000 mark note. I hope you don't try and cash it as it isn't legal tender. It's a good souvenir to add to your collection. Darling, thanks a lot for the package. They are beginning to roll in now and everyone is envious of my wife.

Whenever you fall off I can always tell from your letter. You sound disillusioned and disgusted. Darling, you seem mad at so many people. Please try and get along as best as you can at least until I get back home.

Richard Leitman with Michael Hollander

◆   ◆   ◆

> **New German prisoners are telling American forces they are eager to surrender.**

February 24, 1945   _Germany_

Dear Roz,

Honey, I received two letters from you last night and couldn't answer them. I'm living in a house again and I think we will even take showers again while we are here.

Some stupid German walked right out in front of us and it was as if they didn't think much of our accuracy. Well he didn't take his first step before he met St. Peter. I can't understand them. They know where we are and yet they walk around as if they were drunk.

Honey, you won't read anything about my unit in the newspapers. They don't publicize us any more. We still are in the 3rd Army but we have it pretty easy.

We are getting hot meals again. It was a damn good thing I always carried a mess kit with me as I needed to use it as a frying pan. I think the next thing I will get rid of is my overcoat. It's too damn heavy to carry around. Everything I own must be carried on my back and I'm always looking for some way to make the load lighter. God bless the infantry soldier.

It seems that the brass in our battalion said I had a rest and now I go to the bottom of the officers pass list to Paris. I was practically accused of gold-bricking by certain people who never even see the front lines. Well after I have my say on the subject I guess I automatically go to the bottom of their shit list. However, as long as I'm on the line and others are to the rear I won't take any crap from them. I'm not really in trouble honey - it's just a small dispute.

Well darling, that's about all for now. I'm mailing back the pictures. Darling whenever you feel blue and lonely remember that I'm thinking of you and love you more every day.

Honey, I'm afraid to dream of you at night. Underwear doesn't dry so easily in cold weather. Well so long for now honey, I'm going to sit down and drink my wine.

◆　　　◆　　　◆

German counter-attacks failing.　Our planes blasting communications. Fifth Army widens activities in Italy.

February 25, 1945   Germany

Dear Roz,

Today was a big day for me. I took a shower at last. I just stood under the hot water and wore out two cakes of soap in working up a good lather. My scalp and hair was so dirty the soapy water was practically black. Now I feel like a new man and I'm ready to pick up my daily quota of dirt again.

I received the razor blades which was my first gift from Richard. I'm going to use them tomorrow for the first time. They seem to be a special type of blade which I've never used before. Darling, I sent home most of my pictures of you and Richard as I don't want them to get ruined or lost. They are too valuable a possession. I still keep a few of them to look at every spare minute I get. I get homesick just thinking of you both and always console myself by thinking of how wonderful our first meeting will be. I try to picture what will happen and it warms the cockles of my heart just dreaming about it. Darling, let's look forward to that happy moment when our little family will be reunited again. I warn you if I find I like having a family we may end up with a tribe.

Richard Leitman with Michael Hollander

◆ ◆ ◆

Americans continue to advance through Germany as the third pounds Trier. City expected to fall soon.

March 3, 1945   Germany

Dear Roz,

I know I haven't written for a few days but it couldn't be helped. We were kept a little busy for a while. I now have a chance to write again. It's getting a little chilly now and I feel cold. I have been receiving packages galore now and I never know what to do with the extra things as I keep moving. That's why I say not to send any soap. I can get plenty of that here. I'm black again and I need a shower.

If you have been reading the papers you probably are reading of big advances. I don't know exactly how all this would affect the war but I'm hoping that it doesn't last too much longer.

I miss you very much. Sometimes I wonder if all this is not some type of punishment. It may be true that a man can be without a woman but I can't live forever without you. I hunger for you which can't be satisfied until I can kiss you again and tell you how much I love you. Darling, even our little one keeps me in suspense. I don't know him, wonder what he is like, and long to play with him. I keep wondering what he's like. I'll know some day but the real important thing is to find you exactly as when I left.

◆ ◆ ◆

Germans have been putting up a fierce defense west of Rhine but their efforts are seen as doomed.

March 8, 1945   Germany

Dear Roz,

I know you are worried after reading about all the headway we are making recently. Darling, to begin with, our company commander is on pass to Paris and just when I took over, all the action is taking place. We walk miles each day and my feet are getting sore as hell. March, attack, and dig in the woods every night. Then attend company commander's meetings at night till well after midnight, return back, orient all my men, and jump off in another attack at dawn. I go on one reconnaissance to another and walk all the time. We attack every day and we hope we will be relieved soon. The resistance we meet is very light and we don't have many casualties. When the Captain returns from Paris he'll be surprised at the rapid advances we have made. We started from Prum and are still going strong.

We go ahead on sparse rations. They even find it difficult to supply us as we move so fast and over rough mountains. So far I can say that Germany only consists of mountains as that's all I've seen so far. I hope this is the end of the German army. Maybe the war will end quickly.

I haven't received any mail as our mail system hasn't been functioning since we began our push. I want to hear from you and know that all is well at home. Darling, please don't worry about me as I am feeling fine. I only suffer from weariness and lack of sleep

We ransack all these German towns and take whatever food we found. Our last objective today was a German town. I selected one building as my CP and demanded eggs. Honey, I made myself scrambled eggs. Got three eggs, bread, butter and ersatz coffee. Most of these people aren't hurting too much for food. They don't like to see their villages leveled and they put up white flags all over town. Now that the war is hitting them, all they have is sad tales of how glad they are that the war is almost over. They treat us pretty good but there isn't any other way to act as we take whatever we want. Sort of a reverse situation with the krauts on the duty end of the stick. Our Bn. Commander is complimenting me on the fine manner in which I have been handling the men. So far we haven't lost one man. The other companies lost a few. Most of our trouble is with snipers and if we catch one, we'll shoot his damn rifle up his ass. I heard some good news about some of our soldiers being over the Rhine but that's not official. I haven't heard any news or read any newspapers in days. As for washing and shaving, that's out again. I don't know when I'll clean up again.

We captured one young girl in uniform. I don't think she was over 17 years old. She was scared to death. I'll bet the German soldiers have some good times in their dugouts.

Darling, here it's living, eating, and sleeping this damn war. You can't forget it for a minute. Right now I'm waiting for a messenger to bring up tomorrow's objectives. Which way we move is beyond me. I hope we have things fairly easy. I always wonder what it's going to be like taking our next objective and how many krauts we will hit, how many men I will lose and how I can prevent excess casualties. Sometimes I'm scared, other times I'm not. Today my runner and radio operator requested that I stay back as they don't like to be up front. They think I'm too brave. Well I'm scared to death myself. I was kept so busy running up and down the line straightening out our lines that I forget about being scared.

Darling, I've written so much and still nothing about that which is most precious to me, namely you. Darling how can I begin to tell you how much I miss you. How much I love you. How much I want to be with you again. Last night I lay in a foxhole, it was raining and I tried to keep warm and sleep and couldn't. All I did was just day dream about you and Dick. I've completely forgotten what it's like to hold you in my arms. I miss you darling. I hope that it won't be too long before I'm together with you again.

◆　　　◆　　　◆

Bridge over Rhine is bombed by Germans to stop advance of Allied troops. Advance continues. Foe was unprepared for offensive.

March 9, 1945   Germany

Dear Roz,

Today I received a long letter from you. We are getting a 24 hour rest to clean up and shave. I have a cold and cough which is very annoying. I wish I could get rid of this cold.

Marching with these shoe (packs?) is tough as they have no arches in them.

I received two large boxes of cookies, one from you and the other from Aunt Clara. Both packages were well banged up. Of course both packages lasted about 20 minutes. I received a visit this morning from the Bn. Commander and he liked them very much. I expect our Captain back from Paris today or tomorrow and once again I'll be back as exec and platoon leader.

Darling, I know that you're faithful to me. I trust you with my life. Darling it is only my faith in our love which keeps me going. I love you with all my heart.

◆　　　◆　　　◆

Bombers hit six oil plants, 5 railyards in Ruhr and pummeled Berlin. Very little ack-ack response. Dessau ravaged by fire- most of city ablaze. Fifteenth air force aids Russians again.

Richard Leitman with Michael Hollander

March 9, 1945   Germany

Dear Roz,

Well I'm back with the platoon again and things will be a bit easier now. I can send more souvenirs but I'd have to drag them around and the mail orderly is never anywhere near us. As for sending myself home, you know that's an impossibility.

I hope that you're right about the war with Japan, but after reading the casualty list I know what type of fighting that was like.

I changed back to shoes again as my feet are in bad shape. There isn't any arch in those shoe (packs?) and my feet hurt over these long marches we have been taking.

◆   ◆   ◆

Bombers hit Japan again with damage somewhat less than Tokyo received. Fires reported burning for hours.

March 14, 1945   France

Dear Roz,

Once again I haven't been able to write. We are resting now for the first time and I'm going to take advantage of this rest to get rid of my cold and cough. My cold went from bad to worse and as usual going to the doc is no solution. If my fever is under 100 there is nothing wrong.

Today is a beautiful day and I took out a chair placed it in the sun and I'm writing while sunning myself.

I received my bracelet from Private Leitman and it's a beauty. I wear baby Mike's (Richard's) gift on my right wrist. My fingers must have become slimmer as my ring slides all over. Darling I hope this rest period will not end before the war with Germany *is over. Don't worry darling, I'm not in any danger now and am in good health. Take care of Dick and yourself.*

◆   ◆   ◆

Soviets making a run for Berlin. River crossed at Kuestrin.

March 15, 1945   France

Dear Roz,

The weather is beautiful and each day is a beautiful spring day. I spend the day lying in a field on a GI blanket and my cold is a little better. The doc says I have a touch of bronchitis and I should take it easy for the next 4 or 5 days. Well here we don't do anything and I can take things easy.

We are living in a French town and living the way we are now is really more like a tourist than as a soldier. I hope the weather doesn't change. Tonight we have a baseball game with M Company. It should be a good game.

◆   ◆   ◆

Zossen takes bomb hits. Railroad supplying defenders in Berlin hit by Americans. RAF targets Ruhr again. Red Army targets German headquarters.

March 16, 1945   France

Dear Roz,

Another day of my vacation gone by. Today we had a good movie shown to us. I don't mind this rest at all. I've been trying to catch up on all my letter writing. Darling from your letter you sound terribly worried about me. Please remember that I can

never see as rough days as I've gone through. I came out all right then and I know I'll go through the rest all right too. Darling, don't ever worry about me keeping a smile for you. I'll always have my best one ready for our first meeting. Darling, you're all I live for so just thinking about you makes me happy.

So you want a daughter next. Well I hope we can get settled when I'm home and fulfill your desire. As for myself it doesn't matter. I want to see one grow up from scratch and gain where I lost with little Richard. As you write, Dick seems to be developing some of my habits. Are they the good ones at least? I know he is a big boy now and I won't be too long before he can walk.

Darling, you never wrote me whether you received the money order I sent. Please let me know in a future letter. I've only received one small medicine bottle of liquid. If you sent any more it hasn't arrived as yet. I'm getting packages now which were mailed to my old APO address. I'm also out of writing paper so you can send me a piece in each letter.

◆   ◆   ◆

Strikes reported in Bremen. Witness tells of bloody clashes between SS and hungry workers demanding end to war.

March 17, 1945   France

Dear Roz,

Today has been a bit chilly. I began the day by taking a shower. After that I inspected the company area. That just about took care of the morning. The company went out this afternoon for a parade and I remained behind and slept. Then I woke up in time for supper. That brings my day up to the present.

We were issued new sleeping bags which are much warmer. Once again I didn't receive any mail from you today. The mail seems to be screwed up again around here. We have a new officer in the company now and once again I lose my platoon. I don't know exactly what I'll do but I guess it will be to the 4th platoon which is in a little trouble at present.

Nisei made to take special oath by Army. Must renounce Japan before being accepted. Questioned heavily.

March 17, 1945   France

(Drunken love letter)
Dear Roz,

Tonight I'm writing a letter to my sweetheart. Just what does that word sweetheart mean to me? It represents the most beautiful feeling anyone can know or feel. My sweet, although we are married, and even if we weren't, I would still feel that you were everything in this world to me. Unfortunately, not many people can ever feel the ecstasy of love. Myself, the mere thought of you makes me forget all this turmoil, and makes me visualize those things that are beautiful and desirable.

Darling, I look back and think of those precious moments were spent together. How valuable they seem to me now. I remember our petty quarrels. You would cry and I would feel bad and you, instead of trying to compromise, would only get annoyed. Weren't we foolish acting that way?

My only desire since I first met you was to make you happy. Since I first met you, no woman has ever made me feel as you did. I often kidded you about being able to put my arms around you twice. I can't imagine any feeling more exciting that holding you closely to me and kissing you.

Darling it isn't just our sexual life. Just watching you walk and talk does things to me. When we first met I was so proud to bring my friends up because you were a perfect hostess and completely snowed any other girl they had ever met.

Tonight we received our first whiskey ration of bourbon. I've had more than I should but it made me feel that I've been causing pain to the most beautiful person I know. You know how romantic I get when I drink. However, my love for you darling is so great that I just had to write to you. I hope you find no difficulty in reading my writing.

So far I've just about had 3/8 of a quart. Darling I miss you so much (that) tonight I probably could just hold you close to me and keep kissing you until I fall asleep. Darling, I love you more that I can ever tell you in writing. What you mean to me is the most beautiful thing in the world. Please love me the way I love you as I could never love anyone as I love you. I love you with all my heart.

◆   ◆   ◆

Fires in Kobe burn more than 24 hours. Locomotive and aircraft plants targeted. Dock area on fire. Rangoon hit by B-29's.

March 18, 1945   France

Dear Roz,

Today I spent most of the day playing baseball and in between I saw a good GI floor show. The show was very good and I enjoyed it very much. Being back here in the rear is quite difficult. Our nerves were so strained that we find it difficult to relax. Tonight I guess I'll just have to go to bed early. Remember I wore size 36 pants. Well I've been wearing that size right along and I went to the shower the other day. We usually get clean clothes then. I asked for 36 and they didn't have it. I took size 34 and much to my surprise I found that they fit me very well and aren't snug at all. I must have lost a bit of my rear end somewhere in my travels.

Last night we had a celebration and drank a couple of quarts of real American bourbon. I went to bed early as soon as I knew that I had my fill. I still can't take my whiskey and any attempt on my part in a drinking party usually ends with me being the first to quit. The only bad effect of drinking is that I get terribly *lonesome for you and I must write to you. I keep writing how much you mean to me and yet I wonder if I can even convey the feeling in my heart through a letter. I can't believe it can be done but when I read your letters I know that you're with me body and soul. You know darling there is something very binding to our love which makes me feel that we are closer than any two other people. Here we are miles apart and yet I can't help feeling that it was only yesterday that we parted. This mess seems just like a bad dream and in the morning why then you will be getting my scrambled eggs for breakfast. Does that make sense to you?*

Dad taking a break from the war.

What really keeps me going is that I'm so sure of your love and I know that you'll always be waiting for me. I know that I've made a very lucky gain in having you consent to be my wife. I sometimes wonder what it would be like married to any of the other girls I knew. Let us say Edie or Pauline or any other female. I can't help thinking that I couldn't be as happy as I am now. Even though I can picture myself as some other female's mate I can't help thinking that you're mine. I can't in my wildest imagination picture you as any other man's spouse. Your mine and I'm ready to defend my claim for you. Remember that I can only picture you as the innocent girl I met years ago. I can remember how we sweated out our honeymoon and after the trying moments we had together on our honeymoon I claim all rights to you and all that you stand for. Do you think I'm being a bit selfish? I don't. I will also confess that I have been a faithful husband and will always be that way. Now I'm not placing any halo over my head as there are moments when I've been tempted- you know what I mean.

Lately I've been thinking of those wonderful moments we spent lying down with your warm body close to mine. I will admit that as far as physical attraction you always had me with my tongue hanging out. Physically you always had me beat and I knew it too. Instead of stopping, you would tease me and then it seems as if you were laughing at my physical weakness. Yes, you weren't very fair. I can just see a very vicious smile on your lips now while reading this. I can play a few tricks on you too, such as keeping you busy raising babies and things like that, but I'm too fair a player to do that. Well I think I've said more that I should so I'd better close this letter now before I get into trouble. Don't take this letter in the wrong light. I love you very, very much.

◆　　　◆　　　◆

German's escape route home eyed by Patton. Threatens to follow them.

March 19, 1945   France

Dear Roz,

Today and for the next few days I will be on the range as range officer. I have two assistant 2nd Lt's. who do all the work but I just remain there and assume all responsibilities. Today I finally saw one regimental commander and he seemed satisfied with the way things are run. The weather is changing for the best. It's cold at night and early in the morning. During the day it gets warm and sunny. I've been playing baseball and today I feel sore all over. All my muscles ache.

Yes, we are back to Garrison duty again. Close order drill, saluting, etc. Do I like that? Darling I love that and will accept it for the rest of the war.

We now send officers and men to Nancy, Lyons and Paris. Somehow or other my turn for a three day pass hasn't come up as yet. I would like to go to Paris on my pass. When I was in England and I went to see London. In France I would like to see Paris and in Germany, Berlin.

These French towns are all the same. They haven't changed any in the past 200 years. In front of each house are the manure pits. It seems to me as the wealth of a person depends on the size of the pile in front of their house. I've learned the word for eggs; it sounds something oof. My French is very bad and I can say beaucoup, oof, merci and we. Beaucoup means many and I believe that it will become part of the English slang when we all come home. The other word is kaput which is German and means ruined, destroyed, captured, killed or anything along those lines. Although I know the words for intercourse in French I do not know the German translation. Every American soldier knows mademoiselle, zig zig. Don't get the wrong impression darling, I've been on the front a long time and have no personal experiences myself. Just thought you'd be interested.

I find it very difficult going to sleep at night. The doc gave me some sleeping pills which I take now and then. My cold is still bad and it was diagnosed as a touch of bronchitis however I was told to stay in the sun as much as possible. Tonight when I return there should be some mail for me. Nothing gripes me more than to receive a V-mail letter. There isn't anything to read in them and I practically never use them myself. I wonder what you are doing right now. I just can't stop thinking about you.

Love, Dave

ON THE LIGHTER SIDE

Dear Dad,

It's good to see that you could enjoy a little humor in the midst of all the harshness that you were thrown into. You always did enjoy a good joke. What's interesting to me is that I never heard you tell a joke that had crude language or was based around sex. So, I was a little surprised to see the stories you sent to Mom were more off color than I was used to hearing from you. Your taste in humor, as I knew it, was consistent with the way you lived your life. You frowned upon stories or movies that were too sexually explicit and would switch television channels if a show offended you. In this regard you were definitely more prudish than Mom, or the rest of us for that matter.

> *Question: Why is a honeymoon like a bath?*
> *Answer: You find it isn't as hot once you're inside.*
> *Now that can be taken in more than one way and I hope you find it amusing.*
> *England*   *October 25, 1944*

I didn't like some of your humor, however. The way you teased people, thinking it was funny, I did not find very amusing. I also admit that I always became upset when you did this. I thought humor at the expense of other people was not funny, but insulting and hurtful. I wish you hadn't done that and I wish I had been brave enough to ask you to stop. This was another instance of me becoming a little boy in your presence and finding it impossible to express my own voice. I see this so clearly now that you're gone but I wonder how I would react if we were back in time several years and I was witness to some relative or friend bearing the brunt of your caustic sarcasm. Would I be able to stand up to you?

211

Richard Leitman with Michael Hollander

> *Dear Roz,*
>
> *I'm going to tell you something funny now. We buy rubbers 1 dozen for 4 pence here and we use them for various uses. For example, if we open a can of Nescafe coffee we slip one over the top to keep the aroma in and the moisture out. In this damp weather there are hundreds of uses for them here. In landing amphibiously everyone slips one over their wallet to keep it from getting wet. So you see it has more used than just for intercourse.*
>
> *England*   *September 4, 1944*

Facing reality, however, you are not with me anymore and as I seek to form permanent memories of you in my mind. I prefer to dwell on the more pleasant ways you brought humor into your life. I remember sitting with you on the town dock in Port Washington when one of your friends from the VFW walked up to us. You and he started joking around and before long we were all laughing at some jokes he told. It was a beautiful moment to remember, especially since it was one of the last times we were able to go out of the house with you before you entered hospice care.

I also like to remember the times you taught us to sing silly songs such as, *The First Marine He Ate the Bean, Parlez-Vous?*, or the high school cheer *El-o-men*. These are the songs I taught my children and then my grandsons. They were always surprised when you sang those chants to them. They looked at you in amazement and I could see the silent question running through their minds, "How did you know that?" never realizing it was you who originated those ditties in our family tradition.

I remember the way you joked around at the Passover seders and the way you smiled when you laughed at funny things a child did. You laughed at our friend's dog when she watched television so attentively, and you saw humor in old time television comedians such as Jack Benny, Milton Berle, and Red Skelton. That was your kind of humor. I guess I picked a lot of that up from you because that's the type of humor I also prefer. I also find jokes with off-color language distasteful.

Dear Roz,

Darling, I know that the girl I married had all the qualifications of a good wife. Of course if she is supporting a couple of lovers (gigolos) I can't do much to help that. All I can ask is whether they please you more than I did. As for myself, I sleep with a different woman each night and I find them much more enjoyable than you were. Besides, I'm getting so tired of intercourse that I decided to quit for a couple of years after the war. You might as well look for a new man. My girl friends find me so cold that they have to parade around me in the nude to raise my ambition. What a life that would be if it were only true. I hope you take all this as a jest as my life as far as women goes has been a total blank. Darling, I can wait until we are together again. Please bear with me until this is over, no matter how long it takes.

Luxemburg   *December 15, 1944*

Dad, I want to write about another incident I found pretty funny. A few months before you passed away, Marlene and I came to visit with you and when I came into the house I saw you were sitting in your favorite reclining chair watching television. Unfortunately the television was broken and the screen was only displaying lines and "snow". You said it just recently broke – a few days ago! A few days of watching snow! I took you out to buy a new $1000 Sony flat screen set. We were both excited as we brought it home and set it up. Your excitement quickly turned to disappointment when you had trouble hearing the sound, even though the volume was turned up to maximum. The walls of the living room were vibrating but you couldn't hear it!

Dear Roz,

Another funny incident. We have a company of officers here under the command of a major. Well officers are worse than enlisted men to control and they never fall out for formation on time. Some of them don't even get up for reveille and I'll admit that I have missed it a couple times myself. Well to get back to the story, he gathers us all together in a group and tells us that toilet paper is scarce here and some of the officers are using twelve sheets. Well someone suggested the solution – to only use one sheet, cut out a hole big enough for the middle finger, right hand. The application goes thusly. Place the middle finger through the hole in center of the single sheet. Wipe with finger, first joint sufficient, and wipe first joint of middle finger with single sheet of toilet paper. Simple isn't it. But how the hell did he find out how many sheets each officer uses. That's the army for you, honey.

England   September 6, 1944

Dear Roz,

Here's something amusing. We were standing in the mess line one day waiting to wash out our mess equipment. There are colored boys who keep the fire going. Suddenly one of them heard a buzz bomb coming in our direction and he said, "Lord, give it power." Everyone burst out laughing. If you don't get it, the bomb will never hit us as long as we can hear it. There aren't too many of them anyway.

Belgium   November 13, 1944

The next day I got a frantic call from Mom to come quickly and return the set to the store. Every time you looked at it you became aggravated and expressed your frustration by complaining loudly to her. I thought I had the solution. I bought an amplifier and Bose speakers and hooked them up to the set. With added power the set became marginally acceptable to you. No one could understand what was going on and I suspected dementia. A few days later you saw your doctor for a regularly scheduled visit and he performed a routine ear cleaning. I later heard that the set was now too loud and I should take out the speakers. Problem solved.

Dad, I believe you are finding some humor in the place you are now. But if you can hear me, listen carefully. Please don't use that old sarcastic humor of yours or you may anger the wrong one and find yourself on a very long and difficult journey to a much hotter environment.

Love, Rich

The Letters – (Cont.)

Clergyman in Munich reports city devastated after last air attack. Life paralyzed.

March 20, 1945   France

Dear Roz,

Once again I have a new home. This time however, all the candles I have been carrying are paying dividends. We have no electric here and a candle is our only illumination. This is also a jerry candle burning here and I tried to light my cigarette with it and some of the wax ran on this paper. I scraped off most of it. As I was saying, your latest letters were very interesting. First, I know that you had a gathering for old friends and I know that you showed our little son off. You keep writing how attractive he is. Everyone seems to like him. If he has a pleasant smile he probably inherited that from his mother as she has a very pretty smile. As for his not eating whites of eggs, darling, I didn't know that was a hereditary trait handed down from father to son. You sure he inherits most of his bad habits from me? You try and make me feel as if I gave birth to Dick all by myself. First it's physically impossible, and besides, Dick has a very lovely mother who also contributed very much to our little angel's character.

Please remember that I wish I could see him trying to waddle around and attempt to stand. I know that it won't be too long before he will be walking, hanging on to your skirt. What makes me very happy is that he recognized my picture which you show him as someone whom he should know. Just how bright he is at present, I have no way of knowing. I know you very well, my sweet, and you probably include me in every nursery rhyme which you tell him.

Now for your other troubles. You write that you're not getting along with everyone. Darling I know exactly how you feel. At times I feel the same way myself. However other people aren't really concerned with our personal life and the feelings which

216

they go through are not the same as that which we both feel. In any event, let's try and bear everyone as much as possible.

I get a big kick out of reading that Pop changes Dick's diapers. So he really believes that the baby is a well mannered baby. Now I know that our Richard is really a very valuable possession. I know that Pop must be very proud of his grandson. For that matter, who isn't?

◆   ◆   ◆

Our victories in the Saar big loss to Reich army in Ruhr. Seen to be a big factor for shortening war.

March 21, 1945   France

Dear Roz,

It seems no one knows just what our status is as we go from a two hour alert to no alert daily. This 4ᵗʰ Division is a bastard's outfit. Why we have gone from the 1ˢᵗ Army to the 3ʳᵈ Army and now the 7ᵗʰ Army is beyond me. However, being in army reserve is really wonderful. I can just sit here and relax for the rest of the war.

We read the Stars and Stripes for news and it seems as if the German army is being defeated and yet the war still goes on. I'm beginning to wonder just how true the information is that we read in the papers. I wonder how the home newspapers are writing things up at present.

I hated to leave the 3ʳᵈ Army. General Patton is a good man and the infantry in his army always did have plenty of help. Sure we hit tough places but the tanks were right up there to shoot hell out of everything and we would push forward again. It wasn't like that under General Hodges. In the 1ˢᵗ Army we just pushed with no help. We would wonder whether today we were going to be hit as everyone was hit up there. Somehow, I was lucky. Our company would change personnel every few hours when we could get replacements. That's all water under the bridge and

I believe our brains have learned that it is easier to be passive resistance than to attempt to run into it head on. I know damn well that Patton will practically win this war with his 3rd army. The Germans fear him more than anyone else. They know that he knows how to attack and keep rolling. I really admire him from the infantry point of view.

My old platoon sergeant and squad leaders are both being put in for battle field commissions now. I have the 4th platoon now which is the weapons platoon. We bring up the rear and fire mortars and our machine guns if the riflemen are stopped. It's really a good break. Of course, I'm still exec but that doesn't mean much around here.

Darling, some officers are being reclassified for not doing their job. Imagine an officer refusing to leave Bn. to bring up antitank guns and help us. Everyone in Bn. sits and shivers and thinks how awful it is up ahead and all are too afraid to come up. There are at least 10 officers in Bn. who have no idea what combat is like and yet they wear all the ribbons and get all the rewards. The Captain, Roberts, and myself are just three mules who somehow keep going and make I Company the best company in the regiment. Yes darling, it is. We have lost less men in the last few months than any other company.

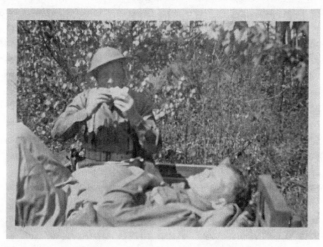

Dave taking a nap during a lull in the fighting.

Sometimes I wonder why? We have seen other companies attempt to take objectives and fail, losing many men. We then get the same mission, shoot beaucoups (French for much) artillery at them and just walk up without firing a shot and the krauts give-up. Is it luck or what? We three have seen other officers come and go in our company, and other companies, and yet we go on indefinitely doing our job. We are veterans and tonight at supper the Captain said that he was going to speak to the Bn. CO and ask him why he doesn't take out rifle officers for replacement at Bn. jobs when vacancies exist. Sort of give the officers who have been doing their job daily a break.

Daring, rewards are easily obtainable. I can't think of very few men in our company who do not rate a reward and yet we are too lazy to write them up. A reward means nothing to us. We just want to get out in one piece. A general may move up as far as Bn. and he'll get the bronze star for exposing himself to enemy fire. I lead the company in attacks for 7 days straight. I was the first man leading. I tried to set the example and if the company Commander leads, every man will follow him into hell and high water. That's the officer's job and we certainly rate awards for that. However, the rear echelon brass hats who approve of the awards will say that what we do is line of duty or just our job. Compree? They have no idea of the fears and courage a man has to show in order to walk towards an enemy machine gun or sniper (these have bothered us but have been very inaccurate).

Darling I'm not trying to set myself as a hero. I'll admit I'm scared. I'll also admit that I still won't go on the parachute ride at Coney Island. You see your husband is a very scared, meek man. If you have been entertaining any thought in your mind as to your husband being fearless, you are totally wrong. I'm just doing my job as best as I can and keep my fingers crossed while doing it. I have learned much and I'd rather use every artillery piece in the rear firing at our target than lose one man and that's exactly what I do. My artillery forward observer always knows that he will get plenty of business with us and yet they always request to go back to our company than go to another. They know that we always use everything the army has in the rear designed to help riflemen. My sergeant just handed me another letter which just arrived. My, this is going to be the longest one I've written in ages.

As for everyone discussing me, I hope that I provide amusing conservations. I know that if my wife lets a few of my private habits out of the bag she'll have everyone in stitches. You wouldn't do that to a fellow, would you? Of course, I can see everyone comparing every move that Richie makes to me. Say, do they ever say he has any of your characteristics? They must have.

Well if he likes rough treatment I'm just the guy to furnish it. You should know I'll probably be gentle as a lamb when I'm home until I get oriented to living with civilians again.

◆   ◆   ◆

British take over Mandalay. Japanese flee from protected fort. Big political gain for Allies.

March 21, 1945   France

Dear Roz,

Guess what, today we received our first ration of canned beer from the States. This beer comes from Pennsylvania somewhere as I never heard of this type of beer before.

◆   ◆   ◆

March 23, 1945   France

Dear Roz,

This morning I was agent officer and paid off the company in francs. I received 543,742, or over a half million francs. That, my darling, is not hay. I'll mail you the receipt which I signed for. After paying off the company I had some doughnuts and coffee. Two Red Cross gals were dishing out their wares right in our company area.

One of the men in my old platoon was court-martialed today. It seems he continually went to the rear in every attack and we would always be looking for him. For misbehaving in the face of the enemy he received 40 years imprisonment today. Last month one man received life imprisonment. Nothing is more drastic than to shag-ass to the rear and leave your buddies holding the bag. Perhaps that one shot which he could have fired would have saved someone's life.

I managed to be paid for January and February and you are once again going to receive $100 more from me this month. Darling, once again I say use it as you wish and buy little things for yourself that all women love to have. What more can I say. I want you to be as happy as possible under the circumstances. I know that you are not enjoying these bitter times with us far apart. I want to think how wonderful it would be to have some money in the bank. Now I can only think in terms of making you happy. Yes darling, your happiness means more to me than anything else.

Did I tell you that in this part of France people speak German? So I manage to get along fairly well with my kraut talk. I'm living with a civilian and three children. Don't get any funny ideas. She is a peasant woman and not very attractive. She has a daughter about 15 years old and all the GI's around here have been trying to make her. They would do anything for a little fun. One sergeant asked me if I wanted to get fixed up, and *would I let him use my room so he could get this gal away from her mother's eyes? I told him he could have the room but to count me out. However, I don't think he got what he expected. Perhaps he couldn't speak German well enough. In any event with all this going on around me I am beginning to feel the pangs of desire going through my veins. It's been a long time for me. However, darling you still mean everything to me.*

◆　　　◆　　　◆

Adolf Hitler calls all Cabinet Ministers and Nazi party leaders to an emergency meeting at Berchtesgaden hide-out. Last-ditch stand to be taken by fanatical Nazi troops in Bavarian Alps.

March 27, 1945　　　　　　　　　　　　　　　　　　*Germany*

Dear Roz,

Yesterday I wrote you that I'm living in another place. This is a new modern house with a bathtub and hot water. Of course I've taken advantage of this luxury. Oh yes, it also has a new type toilet bowl. I actually enjoy the act now. The kraut's are scared to death of the Russian soldiers here and are sweating them out. I never saw any people fear anyone else as much. Exactly why I don't know.

◆　　　◆　　　◆

> *Girls and women fighting U.S. troops in Heidelberg but city taken. Little damage reported. Phone attempts to arrange surrender fail.*

March 31, 1945   Germany

Dear Roz,

I'm sorry I didn't write for the past few days. I've been moving so much it's impossible to find any time for myself. We know less about what is going on here than you do. The lines are fluid as hell and I know that the krauts are changing from uniforms to civilian clothes. Crossing the Rhine was simple. The famous Rhine is fairly wide, about 600 yards where we crossed, but it's nothing compared to the Hudson which is really a river. The more I see of the German civilians the more they realize that they are kaput. They can't actually believe that we have crossed the Rhine. It's the first time their Rhine has ever been invaded. I heard a rumor that Patton was in Munich but that's only a rumor and I haven't seen a newspaper in days now so I really don't know what is up. We have been lucky as hell lately. We still haven't been committed and have had one long vacation but we keep moving around and I call it a vacation because no one is shooting at us. I hate like hell to be so optimistic but my guess is that the 3rd Reich is kaput. I imagine that because of the lack of a government willing to surrender we will have to keep pushing across Germany until we meet up with the Russians.

Love, Dave

STILL NO MAIL

Dear Dad,

Your frustration with the mail during the war is very clear. I can visualize your situation; being alone in a foreign country, miles from home, with fear of an uncertain future, and missing your new wife and baby at home. The thin thread that anchors you to your home is a letter, containing fresh news of your loved ones, news that all-in-all simply says I love you and I'm thinking of you right now. How sad it was that you had to go weeks without a letter from home. When the mail finally caught up with you, your situation had changed and you found yourself responding in your letters to questions Mom asked about a completely different situation, the old one already a fading memory in your mind.

Dear Roz,

Honey, still no mail from you or anyone else. I wonder why so called 4F's couldn't be drafted to be used as mail clerks to ease the mail situation. I can't think of anything worse than no mail.

Germany   November 19, 1944

Honey, the hardest thing about this war is not receiving any mail from you. Darling, I do want to hear from you and when the mail arrives and when there's none for me it's hard to take. As soon as you received my new address, I hoped you would write immediately.

Germany   December 9, 1944

Today I received a letter and a telegram both from you. I don't have to tell you how happy I was to receive them. I've already read the letter three times and I'm going to read it more yet. It's the second time I received mail in two months or more.

Luxemburg   *December 21, 1944*

Darling, please write to me about yourself. Let me know how you are and what you are doing. I want to read about you and I demand at least 4 pages in each letter just about yourself. Won't you let me read about the most important person I know?

Luxemburg   *December 25, 1944*

Say how come I don't hear from you so often? I receive a letter with a gap of about 30 days between that one and the last one. I hope the enemy who captured my mail got as much enjoyment out of it as I would have.

Luxemburg   *January 16, 1945*

I received about 4 letters from you today dated 6 November to the 10 November. Of course the letters are old news and you still think I'm in England but at least they're letters which you wrote and are always welcome.

Luxemburg   *January 13, 1945*

In today's world of cell phones and e-mail it is hard to imagine how you depended on the simple written note to keep it touch. When I get lonely or need some information I pull out my cell phone and make a call; in seconds I'm connected. When Marlene arrives at a destination late at night she calls me and I know instantly that she's okay. Sending a letter just isn't an option, yet that's what you had to do.

225

Dad writing a letter to Mom in a tent.

In one letter Mom tells you I was sick. Three weeks later she gets your reply asking if I am getting better. She doesn't think to update you right away, and six weeks from the original news she replies to you and you find out that everything is okay. That just doesn't seem to work. You had enough on your mind taking care of yourself in the war and it was sad you had to put up with this inefficiency in communications.

I can see why you disliked V-Mail. When you finally got a letter from Mom the writing was too tiny to read and the space for writing was limited. If you wrote two V-mails and sent them as pages 1 and 2 of a letter, it wasn't certain they would even arrive on the same day. Although they seemed to arrive faster than a letter in an envelope, you made your choice very clear; you wanted full letters from Mom and that's what you sent her.

Dear Roz,

Darling, how are you and the little one getting along. I suppose you still have to get up early to feed him and the daily routine with the baby probably keeps you busy all day long. I imagine he is down to a normal eating schedule so you can regulate his diet. What does he look like now? Is he still long and thin or has he filled out? What about yourself honey? How does my angel look these days? Still smiling or do you wear a hard look? Still thin and wiry or are you gaining weight? Still miss me or doesn't it matter? So many questions to answer and yet I hear nothing. Darling I miss you terribly. If only I could see you and Dick again I would be very happy. I need you darling and always will need you by my side. Someday we will gather with our new family and look back over the hard days we had in the past.

Germany   *November 17, 1944*

I am amazed how diligent you were in writing to Mom nearly every day, and sometimes two or three times in one day. No matter how uncomfortable you were or how tired, somehow you managed to get a letter out to her. You sent her money orders not knowing if they would get home, sometimes only finding out months later. This behavior is exactly how I remember you. You made sure you did what you thought needed to be done for your family and didn't get discouraged that money might be stolen. Your situation was never too difficult to carry out your part of a bargain. This is an example of the importance of integrity in your life.

I'm not sure if the army could have improved the mail situation given the circumstances and the technology at the time. Judging from your letters, however, the morale of our troops would have been greatly improved if they had given it a little more priority.

Love,   Rich

The Letters – (Cont.)

Third Army attacks Liepzig and cuts off last large industrial area from Reich. 30,000 Germans trapped. Next objective is to split Germany as Seventh Army turns eastward.

April 2, 1945   *Germany*

Dear Roz,

Well I may have a chance to write a letter now. We still are moving quite rapidly and I don't always get a chance to write. As for mail, well we just don't receive any. It seems as if the mail can't keep up with us. This last house I'm living in now had a motorcycle so .... I will admit it's a lot of fun. I always did want one. We caught a few fish in a nearby stream. Trout. All we do is throw a few hand grenades in the water and catch the dead fish when they float to the top. Of course I'll admit that it isn't exactly sporting but it works.

◆   ◆   ◆

Tokyo radio tells Japanese people for first time that Japan may fall. The Okinawa invasion has turned them pessimistic. The war situation grows more serious with each added second.

April 3, 1945   *Germany*

Dear Roz,

Yesterday I took a haircut and the soldier cutting my hair told me that I'm getting a few grey hairs. I guess I'm getting older without realizing that I am.

◆   ◆   ◆

Poles say their envoys to Russia have vanished. Not the first time this claim has been made. British are skeptical.

April 7, 1945   Germany

Dear Roz,

I don't know how to begin writing this letter. I haven't written for days now but not because I didn't want to. First it's moving forward every day by foot and sleeping in woods and fox holes again. Today we took a town but I haven't got my Musset bag with me and I can't carry more than is possible. I've finally been able to borrow some paper and write this letter to you now.

Darling, your mail has been reaching me with my K rations every night. I notice that you, too, are beginning to be very neglectful in writing to me. Your letters also lack the spirit you always possessed. Darling, I don't want to believe that you are as lonely and blue as your letters signify. Please try and take these trying days a little better. I want to read a little laughter in your letters so please buck up old girl. As for myself, I've been getting along fairly well and am in good health. Darling, I think of you all the time and miss you even more.

◆   ◆   ◆

ROOSEVELT DIES; TRUMAN IS NOW PRESIDENT. President dies at Warm Springs. Everyone, including his family, was unaware of his serious condition and surprised. A cerebral stroke proved fatal to the four term President. He was 63. Cabinet members will keep their posts for now. Funeral is tomorrow at the White House. He will be buried at his home in Hyde Park . Capital stunned.

April 12, 1945   Germany

Dear Roz,

Today I received the package with the chicken dinner in it and cranberry sauce. Of course, we had a little celebration. I certainly haven't been hurting for food since I've been in Germany. I didn't sleep so well last night. I don't know why. Just tired of it all I guess.

Darling, I miss you. I have nothing to look forward to here but to beautiful memories of our past. I wonder just why? Why do we have to keep fighting from day to day? It wouldn't be so bad if it wasn't for the same ones doing all the fighting all the time. One of our sergeants was busted because he failed to salute a colonel in a rear area. They are fighting a different war than we are. Yesterday we were relieved and of course the men were billeted in barns while all the rear echelon boys who never fight live in buildings. Darling it isn't right this way. I believe that nothing is too good for a fighting infantry soldier. These high ranking armchair commanders can only picture us as a symbol on a map to be pushed one way and then another. You will do this. You will attack that objective. Why haven't you jumped off as yet? Things like that and they all get their ribbons and awards from the work which we do.

I lost some good men yesterday. They were only wounded and I knew them all very well. They were casualties because we were obeying an order which never should have been given. I kept thinking about it and I'm feeling pretty bad right now. Yes darling, I've been with these men a long time and combat men have feelings which never become hard and coarse as the newspapers so gallantly describe we veterans.

Honey, now that I've written this to you I feel better already. Just writing to you is just like a tonic. I keep thinking how lovely it would be to have you in my arms and just be with you. That is the most precious thought I have. Darling, I love you and Dick with all my heart. With you at my side I could take anything. Please don't ever let anything ever change that.

◆   ◆   ◆

Himmler has ordered towns not to surrender. Gestapo Chief calls for house-to-house fighting with only death as alternative.

April 13, 1945   Germany

Dear Roz,

No mail today for me. However the eagle S—T today and in marks. I've given 500 marks to the mail orderly to convert into a $50 money order. As soon as he gets it I'll mail it to you. Yes darling, I want you to know it as petty cash for your own personal desires. What you receive in allotment is for you to live on and save. What I send you in money orders I want you to use as you like to. Don't write me and tell me that you intend to save the extra money I send. I still have $30 left for my own personal use.

I sent a couple of swords home. I don't how long it takes to reach you but it should arrive in about a month or so.

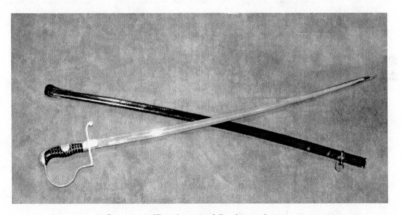

German officer's sword Dad sent home.

The news about President Roosevelt was shocking. I think that things will work out all right. The war seems to be rolling along except in our sector where we meet a little resistance. However, it isn't too much to worry about.

I took a shower today and for the first time in ages I'm wearing summer underwear again. I feel as if I'm naked without my long handles on. It wouldn't be so bad if you were with me. I like being bare when you're around. I've been thinking that my next pleasure after kissing you will be to take a real hot bath and you will scrub my back until I know it's clean. I just can't seem to reach my back myself and today my first shower in a month ended in failure as far as washing the back of yours truly. If you are real good at it I may even consent to wash you.

I read a very good article about the infantry. I cut it out and am mailing it to you. It's very true about the infantry. The weather has been very good. It hasn't rained too much and it's usually warm.

◆   ◆   ◆

Adolf Hitler has asked the Pope to aid in surrender. Nazi slayings are reported as a morale booster to people.

April 15 1944   Germany

Dear Roz,

I started to write Dear Dave. I was talking to one of the men and I wasn't thinking. I'm still moving around a lot. I received a package from you today with the Brown's cough medicine. There wasn't any letter for me from you. I haven't heard from you in at least three days. However, I'm still sweating out a good letter from you.

My gas mask carrier is loaded with all types of food including the mustard you sent. Back in the States we were never permitted to carry food in it but here everything goes.

We passed a captured German airport today with a few planes shot up. Lots of German towns which offer no resistance are still in good shape. Where they decide to defend the town is always shot up and left burning. I'm living in a barracks now and it isn't anything like ours are back in the States.

Well darling, thanks a lot for the package. I keep looking forward to them regularly.

◆   ◆   ◆

Truman sworn in as 32nd President.

April 17, 1945   Germany

Dear Roz,

They tell us during lulls in fighting to take care of ourselves and our equipment. I just moved into a new town, ate scrambled eggs, bread and butter, and milk. Then I washed and shaved. Yesterday the Captain and I had to seek cover behind a manure pit when jerry threw a little artillery. After it was over we both noticed small crab like insects crawling all over us. Today I completely deloused myself with delousing powder. Of course they managed to have a good meal on me until I was able to apply the first aid. I itch in a couple places but I'm still okay.

I made new handles for my 45 pistol out of the Plexiglas captured from a jerry plane. It's transparent and I carry Richard's pictures on both sides. I'm using the pictures with him in the bath tub and one of him completely nude. Of course everyone notices my pistol..

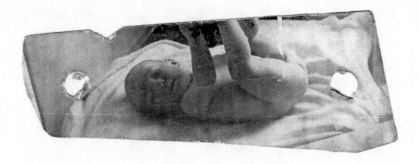

Pictures of Richard that Dave put in his pistol handle.

Dave's pistol with Richard's picture in the handle.

I believe I told you that I was issued a 17 jewel Waltham wrist watch. Well I let one of the men use the one you gave me and he was wounded way back when we jumped over the Auer River into Germany. He was wounded and returned the other day. Now I have two watches again. Of course it doesn't run right since I took the trip on the Ile de France. I don't know why. I guess the salt water moisture caused some part to rust.

I don't have any idea what the latest news is. I hear rumors that armored units are running pell-mell all over Germany without much opposition. I wish I could say the same but I can't. Some day remind to tell you about XXI corps trying to make a truce. I can't tell you more in a letter now. Enclosed you will find a volkstrum band which marked a German civilian automatically into a soldier.

◆   ◆   ◆

British and Americans gain in Bologna push. Argenta captured by Brits. Americans reach Pianora. The coastal advance continues.

April 19, 1945   Germany

Dear Roz,

We still are chasing these krauts and every now and then we run into some rough places. I'm dead tired from walking and every time I get a chicken or duck frying we get the order to move up. Excuse me -----.

Back again darling. I began writing this letter hours ago. Now I'm in another strange town. My poor aching feet. If ever a pair of dogs are barking mine are those. We still are chasing the krauts and by God it isn't an easy job. Every one higher up keeps pushing us forward and all is well until we run into a place that the damn krauts have decided to defend. Then things begin to happen. *Oh what a life this infantry is. I'm tired of fighting and having everyone right behind us. They can't wait until we take a town so that the entire motorized army can ride in and select the best buildings while we get kicked in the pants and are told to take a new objective.*

Love, Dave

FINDING THE FATHER

My friend, this body offers to carry us for nothing - as the ocean
carries logs.
So on some days the body wails with its great energy;
it smashes up the boulders,
lifting small crabs, that flow around the sides.

Someone knocks on the door.
We do not have time to dress.
He wants us to go with him through the blowing and rainy streets,
to the dark house.

We will go there, the body says,
and there find the father whom we have never met,
who wandered out in a snowstorm the night we were born,
and who then lost his memory,
and has lived since longing for his child,
whom he saw only once...
while he worked as a shoemaker,
as a cattle herder in Australia,
as a restaurant cook who painted at night.

When you light the lamp you will see him.
he sits there behind the door....
the eyebrows so heavy,
the forehead so light....
lonely in his whole body,
waiting for you.

—by Robert Bly

LIFE IS GOOD

Dear Dad,

I read these lines you wrote from Belgium and I remembered how you used to say similar things to us all the time. No matter what you had you always thought yours was the best that could be had. The wall air conditioner in your living room got the house colder, faster than any other unit sold. The fact that it was 20 years old didn't matter to you. It was yours and therefore it was the best, and yes, it did get the house very cold in no time.

> *Dear Roz,*
>
> *Did you ever believe all this would have happened to us when we first met? It's hard to believe it's happening now. Most of my life since we were married has been like a dream. I have to pinch myself to be sure it's true. I know I'm married and am a father but, and it's a big but. Like a dream I had last night. A beautiful dream with wonderful memories. I wonder if you think I'm going batty writing this way but I'm not darling. I want you very badly and I'm writing the way I feel now.*
>
> *Belgium*   *November 15, 1944*

There was no better place to live than Port Washington, NY. Situated on the north shore of Long Island, you had the town dock which really was a truly beautiful place to sit and look out over the bay. Main Street had all the shopping you could ever need. Even the beaches were the best, although they were polluted and you couldn't swim there. But who wanted to swim anyway. They had beautiful park areas to sit and read by the water and a pavilion where the town provided live music and dancing during the summer months. What more could anyone want?

Dave with his sister, Ruth

You didn't seem to mind the endless traffic on the roads, and store parking lots that were so tiny and congested that they could rival professionally designed obstacle courses. Nothing could detract from that fact that it was your town and therefore the best. Your fifteen year old Sable was peppy and drove smoothly. This was a pattern that covered just about everything you had.

It goes without saying that you had the best wife. You loved Mom more than anything, and although I never heard the word love mentioned, you often said she was a beautiful woman and that she was the best.

I'll admit that I got tired of hearing you talk about how good everything you had was. It's not because I minded what you were saying, but you said it so often. I wondered why you found it necessary to repeat these bragging statements all the time. Sometimes I thought you were really very satisfied with your lot in life and repeating things was just a habit. Then I would wonder if you had an inferiority complex and had to state how great your things were to convince yourself and others. I'll never know what was really going through your mind, Dad, but I suspect that you were very satisfied and happy and you wanted other people to know it.

I wish you could have enjoyed being who you were, and what you had, in a more personal way; that you could feel good just by thinking about how lucky you were, but that wasn't enough for you. You had to make sure others knew it. If it were possible for me to relive some of the past, I would have tried to enroll you in my men's group, The Mankind Project, where you would have had the opportunity to explore this personal shadow. This would not have been an easy sell though, because you were against any kind of therapy, self-improvement exercises, and admission of personal weaknesses. In fact, I didn't even tell you about my association with MPK because I thought you would laugh at me and say it was a waste of time, although Mom did know about it. That's too bad because it erected another barrier between us.

Dad, I know you are happy in the peaceful place you are now, and I think you finally understand that it wasn't important what everyone else thought. What mattered is that you believed it.

Love, Rich

The Letters – (Cont.)

Patton turns flank of enemy in drive to capture Hitler's redoubt. Bremen on fire after Germans reject ultimatums to quit. Tanks covered 53 miles in hard drive southward.

April 24, 1945   Germany

Dear Roz,

I received another package from you with whiskey and crackers. It really was a good package and hit the spot. Thanks a lot honey. Your packages arrive very often now. Speaking of money, I also sent some through government channels, PIS. I believe you told me that you received that.

Before I forget we have a Japanese field artillery with us now. My forward observer is with me right now.

I believe that passes to the Riviera will commence soon so perhaps I'll get a chance to go there in a few weeks. Oh yes, before I forget too, we have liberated beaucoups of concentration camp personnel. The people are so happy they just keep running around us admiring us just as if we were freaks at a side show. Many pack all their belongings in a bag and hit the long refugee trail back home.

In regards to that article you read on officers, I was asked whether I would like to get a regular army commission. My answer was emphatically no. The reason being that I had enough of army life to last me a lifetime.

◆   ◆   ◆

Hitler's redoubt is eyed as target by Third Army. The fortress is offering little resistance as Americans close in near the Danube city of Regensburg. A huge explosion reported caused by our planes.

April 25, 1945   Germany

Dear Roz,

I have a few minutes to write a short letter. I'm in a new home again and getting my company set up. I found another type of insignia which I am sending to you. I've caught a slight cold and my nose is running. However, don't send me any medicines as it doesn't help any.

◆   ◆   ◆

The Po river was crossed today despite heavy resistance.

April 26, 1945   Germany

Dear Roz,

Well here I am still moving along and this time I had a real experience. I never rode tanks before and my company spearheaded an attack. We went right through the German lines and kept going. Our destination was a nice size town and we are waiting for the rest of our Bn. to catch up to us. I Company was a task force all by itself.

My First Sergeant shot himself in the leg yesterday. He was always a highly nervous person and I expected him to crash but I didn't think he had the nerve to shoot himself. I know that I could never do a thing like that. Outside of that we didn't lose a man. We ran across a group of German soldiers and the tanks just shot the hell out of them and we kept rolling.

God have I been walking lately. I have blisters on my feet and they are sore as hell. The men are all saying that I walk too fast and they can't keep up with me. I can't help that as we have to cross much open country. When I know that the jerries are looking right at us I know we have to move fast so they can't get too good a target. However, my greatest ambition is to save as many lives as possible and let the men walk a little faster. They appreciate it when we get there.

I'm losing a little weight. Believe it or not size 34 pants are getting too large for me. We begin attacking at dawn and continue till sun down. Then there are a million things to do like getting the men billets, setting up all around defenses and outposts and then I try and grab something to eat. At around 11:30 PM I'm called up to a company commanders meeting to plan the next day's attack and I usually receive the attack orders and plan how we will go about it. It usually lasts about 2 hours. I then return to my company, wake up the platoon leaders, and give them the poop. At about 2 am I get to sleep and am up at 6 am. So you see honey, it really is rough and over a long period of time it gets a man physically.

We walk at least ten miles a day, reach our objective and then the cycle begins again. Isn't it a great life? Add to that the Germans shooting at us and you have a good mental picture of modern warfare. What I sweat out most of all is having a town as our final objective for the day. If we wind up in woods it means digging in for the night and no smoking as we observe strict blackout all the time. Oh well, why I write all this to you I can't really understand myself. I've always been truthful with you and I'm not telling all this so you can worry. I'm just giving you a picture of what is going on.

I'm hoping that all is going well with you at home and also that this damn war ends soon. I miss you all very much darling and am looking forward to a swell reunion.

◆　　　◆　　　◆

Fighting between the Gestapo and German citizens reported in Berlin. Sewers become battlefield. Corpses seen in street.

April 29, 1945   Germany

Dear Roz,

Honestly my feet are in very bad shape. Yesterday we walked about 15 miles through woods. It rained like hell and we were soaking wet. Keep pushing is all I hear all the time. Why have you stopped? We got to keep going. I get all this over my radio and I get pissed off. We don't even get enough time to cook a K ration. As soon as we take a town why every rear echelon unit is there and we get kicked out.

◆   ◆   ◆

Mussolini slain in northern Italy by partisans. His mistress was also killed with him. The dictator was executed after a trial in which he begged for his life. Others killed too. The Vatican has mixed feelings about the slayings. Bodies on display in Milan.

April 30, 1945   Germany

Well I finally found out why I'm not receiving any mail. It seems that the mail has no priorities in this fast moving situation. Today we did a few more miles on foot. I was able to see the Alps for the first time. They are immense mountains capped with snow. From the artistic point of view it's beautiful, from the soldier's it means hard rough fighting in cold mountainous country.

So far I've been doing fairly well as company commander. I haven't had any trouble with any of the men.

My right foot is very sore. I have my ankle all taped up but these long walks over rough country is hard on my feet. Fear is a wonderful strength producer. Yesterday I crossed a flat field 4,000 yards wide. It was raining and we were supposed to take *a town on the other side of the field. Well I looked around and could find no concealed route so I sent a strong patrol and a radio ahead to feel out the town and see if they get any fire on them They were about half way over and called back that all is well and they could see white flags flying signifying that the town surrenders. I led the main body and we followed. About half way over I noticed a group of artillery guns about 3,000 yards to my left and people were walking around them. I knew they weren't ours as we were far ahead of our own artillery. I looked through my field glasses and could recognize the guns but I couldn't recognize the soldiers. It was raining and cold but I still broke out into a cold sweat. I passed the word back 50 yards between each man and I shagged ass forward. My aching foot didn't hinder me any then and we made it across in record time. Later I found out that it was civilians milling around and the guns were knocked out. It's little things like that which give me grey hairs.*

I don't know how I would feel if I ever walked the company into a trap. I honestly believe that I would crack if that ever happened. I try and use all the safety precautions I can but higher brass is always on my neck why I'm not moving faster. No one of them ever comes up to see what is happening. I have more combat time than all the officers in Bn. headquarters added together. They have been in so called combat longer but not in the rifle companies. Here the word combat means just that. I will admit that I'm not too brave myself. I hear shells coming in and I'm looking for a hole somewhere.

I'd like to go to sleep but I can't. I have to get many things done yet before I retire. I'll get 15 messages too about the company at different hours or to report to Bn. at 2 am. Anything to keep me from getting a good night's rest. My headquarters men kid me about bucking for captain. I don't buck for anything except getting out of the infantry. I'd trade all the prestige that goes with being company commander for a private's rating in ordnance or quartermaster in the States. Oh well. I guess I've given you my daily complaint. I still manage to get by somehow. Today I ate 10 eggs. I can't eat K rations anymore. I'm too tired looking at them and eating them. I'm never lazy enough to cook a good meal.

◆   ◆   ◆

The German Annihilation Institute in Kiev executed 140,000 people unworthy to live, according to Dr. G. Wilheim Schuebbe, during his nine month tenure there.

May 1, 1945   Germany

Another day gone by to bring this war closer to an end. My poor aching feet are swathed in miles of tape. We run the remaining krauts back to the mountains and from here on I believe they are going to get a little rough. There can't be too many because of the number of prisoners we have been taking.

I keep thinking how wonderful it would be to be at home with you. Darling I miss our home more every day. I'm really tired physically and mentally. I lost a little weight. I go without eating as we don't stop long enough to heat up a K ration. Believe it or not my 34 pants are getting large on me. The old Leitman 'can' just can't be there any more. We are resting here for a few hours and I took a shave and haircut. I needed a haircut badly. We have only had two hot meals in the last ten days. It's very difficult to bring up the kitchen. Even the mail is slow in arriving. I haven't heard from you in days now and miss your letters.

I had a run in with some rear echelon signal corps captain yesterday. After walking from 7 am until 6 pm we were ordered to halt and await further orders. It began to rain and I told the men to go into buildings which some signal men had put their reserved signs on. They tried to kick us out and I told this particular captain of the signal unit that anytime fighting men who walked as far as we do can't move in a building that has a reserve sign on it for troops that never fight, and ride, that will be the day. I told him that he could have my job if he wanted it bad enough. I would gladly change places with him. He threatened to call some colonel which I told him was fine. I told him that I'll tell this colonel the same damn thing. I know who is fighting this war and I'm not taking any crap from the rear.

The final windup was that he apologized to me and all was well. We stayed.

Well darling, that's just an incident in my daily life. So long for now honey. I'm tired and will attempt to get some sleep while I can. So long for now and kiss Richard a special kiss for me.

◆　　　◆　　　◆

The Big Three have agreed that France will share in the Reich surrender. France will be part of the German capitulation.

May 2, 1945   Germany

Dear Roz,

Another day gone by and many miles passed under our feet today. Darling, I get disgusted with this infantry life more every day. Today I walked through miles of swamps. No hot meals, no mail. I've had three eggs and a cup of coffee for all day today. I spoke to the Bn. Commander and he tells me that I'm bitching too much. He rides everywhere, never sticks his nose where there is the slightest danger and has his kitchen truck follow him everywhere he goes. Just what they expect of a doughboy is beyond me. We expect hardships but we also expect people to think of us other than to receive attack orders.

It snowed all morning and was cold. I've changed to summer underwear and know that we are in cold country. I'm not dressed for the occasion.

Darling I miss your letters very much and am looking forward to some of your mail arriving soon. I just had three letters handed to me. It seems that some of the mail did come through. One of the letters, however, was mailed in December and just arrived. Of course after reading your letters about Richard I just can't help feeling the part of the proud father. I wish I could see him darling. I keep wondering what he is like. I tell myself time and time again that he looks like you and me, and then I begin to wonder. Of course my greatest desire is to be with you. I miss you so much. I could just lie in bed with you and hold you close to me for days.

One of the men just told me a report came over the radio that Hitler was dead. Also the German army in Italy had surrendered. I don't know how many prisoners we have captured these past few days. We got at least 900 today. I line them up in a column and they follow me. More krauts come hopping out of the woods and just form in line behind the POW column.

However, the war still goes on and I don't know what to expect. Right now there are large mountains ahead of us. I'm sweating them out. Well honey, that's all for now. I have you on my mind always and love you more than ever.

◆   ◆   ◆

HITLER AND GOEBBELS DEAD. Truman said he believes the fanatical dictator of the Reich died by his own hands.

May 3, 1945   Germany

Dear Roz,

Today is the 3rd of May and it's snowing. I can't figure out this climate but if it weren't for this time of the year I'd swear it was winter. I'm deep down in Germany now and well in their inner fortress. Believe me I can see why it's called that as every time I look at those damn mountains I can see rough walking, let alone fighting. One of my nom-coms from my old 1st platoon was hit by a truck speeding through this town. Darling, I could have screamed when I heard that. He was one of my better non-coms and he was banged up and refused to be evacuated. I'm going to let him stay with the kitchen today. Speaking of the kitchen, we had a hot meal today and it runs right through me. I don't seem to be able to hold food in my stomach. I guess that after eating regular again I should get back to normal habits. I know I can get into size 32 pants as the 34's I'm wearing now is very baggy.

How am I doing as Company Commander? From the military point of view I have taken every objective given to me so far. My casualties have been very few. I'm really doing fine however there are so many little things to be done. For example, in the middle of an attack I receive a radio message for the names of three men who have a GI license and can drive a truck. Well my company was spread out over a long area and I had to send messages up and down the line to get the info and call it back over the radio. I'm really pretty handy with the radio myself and do well with the set. I'm getting to be a very versatile individual.

Today Stars and Stripes carried three inch headlines that Hitler was dead. It didn't mention how he died. Well perhaps that will be the end of all organized resistance now. I hope so. Refugees and prisoners we have liberated come begging (to) us for food. We give them a little of our K rations and some of them just keel over and die. They haven't eaten in so long that decent food kills them. How these Germans can expect any sympathy from us is beyond me. They aren't civilized from the way I look at them.

Darling, the horrors of Germany are well known. I've seen some of them and also I know the horrors of modern warfare. All weapons designed to kill are designed to kill the infantryman. He is the one with the least protection. He is the one who must come out in the open to reach them. Before each attack I always get a nervous feeling. All we ever do is attack so at the end of a month's fighting everyone is on a razor edge mentally. We still laugh and joke and kid around ourselves but we all know the seriousness of an attack. We know that if we are lucky we will have light casualties. We do know that some one always gets hit and the old question of who it will be always causes the fear. I'm getting exhausted physically and mentally myself.

I pickup up a few million marks of old German currency. I'll send you some samples of it in this letter.

Well darling, that's all for now. I'll let you know how things work out when they take place. So long for now.

Love, Dave

Old German currency that Dad sent home.

About Whiskey

Dear Dad,

If a stranger were to read your letters he would think that drinking alcohol was a major part of your life. You wrote about when the whiskey rations were given out, and how you anxiously awaited their arrival. You wrote of bouts of drinking and hangovers. I laughed when I read about the milk of magnesia bottles Mom sent to you that were actually filled with whiskey. I write this letter to you because I have a feeling it is important to explore your interesting relationship with the drink if I am to understand who you were. You were certainly not an alcoholic, by any means, but were you an abuser of the substance? Were you prone to drinking in excess once you started? Did alcohol have an effect on you and did it shape parts of your life?

Dear Roz,

I know that you can send packages to me and I'll get them quickly now. I still can use the medicine in the milk of magnesia bottle.

Luxemburg   *January 24, 1945*

Dear Roz,

I know that you can send packages to me and I'll get them quickly now. I still can use the medicine in the milk of magnesia bottle.

Luxemburg   *January 24, 1945*

There is no question in my mind that you enjoyed drinking while in the army and I don't think that is strange. Under the circumstances I could see looking forward to the diversion myself. It was an escape from boredom which you faced much of the time. It served to quiet your fears and numb the horrors of death while on the front lines. It was an innocent form of entertainment, sanctioned by the army and supplied in regular rations to you as an officer. A pass meant a chance to let loose, which meant whiskey was called for. What else was a soldier to do for entertainment?

Dear Roz,

I received my latest whiskey ration and it consisted of one bottle of scotch and a half bottle of gin. From my letters you must think that I get bottles of liquor and just sit and get drunk. Actually I give away most of my hooch and drink very little myself. All the whiskey I've been getting lately is a back issue. There were many places where it was impossible to bring it up to us. Now that things are a bit easy they are making up for all that we missed.

Tomorrow on my pass I think I'll get a little high. It's been a hell of a long time and I'm anxious to see what it's like. I sure wish you were with me and we were going out together. Honey, when I'm home again you and I will steal an evening for ourselves and both of us will get piss-eyed. I will probably get drunk first and the evening will wind up with you taking home a drunken ex-soldier. At least I know that you will put me to bed.

Luxemburg   *January 14, 1945*

In some letters to Mom you talk about wanting to get drunk and in others you say you do not abuse alcohol. I think the former more accurately describes your interest in drinking in those days. However, that conflicted with your image of a responsible husband and father and every now and then you made an attempt to convince yourself that whiskey was just not that important to you. You did not convince me and I don't think you convinced yourself, or Mom. That's not to criticize you, for after all, you deserved any form of enjoyment you could obtain, but I am just searching for your truth.

Dear Roz,

You seem to think that I write better letters when I'm drinking. I get more passionate and romantic them days. Drinking sort of brings out my inner feelings. God help the German maedchen. I have ample opportunity to indulge in a little Dutch intercourse. The boys tell me that these kraut women are very passionate people. As for myself, I really am hurting at present for a little bit of that but I always felt that your whosis was the most precious and most desired asset as far as my sport and pleasures went. Are you laughing as yet? Don't worry hon, I'll be good. But when I get home beware. I can think of certain parts of our anatomy which will subject to much wear and tear (mostly wear).

Germany   *April 15, 1945*

Drinking obviously did not interfere with the job you did as an officer and infantryman. Your performance was that of a hero to me. The men under you knew it too. They respected your knowledge, clear thinking, and concern for their own safety and followed you diligently in charge after charge against the enemy. Your use of alcohol was apparently no concern to them and not out of control.

Dad had a beautiful smile.

It does sound like you were an abuser, though, and did not know how, or care to control how much you drank when you did. I don't understand why you would drink enough to get a hangover the next day when you know how awful that felt. Why wasn't more moderate drinking adequate for you?

I talked to Mom about how it was when you returned home. Her response was surprising to me. I expected that you would have returned as a grateful, loving husband, anxious to get on with your life in a more normal way and put all the war stuff behind you. Her response was short and to the point, "It was hard because of the drinking." How sad this must have been for the two of you. I was too young to know what was going on but I'm sure I was affected in some way too by your weakness for alcohol.

But I wonder if this wasn't to be expected. How did the army prepare you for the return to civilian life? Did they provide training classes like they did when you were sent overseas? Did they offer sessions with a counselor or therapist to see what the nightmarish experiences had done to you? Did they just turn you loose to fend for yourself as a civilian after five years of living under strict rules and guidelines?

Yes, you were prone to alcohol abuse and with your newfound freedom you took advantage of the opportunity to drink to excess. Mom's memory is not strong enough now, nor is her will, to remember the details of how you got over this damaging habit and how your family life settled down to a more stable situation. I know that it did because I don't have many recollections of your alcohol abuse while I was growing up. Sure you liked to have a Tom Collins or a vodka and orange juice in the evening, or while sitting on the porch on a hot summer day, but I don't remember you having more.

> *Dear Roz,*
>
> *You wrote M. gets drunk as hell every chance he gets. Darling, I think your brother just grew up too fast. He travels in fast company and if he thinks that getting drunk is the solution of a good time he's mistaken. However, it's a bad habit to form. As for myself I don't go in for any excessive drinking. There is plenty of Schnapps here but I don't care for it. I hope Richard never gets any craving for the stuff.*
>
> *Germany*   *May 24, 1945*

You had some interesting drinking habits. You didn't drink beer except on rare occasions and then only one or two. The only wine I was familiar with was Manischewitz and we drank it only on religious occasions such as at our family Passover Seder. I didn't even know that Merlots, Chablis, and the other finer wines existed. You told us never to go to a saloon to drink but that if we wanted a drink it was okay to have it in the privacy of our home. You considered drinking in a bar very low class. I must say that I got through all my college years without going into a bar or sitting on a barstool in a restaurant until after I was married because of what you taught me, and even to this day I am not comfortable with it, although I do find it quite natural to have a drink with my meal in a restaurant.

Although later on in life you were not a real abuser of alcohol, you did like to make a big deal over having a drink in the evening, even as you got much older. "Roz, give me a shot of bourbon," or, "Give me some whiskey and don't be stingy," were said dramatically as if you were flaunting that you could drink. I always thought it odd because sometimes you never even finished your drink. I think you did it more for the effect than because you wanted the alcohol.

When you were in your last year of life you complained to me that you were upset that you couldn't have a drink. We talked to your doctor and he gave you permission to have one drink a night. This made you very happy. We asked you often if you wanted something to drink and you rarely did. When we

255

offered you some alcoholic beverage you rarely took more than one sip. I think you just wanted to know that you were not being denied yet another thing, and you got back a little more control of your life.

Dad, you know that alcohol is not an important part of my life and I rarely drink it. I learned some healthy habits around drinking from you and I'm glad you got over your abuse of the substance early on so that it did not affect our family life.

Dad, I think I'll have a drink tonight and make a toast to you. I miss you.

Love, Rich

The Letters – (Cont.)

Hitler's charred remains found by Russian soldiers.

May 4, 1945   *Germany*

Dear Roz,

Another day gone by and I'm still in the dark as to just what is going on in this war. Is it over here or not? I don't know. We could be in reserve as we are having a two day rest now. I've caught up on my sleep and am eating well again. The officers have been receiving whiskey rations and we never had a chance to drink them. Last night I took my bottle of gin and got some grapefruit juice from the kitchen. It really mixes well and is very tasty. We also had scotch and bourbon. I don't care for it and still do not drink very much. It's not too hard to get cognac and schnapps but those drinks do not satisfy my sense of taste either.

The family is complete: Richard, Roz, Dave, Mark, and Susan
holding sister Sally.

There are many refugees here from bombed out cities and all the small country towns are loaded with them. They tried to run away from the war but no matter which way they went they still had the war come to them. There are hundreds of people who left the Dachau concentration camp near here and they are practically walking dead.

In the next town where I have some of the men, these ex-prisoners slaughtered a cow, cooked it and ate so fast six of them died. Life is cheap here and when people flop down dead in the streets it's just another every day incident.

The Germans were told that we would kill their babies and be very brutal to them. They were terribly afraid of us when we first entered. Now they have lost their fear and hope we remain. They know that as long as the Americans are here the SS will not return. People of all nationalities roaming around from town begging for food. We can't feed them as the word gets around and we'll have hundreds at our kitchen door. It's hard to chase them away but there is nothing we can do. Not many Americans back home can realize the hardships which these Nazis have caused to so many people. The regular German army has already surrendered most of their men. The SS fanatics still believe in dying for the cause. I can't understand them unless they consist of dope drugged addicts.

I received a letter from you yesterday. Darling you seem so downhearted. Please try and buck your spirits up a little. When I'm in a rest area as I am in these past two days I am so relieved to be off the line that I'm actually happy. It means two days less of fighting. Two days in which no one is killed or wounded. That is the most we can pray for and hope for.

I think about our home, scrambled eggs for breakfast, my frau and sohn and I'm day dreaming in a different world. Then my mental picture takes in both of us lying on the couch listening to the radio, Richard romping around on the floor, and I see the perfect American home. Darling, America is a wonderful country and what we have there can't be described in words.

My dear, perhaps it won't be too long before we are (with) each other again. It won't be long before it will be a year since I last saw you. One long year which seems like ten. So much has happened.

I read an article in the Readers Digest *how people are going to treat us like freaks after this war is over. We don't want to be treated that way. Just let it seem as if we left yesterday and returned today and nothing happened. That's the way we would want it to be. Well darling, that's all for now. I hope this letter raises your spirits enough to smile. Yes darling, please smile while reading this letter so I know that it has done some good. Darling, so long for now. I have you and the little one on my mind all the time.*

PS How about some more pictures of you and Richard?

◆　　　　◆　　　　◆

Contact between the U.S, and Russian soldiers has been friendly. Little animosity seen.

May 6, 1945   Germany

Dear Roz,

I've already written one letter to you today. However, tonight I received three letters from you so I believe you have another letter coming to you. First of all, on the money I sent you, you should have received some through P.T.A. and also I sent one money order. I gave the mail clerk $50 and as yet I didn't get it back so I couldn't mail it to you. I'm going to send all of my next pay through P.T.A. That seems to be the only way to send money. They are checking up on all money sent home and no one can send home more than he earns unless he submits a statement saying how he got it.

I really don't know what I need for my birthday. Actually I need nothing; however, if you can send me a good box of chocolates I'd appreciate it very much.

The more I think of it the more I realize that my son is changing one hell of a lot. He is getting bigger even though in the photo his pants are dragging on the floor. However, you were on one picture and that picture received beaucoups of my undivided attention.

Honey, that beautiful feeling you get in my arms will be yours again. I'm in good health; however, now that I get a good chance to eat hot meals and get plenty of sleep I'm sure to gain weight. Darling, you won't be disappointed when you see me. However it looks as if I will be in the army of occupation and that may take a little time before I'm home. I can't kick about this job honey as at least it means that much less time before I can be sent to the other front.

Darling, you read about four or five year men being discharged. You get yourself too worked up honey, as to begin with, I'm an officer and we don't operate the same way as enlisted men. There is always a shortage of infantry officers and I'm sweating out someone deciding that I have a world of combat experience and put my experience to work.

So you see only the end of the war brings total peace. Then of course I have to find a job. That ought to be easy. However, our family will always be intact.

By the way, does the car still run? If it does, then that 35 Plymouth is a miracle all by itself. However, I could understand getting a flat with those tires. I surely expected the tubes to be sticking out the sides of the walls by this time. I hope that Richard likes rough treatment as you say as I'll probably be very hard with him myself. I just wouldn't know how to play with a baby.

Dad with his 1935 Plymouth.

I'm going to return the pictures you sent as I'll only lose them anyhow. I'm also enclosing a picture of a priest. I stayed in his house with my CP group. He thought we were so nice there was nothing too good for us. I told all the men that there would be no looting. Usually we hit a house and everyone is hunting in closets and drawers. The place usually looks like a tornado hit it.

Well darling, that just about covers all I have to write. Take care of yourself and don't worry. I love you both very much.

◆　　　◆　　　◆

Berlin's short wave radio stops transmitting.

May 6, 1945   *Germany*

Dear Roz,

Well my fright is over for the moment. When I was beyond Munich and saw those Alps I could see rough fighting ahead. When we were rolling toward Nuremburg and Munich I could see hard street fighting as we had in Augsburg when the Captain was wounded. Instead it was easy and the steam roller moved in. Now we are in a new area. Strong rumors persist that we will be part of the army of occupation. I don't even know at present if this war here is over as news is slow in arriving.

Darling, both of us are wondering just how long before we see each other again. I think of that myself for many an hour. However, I know what is to be done first before we go home; for one thing, the war in Japan, the other, the army of occupation. Which of these two evils is worse? Having been in combat the answer is very clear to me. I hope and pray that I will remain here and not go to the Pacific. Darling, I'm certain that there will be an increase of leaves and furloughs from Germany when things quiet down. Right now I'd rather look forward to that than a 30 day furlough to the States and off to another war. I could never begin to tell you everything that an infantry soldier goes through in combat. Aside from the fighting, the living is the worst imaginable... filth, dirt, water, mud all of which we have to endure. The thought of going to the pacific and going through the same and perhaps rougher living doesn't fill me with any joy. Yes darling, being in Germany is the lesser of the two evils and I hope my wish comes true.

The weather is bad. It's been raining now for two days. My clothes are damp on me and I'm trying to dry up. First thing I'm going to do is gain some of my lost weight. I don't feel right this way and am a little weak.

Darling, I'm looking forward to your mail arriving soon. It's very slow in coming, being that mail has no priorities. I'll keep writing darling, when I can, and you'll always be notified of my being. This month I'll be 26 years old. Five years of my life gone. Well darling, that's about everything I have to write about now. Take good care of yourself and don't worry about me now as there is no shooting where I am now. I love you with all my heart.

◆   ◆   ◆

Russians pushing hard to take as much territory before the Americans. Increasing opposition of west cited.

May 7, 1945   Germany

Dear Roz,

Well my short term as C.O. is over. The Captain wasn't hit too bad and returned quickly. Instead of removing the shrapnel they decided that it was better to let the wound heal as that would not require any cutting. This is frequently done as at times it is necessary to make large incisions to probe for a small piece of shrapnel. I am glad he is back, now I can relax a bit and revert back to my job as exec.

Today we went looking for a car, which we found, and went for a spin. These cars here haven't got the pep that ours have. The battalion CO has Goering's special car. He is living in his house at present. We took a ride to a nearby castle and looked around there. It's just like a museum with many old family relics.

The castle belongs to some baron who was a Nazi and was taken back for questioning. His wife and servants are still there and she acted frightened but we just walked in and looked over the place. They had a family tree on the wall which dated way back and continued back to 1700. Many castles were bombed but that is strictly T.S. (Top secret).

I don't believe we will remain here very long as I don't see what we can guard here. It's a sort of a resort here and I can't actually believe that I am on a vacation. Even so at night I don't feel right unless I black out the windows. It's hard to believe that the war is over. I still can't sleep at ease at night unless I know that there is a guard on during the hours of darkness. One doesn't just get over combat mentally so quickly. Honestly, honey, I just can't believe that the war is over.

Darling, please don't write so often about me going home so that I don't feel too bad. I really don't expect to go home so soon and I don't want you to feel too disappointed. Darling, I am so happy to have survived combat in one piece that I can't expect to have all the fortunes of luck on my side now. Well darling, so long for now. I have just about covered all the latest news. No need to worry any more so concentrate on yourself and Richard.

◆　　　◆　　　◆

END OF THE WAR IN EUROPE!
Unconditional surrender by Germany. V-E Day proclaimed.

May 7, 1945   Germany

Dear Roz,

Well it looks as if we begin the second phase of occupation now. We already are beginning the preparations necessary to function. We have a good set up and my CP is in a nice hotel with electric lights, radio and a nice soft bed. What more can I ask for? I'm hoping that I remain here as I'm not too keen about going to another theatre of operation. We are pretty busy now taking inventory of everything in all our buildings. In our hair, we have hundreds of women and children who were evacuated from bombed out cities in Germany. Exactly what happens to them I don't know. In any event I have women crying on my shoulder all day long telling me that their husbands are all dead or missing and they have two or three children and no place to go. Darling I was lucky as hell to get through what I did unscathed. I was the (only) officer in the history of our company who did not get the Purple Heart. Darling, I don't know what more to write. Well darling, that's about all for now. I'm going to take a hot bath and go to sleep.

◆   ◆   ◆

Truman says victory is only half won. Urges the Japanese to quit.

May 9 1945   Germany

Dear Roz,

Well they still say the war is over and I still can't believe it. Today was inspection day for us and passed with flying colors. Considering the buildings which we had to clean up we did an excellent job.

It looks as if we will be moving around a bit more before we finally get settled. Of course the big talk here is when and who will go to the South Pacific but we haven't heard a word about going ourselves, not even a rumor which makes me very happy.

We tried to get riding horses so the Burgomeister (mayor) took us to a house but all they had there were truck horses. Of course this non-fraternizing policy of our army doesn't help any as there are many pretty maedchen around here; the real sharp stuff which left the big cities as they were being bombed. Of course some of the officers seem not (to) be bothered too much by army policies and they say that these babes are very obliging and willing. They are very disappointed in themselves as they have been eating K rations so long that the will is there but the everlasting power is gone.

Love, Dave

THE SIGNIFICANCE OF A WATCH

Dear Dad,

When I read this letter about your watches a soft sadness overcame me and my eyes got teary. Your words drew me very close to you for I know how important your watch always was to you.

Dear Roz,

The watch I bought on the boat was a cheap one and it stopped already. I had to wind it every morning and night. I was firing a rifle and the recoil of the gun stopped the watch. Now you see why it is important to have a shockproof watch in the army. I believe I told you that I had my old watch fixed and now it is running in good order. That was an excellent watch.

England   *September 11, 1944*

Several years ago you were ill and had to stay in the hospital for awhile. I think it was when you fell and broke your shoulder and wrist. You were very uncomfortable and in a lot of pain. You were also extremely aggravated that your watch had stopped working and you asked me to buy you another one right away.

I wanted you to be less agitated so your mind could concentrate on healing your broken bones, so I went right out to the drug store and bought you a battery operated Timex watch for $25. It was very plain but had a large round face and large clear numbers so you could see it easily.

You loved it and you put it on your left arm as soon as you saw it. You did indeed relax more now that you were back in the business of telling time. Yes, you loved that watch.

Every time I visited you was an occasion for you to tell me how much you were amazed at that watch because it never stopped running and always told the correct time. This was one of your rituals that you performed faithfully, whether you were sick or well, lucid or dealing with a bout of dementia. The operation of that watch became a foundation of your life and it never disappointed you.

When you were in your final days and under the care of your hospice workers and aides, we took the watch off your arm because we thought you would hurt yourself with it as you tossed your arms around in your bed. At one point you woke up from your medicated doze and realized the watch was not on your arm. You were angry and demanded we put it back on, which we did.

I wonder why the watch was so important to you Dad, and what it signified. Was it just a convenience so you could always tell the passing of the day with a glance, or did the steady, accurate movement of the hands signify the very existence of your own life; that as long as the watch was alive and ticking, your days were not yet over?

I like to tell myself, though, a different story. I think that it was special to you because I bought it for you. I believe you saw my giving of this gift as an act of love towards you, a love that was never clearly expressed in words by either of us. It was a love that had to be satisfied with expression through gifts and actions but could not and would never find a spoken voice or an intimate touch or hug.

Dad, when I saw you for the last time at the funeral home before your burial I placed the watch on your wrist for one last time. I think that watch is still ticking away. May it always remind you of my unspoken love for you.

Love, Rich

The Letters – (Cont.)

Gains being made in Okinawa. Mud making push difficult.

May 10 1945   Germany

Dear Roz,

Today I hit the jackpot on mail. First I took another reconnaissance in a ¼ ton to look around. I find that many towns are completely ruined and no civilians live there any more. This afternoon I spent the entire time sleeping and after supper I went on a bicycle ride. Now I'm back again. I eat like hell and know that I'm gaining weight fast.

So you received the little insignia I sent you. Yes it is made out of chop metal however the swords I sent is a military necessity for an officer and is made out of better steel. The flag I sent my father is a big Nazi flag.

So you did receive the $100 check. That ought to boost up our finances a bit. If I find I can get along without much money as I have in the past, why I'll continue to send you more money. Yesterday I sent you a money order for the amount of $50. I've given the mail man 1200 marks ($120) to make out another money order for me. When he gives that to me I'll mail that home too. That's in addition to your allotment. Yes I was a little lucky in cards.

◆   ◆   ◆

B-29's caused giant fires in Japan in attack by 100 planes.

May 11, 1945   Germany

Dear Roz,

Darling, I received one letter and also a package from you. The army is hot on an education program. I'm education officer in the company, imagine that. By the way, the Captain returned back, he wasn't hit too badly. Before I forget, if you can get any 120 film send it to me. We have a camera here and no film.

You asked me in your letter to write at least once a week. Darling, I doubt if more than one week has ever passed that I didn't write. I'm sure that when your mail does arrive it will come in bunches.

I don't see why you have to work for Mr. Brickner as I think I send you enough money. I don't want you working at all. It seems to me as if you shouldn't have the time to spare.

Honey, tomorrow I'm going to take my German pistols out and do some shooting. I have a German luger which I know I can get $100 for but I'm keeping it as a souvenir. Remember what I told you about always having a pistol at home. I have cut my collection from 6 to 3 pistols all of which I consider very essential. I will not feel right unless I was carrying a pistol with me. I have a small one which I can wear under my arm. I believe I'll keep that always with me.

Today I was riding through some woods and saw a deer. I fired and missed. Piss poor shot, that's me. Oh well.

◆   ◆   ◆

Richard Leitman with Michael Hollander

Truman talks with U.S. delegation heads and Senate leaders about German reparations.

May 11, 1945   Germany   To His Parents

Dear Mom and Pop,

Well the war is over and we are resting and taking things easy. It looks as if we may be part of the army of occupation. I like that myself. We eat good hot meals and I'm gaining back a lot of the weight I lost in combat. I can't begin to tell you how happy I am not to be in combat. For six months all I saw was men being killed, wounded and torn apart by artillery. Many is the time I had artillery and mortars land right along side me and no shrapnel hit me at all and yet those near me were wounded. It's hard to explain why, or was it just luck? I don't know but I was beginning to get very scared. I was the only officer in our company who wasn't wounded and I spent the longest time on the line straight. I knew that sooner or later I would be hit too as it happened to everyone.

When I first joined in Hurtgen back in November the fighting was so horrible that half the company was hit every day. At that time I knew I couldn't last too long and yet somehow, even when the company was whittled down to about 40 men from 140, I was still amongst the fortunate few and yet I would ask myself if I was fortunate to have to go through the same thing tomorrow.

A bombed German building.

During the breakthrough we were totally surrounded for six days and we wondered just how long we could hold out and just how long our ammunition and food would last. Living in the winter was rough. We would dig holes in the ground covered with snow and just shiver through the night. I can't begin to tell you how horrible war is and why I feel as if I'm lucky being here and not in the Pacific. If I stay here a while and miss any more combat I'll be very lucky. I've walked across most of Germany, as far as the Alps below Munich. Walking and fighting, always attacking. Now that the war here is over we can't believe it. We can't believe that as we walk down a road a jerry sniper isn't getting his rifle up to his shoulder ready to fire at us. It will take some time before I change mentally back to a normal way of thinking. I never wrote you much about warfare as I didn't want you to worry. Now it's over and there is nothing to worry about any more. I too wonder when I will go home again but if I have to stay here for a while and not go to the Pacific, why I'll gladly stay here.

We have a few million men overseas and back home every one thinks that all these men are constantly in danger. It isn't so as I found out. Sonny B. was overseas a long time but his job was a good one and the only danger was from an occasional enemy plane. The front line riflemen, who are a very small percentage of this army, actually are the ones who see the fighting and do the fighting. Every weapon designed to kill or maim is directed against them and all they have to protect themselves with is a few prayers and a hole or depression in the ground. This is warfare.

Well I've given you the worst picture of war today. Now that it's over I want you both to relax and just take care of yourselves. I'll be home again and will be able to take up my life where I left off. Don't work too hard.

Love, Dave

P.S. I sent Pop a big swastika flag.

♦   ♦   ♦

> *Advance in Okinawa facing heavy fighting. Chocolate Drop Hill important to foe. Japanese counter-attack repulsed by marines.*

May 16, 1945   Germany
Dear Roz,

I move again and this time my home isn't as nice as the last one on the picture I sent. I went ahead and stopped off in Nuremburg. There is a city that just isn't any more. Everything is bombed out there and it's amazing how people managed to live through all they took. The streets are just rubble and ashes. Nuremburg was at one time one of the prettiest cities in Europe, full of medieval castles. I tried to get some army folding cots to sleep on for the men. I'm sending you a picture of the last town I stayed in. It was a pretty little town and had a castle there which we used as a kitchen. It was the property of some Baron.

This place I'm in now is just a farm village with the usual manure piles in front of each house. The weather is good here and it isn't too hot and at present I'm trying to hunt up a good swimming hole somewhere. Say, if you can manage to get hold of some 120 film send them to me. Of course we get films in our rations but they are grabbed off before they get down to companies. Every one around here is talking about points and going home. Darling, the point system does not affect officers and they aren't discharged as quickly. Of course, under the point system as it exists now one doesn't get a damn thing for being in combat. So you see once again the combat soldier gets -----. They said that they came to this conclusion after questioning many soldiers. Oh well, I'm not included anyway.

Darling, every time we move the mail stops. I'm trying to figure out why so many days have to pass by before I can get a letter from you. Goodness knows, things drag along as it is now without hearing from you.

◆   ◆   ◆

Richard Leitman with Michael Hollander

Our forces win four important objectives: Mindanao Air Base, Luzon Ipo Dam, Tarakan, and Wewak.

May 19, 1945   Germany

Dear Roz,

Today I got the sudden urge to try and get a movie for the company. Well I hopped into a jeep and rode to 3rd Army HQ. There I saw the special services officer. Result ...a movie tonight. We saw Edie was a Lady. It was strictly slap stick stuff but the men all enjoyed it. Of course when Bn. finds out I went over their head and not through channels, certain people may get mad but who cares. You know me when I get a buzz in my head. The result is that I Company, 12 Infantry is on the 3rd Army circuit. I asked them there to keep it under their hat and they said for me to do the same as they aren't permitted to show us any films.

Well as usual and just as we expected we are swamped with paper work. Instead of just calling us on the phone everyone of Bn. wants written reports on everything. We keep two typists going all day now.

The news of officers is still hazy here and I have no definite news to give you. I'm waiting for an accurate check on my point system at present. I'm not too sure of the number of combat stars I have. I know I have 75 points now and that is fairly high even in our company. We have only about 15 men with over 85 points. I'm hoping that I have enough to keep out of the Pacific. I believe I should have enough for that. Darling, I didn't even know it was Mothers Day until I received your letter. Darling how could I ever have forgotten the sweetest mother in the world. The mother who keeps the home fires burning in these trying times. Darling, I love you as a wife and as the mother of my son. I know that if Richard could understand, he too would agree with me.

◆   ◆   ◆

> *Trapped Japanese are being targeted east of Manila. Heavy fighting at Mindanao airfield.*

May 20, 1945   Germany

Dear Roz,

A bulletin was published; we can now say where we are. I am located in a small town by the name of Markt Erlbach. It's about 10 miles west of Nuremburg. It's a small bauer (farming) town. Of course I live in a big house here. We ran all the krauts out. All day long I have refugees of all nationalities coming to my door trying to get home. I hear every type of excuse under the sun. One man about 50 years old asked me to put a guard near his house. It seems that another man about 60 comes to visit his wife every night about 1 am. He sleeps upstairs and she sleeps downstairs. Of course the only interest I have is that the 60 year old lover is breaking curfew. Of course I placed a guard at night figuring that if we see him we will fire a couple of shots into the air and frighten him. So far we haven't caught him. The men call it the "whore house" guard and get a good laugh out of it. They say if any man 60 years old is still interested in romance we ought to help him.

I ride into Nuremburg quite often and take a look around there. It will take years to rebuild Germany again. So far as I know we haven't had any cases of sabotage. However, at present many prisoners are relieved and are returning to their homes. It's really an odd feeling walking on a street and along comes a group of kraut discharged prisoners. They look at us and we look at them and walk by each other.

The Russians are being sent home by truck. We see long columns of 2 ½ ton trucks loaded with Russian ex-slave labor. They are singing, happy, and every truck sports a big red star flag. The war is over for them and they are on the way home. Europe is really in a tangled mess now with many loose strings dangling. It will take a while before everything is smoothed out.

◆   ◆   ◆

Truman seizes foundry making tires needed for the war. Army to operate North Carolina plant replacing striking workers.

May 21, 1945   Germany

Dear Roz,

Another busy day gone by. It's 10 o'clock now. All day long we kept banging out endorsements to everyone. Now we are up to date on all our work and until tomorrow I can relax. We are getting more men each day and night now. We have more men than we ever did have.

I received my total number of points. It's 78, and they say there may be another award for the breakthrough. However I'm pretty high amongst the officers in the rifle companies. In fact I believe I'm highest in the rifle companies.

Mom and Dad on the dance floor.

Yes darling, I do know how much you longed to be with me as I know exactly how I felt in all this time. No, you needn't worry about bullets any more. It's all over now. You always write and make me into a hero. Actually I'm just Dave Leitman. I can't think of anything outstanding that I've ever done in my entire life outside of marrying you. However, confidentially I used to think about you a lot in combat and believe me the urge to see you often gave me the necessary strength to keep moving when I was exhausted, and escape danger.

I've never written about this before but at one time I was really in a tight spot. A jerry machine gun was firing right at me and I couldn't figure where it was coming from. I saw a depression in the ground and kept crawling towards it. The bullets were hitting all around me and believe me I was scared and tired from crawling. However, I made it to the depression and then I thought to myself that I would see you again. Darling, I've led a charmed life. I know we were destined to be together for a lifetime. I love you very, very much my sweet so keep your spirits up. We will be together and continue our happy life more in love than ever.

◆　　　◆　　　◆

German records show Goering telling Hitler he urged stripping Allied fliers in snow. This contradicts his latest statements to reporters that he did everything he could to assure correct treatment of prisoners.

May 23, 1945   Germany

Dear Roz,

I had given the mail clerk 120 dollars and they were slow in getting it into a mail order. I withdrew $20 to get some clothes. Today I received the $100 mail order and I'm mailing it to you in this letter.

The weather has changed a lot here and it suddenly got a little cool. No swimming for the past few days. Hundreds of people come to our door each day with their personal problems. I'm getting tired of hearing them. Things are still all upset here, refugees running back and forth. Small groups of Russians and Polacks are looting German homes. We try and catch them but haven't as yet. It's really amusing to watch the krauts cry on our shoulders. Oh well that's what's coming to them now. A lady comes to us today and wants me to look up a relation of hers in the US army. I quickly told her where the door is located.

I know my handwriting is getting worse now. I write too many business letters during the day and I've signed my name so many times that I can't even read it back any more.

Love, Dave

MY KEEPSAKE

Dear Dad,

Imagine how surprised I was to read this in one of your letters. It was like having an antique clock sit on the mantle for years, and then one day, finding a letter In the attic that documents the clock was given to Grandma by Mrs. Roosevelt or some other noted person in history. How much more valuable that old clock would instantly become.

Dear Roz,

I haven't received any package from Aunt Clara. I'll keep the wallet or send it home but the wallet I have now is the one I'll keep. It still has the medal you gave me.

Germany   *February 16, 1945*

A few years ago I asked Mom if she had some keepsake that she could give me to wear around my neck. I never wore any jewelry except for my wedding ring, and before I acquired my cell phone, a watch. I wanted some way of feeling closer to her and I thought that wearing something of hers would do that. She looked through her jewelry box and pulled out a small pendant with a portrait of Moses holding the tablets on one side and an inscription of a Hebrew prayer on the other. It is oval shaped and no more than half an inch long. She told me that the pendant was given to her when she was a little girl by a family friend. Just before you went overseas Mom had sewn the pendant into your wallet to keep you safe. You carried it throughout the war and it seemed to have been effective, as you came home safely and physically unharmed.

It was exactly what I was looking for. Not only would it be a reminder for me of her, but it also had a special connection to you.

I had the pendant mounted in a thin gold frame and bought a gold chain so I could wear it around my neck. I never take it off. It's one of the most precious things I have.

Now reading through your letters I was fortunate enough to see you refer to this medal. It was special to you too, and you did not want to exchange your old wallet with the sewn-in medal for a new one. What a wonderful find. My keepsake just jumped through the roof in sentimental value.

Love, Rich

The keepsake Roz gave to Richard.

The Letters – (Cont.)

The Soviets said they will not alter their policies or be bribed by U.S. for assistance. They need loans for recovery projects.

May 24, 1945   Germany

Dear Roz,

We just took another town and at last I have a chance to write to you. Things have been rolling along very fast. They are trying to finish off the Germans but the damn krauts still keep withdrawing and shooting at us.

Yesterday the Captain got hit in the leg by shrapnel. It wasn't too bad a wound. I'm company commander now and probably will have this company until he returns from the hospital. This makes two purple hearts for him. I don't particularly care to have a company but I've got it just the same.

The weather changed suddenly and it got very nasty here. We were soaking wet. We lived on trucks for two days and followed tanks until they get stopped. Then we go into action.

◆   ◆   ◆

Eastern Europe poses the first serious and difficult problem facing post-war Allies. The Soviets seek a buffer in the Balkans between themselves and the west. Moscow is using Lend-Lease and UNRRA Aid to establish Cordon Treaty aimed at all potential foes. The rival ideologies of Britain and the U.S. on one hand and the Soviet Communists will face each other in the Balkans.

May 25, 1945   Germany

Dear Roz,

I found the colored paper and being that today is my birthday (26 years old) I decided to change off. Darling the years are going by too quickly. I'm getting old too fast and am not living as well as I should have been.

First I have some good news. The Stars and Stripes came out with an article giving us two new awards. One for the breakthrough in December, and the other for the east of the Rhine. Darling that gives me a total of 3 combat stars and bumps my points up to 88. So far we haven't heard anything official about this but I'm sure it will reach us through channels soon. The Stars and Stripes is the official army paper and they would not print anything like that unless it was true. So now I'm sweating out more information. We still haven't heard anything definite as to who goes home, who goes to the States for discharge, and who goes to fight the Japs.

I know that this entire 1st Army is on the way to fight the Japs and four more divisions were mentioned in the paper yesterday. Ours was the first division to land on D-Day so I don't believe it will go to fight anywhere else. Well the Captain is back again so once again I'm back to exec.

◆   ◆   ◆

Secretary Wallace said there is nothing irreconcilable between the World's two greatest powers and urges Soviet-U.S. amity. See the two great nations working together to help backward areas of the globe and stresses trade.

May 25, 1945   Germany

Dear Roz,

You finally broke down and bought yourself some clothes. Well all I can say is that it's about time. Why didn't you buy clothes right along. I know that you're doing this only for me. You act as if you're apologizing for spending the money when you've no need to. A few days ago I sent you another money order for $100. That should cover your initial clothing cost.

In your letter you mentioned that the saber finally arrived. There is no story that goes with it as German officers do not wear sabers in combat. However, for Richard's interest, there will be one.

My classification is 88 points under the new system of receiving 3 combat awards.

52 points	*Straight army time*
9	*Time overseas*
12	*For Richard*
15	*3 combat stars*
	Germany west of the Rhine - Hurtgen
----	*Ordinance when I was cut off for a day*
88	*Germany east of the Rhine*

◆ ◆ ◆

The army has limited news coming out of the Reich after the Goering report was released. Reporters are now guided by stricter censorship in interviewing enemy officials. Passes are required for visits to hidden factories and internment camps.

May 27, 1945   Germany

Dear Roz,

Today is Sunday and our day of rest. Every day is a day of rest for us. It's been a little chilly lately and it's necessary to wear a field jacket during the day. We have moving pictures a few times a week and this is the majority of our recreation. We are trying to make a ball diamond of our own and start a real athletic program.

Say, one of the officers received a package from home with some canned oysters. They really are good and I was wondering whether you could send me canned oysters or clams in a future package. Sort of a treat.

Well, we finally have a full quota of officers and the jobs are equally distributed. The Captain is back again and my days of arguing with an inconsiderate staff are over. The Captain is very much disappointed to find that after returning, instead of finding a unit, who after being in combat so long, would try and take advantage of this set up, to cooperate, and try and work together, the exact opposite prevails.

A handsome couple.-Mom and Dad.

Of course there is no shooting here and all the heroes in battalion who I have never seen on the line are running around gigging all the men for not saluting and other petty things like that. Every day three rifle officers must ride around in jeeps and visit each company area and look for someone who violated one of their forbidden orders. I get very amused at all this and it seems to me that the infantry has the most unintelligent office(rs) in the service. The higher the rank the worse it gets. The first thing each battalion commander looks to see is if the company's officers live in a better house than him. If he is satisfied that his shack is better, his ego is satisfied. If he finds that his house isn't as nice, we move and he moves in. Sort of childish isn't it. And yet all the high ranking officers in the infantry think along those lines. That's why I say that it's all very amusing to watch these so called intelligent men try and outdo each other.

One thing I am thankful for and that is we have an intelligent captain. He is well educated and when he speaks to these prima donnas he used terminology, which although none of them can understand, all are ashamed to admit it, and he manages to keep them snowed under at all times. I am very happy amongst our officers as we all are of the same type and think along the same lines. Of course various people may criticize us but after being in combat we know the score and we can always prove that our company has had less casualties in the last six months since Captain Davit, Lt. Roberts and myself have been with them than any other in this regiment and the reason for this record is that we think along different lines.

My typing is very bad in this letter, the excuse being that I am using a German captured machine and the keys are located in different places

◆   ◆   ◆

Fighting is spreading between the French and Arabs in Syria with more than 200 casualties reported in Hama. Hope rests with U.S.-British intervention for peaceful solution. Egypt expresses concern to U.S.

May 29, 1945   Germany

Dear Roz,

In the line of packages, I wonder if you can get a few cans of clams and oysters and horse radish and ketchup and send it.

For the past few days I've been Bn. Officer of the Day. In addition to being responsible for the guard it also includes patrolling of our entire area by jeep and see if all the regulations are complied with. Today I entered in town about 20 minutes after 4 Polocks had looted a civilian house. Well I went tearing down the road and picked them up. There isn't anything I could do outside of throwing them in the clink.

I hope the tailor does a good job on your clothes. I know you have neglected yourself for a long time now and I hope everything you buy looks real good on you. It's really amazing how you figured out my points right on the nose without my records. I doubt whether I could have done the same. However, now you know that I have 88, although it still hasn't reached us through channels official.

Darling, where did you even get the idea to stop sending me packages? I'm looking forward to receiving them again soon. I still do not have any idea as to the officer's situation.

Everything we are told is all indefinite and so far I know just as much now as I did two weeks ago. It all depends on who they want and how many. If they take rifle company officers I stand a good chance as very few have more points than I. We just didn't last long enough to accumulate many points.

So you finally did go to work for Mr. Brickner. Tell me do you really enjoy working so much. If so I'll stay home with our children while you go into the world earning a livelihood for us. Sounds like a good idea to me.

◆   ◆   ◆

> *Nearly all of Yokohama is destroyed by B-29's. City in blazes. Japan reports three leaders are missing.*

May 31, 1945   Germany

Dear Roz,

Darling, I knew that Rich needs lots of new clothes as he grows out of his old ones. Just keep buying him everything he needs and all is well.

◆   ◆   ◆

> *The Soviets are said to be liquidating the upper crust of the Reich in an effort to communize the country, according to a team of U.S. Senators returning from a visit to Europe.*

June 2, 1945   Germany

Dear Roz,

Darling, after reading your letters over I realize that you are having a tough time now. Trying to bring up a baby, work in the store and take care of the house is strictly one full time job. Of course, with Milton gone now there is that much more work to do. I want to say for you to take it as easy as possible but it sounds silly when you've so much to do.

My biggest job is trying to run down all cases of theft and looting in the area.

◆   ◆   ◆

> *The U.S. is trying to ship food to a hungry Europe but efforts are hurt by a lack of ships. Policy changes are also needed.*

June 3, 1945   Germany

Dear Roz,

After dinner I went swimming with the Captain. We go swimming in a shallow lake. The water isn't higher than my head but at least it's cool and refreshing. Of course I took a good look at all the women in their bathing suits. Darling, when I first arrived here the women looked awful. Now they seem to be getting better looking. I'm really love starved by this time and am sweating it out. It wasn't so back in combat but now there is plenty of time to think about things like that.

I took an entire roll of film and sent them to be developed. After supper I played baseball until 8 o'clock and now I'm writing to you. Tomorrow I should feel plenty sore.

I feel guilty about not writing home so often but I don't know what to write (to) Mom and Pop. In fact darling, I can only write to you now. I seem to have lost all my ambition. Darling, I miss you very much. I find myself day dreaming all the time and at night. Why, I relive our latter part of our honeymoon. (Remember Superman). Well I don't believe I have superman qualities anymore. This war should have taken something out of me. Right now, as usual, the conversation is still the same. Women in the officer's lives. The trouble is we just talk about it. Well daring, I'd better close before I get myself worked up in frenzy.

◆   ◆   ◆

June 5, 1945   Germany

Dear Roz,

Of course the army still is a complete mystery for me. I was seen by our Bn. CO riding in a jeep not wearing my helmet liner so now I'm in for a $50 fine. I just finished answering a letter why I wasn't wearing it. Honestly honey, the longer I stay in the more the more disgusted I get. In combat when we were fighting, why every one was right behind us cheering us on. Sure we were the ones who were killed. The figures were released on casualties and the 4th Division rated 5th in casualties. The other four were the 3rd, 45th, 36th and the 9th Divisions. These 4 fought in Africa. Our fighting started on D-Day. We had 21,000 casualties (and) that's a lot when you figure how few men actually do the fighting. Yes darling. We were lucky again. I could never describe what things were at its worst.

Well darling, still nothing new to write about other than we may get a Presidential citation for the defense of Luxemburg.

Do you think that I'll have any trouble trying to get into Richard's good graces? You say he needs a father and yet I wonder how good a father I'll be. Remember when he kept us up all night and I said let him cry.

◆   ◆   ◆

June 7, 1945   Germany

Dear Roz,

The Captain was evacuated again and I've been very busy. I am using the jerry typewriter again so don't be too critical of my errors. Things are popping again and it looks as if we are on the move again. This time however, all indications lead to us being home in a few months. Of course it's hard to say exactly what is going to happen but I honestly believe that we will be going home shortly.

If any one actually gets out, it will have to be in the States. I may not find the time to write so often darling, as for one thing, we may not be permitted to write, and for another, the mail may not be going out. If you don't hear from me please don't worry as it's all for the best.

◆   ◆   ◆

Belgium indicts 180,000 people as pro-Nazi.

June 7, 1945   Germany

Dear Roz,

Of course now all I do is daydream about you and the baby. Darling, I can even predict our future argument when I get my first leave. Of course I can see you arguing that you want to go out all the time as it was so long since you had a good time. Darling we will have a lot of fun but confidentially (spoken in a whisper) what I would like to do is go to sleep early every night and catch up on all our lost loving, at least until my physical capacities stand up. I know that I'm not the man I was when I left, as I'm sure that K rations took some of my poop out of me. Don't worry honey, I'll do my best and won't let you down. So brace yourself darling.

◆   ◆   ◆

> *Japanese defense headquarters were targeted by marine planes dumping thousands of gallons of flammable liquid into a valley along with hundreds of rockets. Flames engulfed the area.*

June 15, 1945   Germany

Dear Roz,

Once again I have failed to write for a few days for no other reason other than I don't know what to write. Things are so uncertain here that I still can't write anything definite. The weather here has changed for the worst with rain every day. It still hasn't become too warm and I'm wondering whether this is the normal summer weather.

At present I'm afflicted with a bad case of the runs which is one hell of a nuisance and I can't seem to get rid of it. I am taking seven pills at a time and have orders to stay off food for a day. Last night I spent a rough night going back and forth to the latrine.

We are still living in tents and it isn't too bad even though the weather is bad.

◆   ◆   ◆

> *British proposals for greater Indian autonomy will be subject of Simla conference. Gandhi may attend with other Indian leaders.*

June 17, 1945   Germany

Dear Roz,

Today is Sunday and it's a beautiful day here today. Last night the officers played a baseball game and I am a little sore physically. I still haven't received any mail from you and now I am almost sure that the mail is being held up somewhere. It could be that it is going to our next destination to meet us there. I am almost certain that we are going back to the States now. We have sent two enlisted men ahead as an advance detail. I don't know when we will move but it should be in the near future. Of course rumors have it that we will get 30 day leaves when we get home. Darling need I tell you how anxious I am to see you and Richard. I have written so much on this subject that I hardly feel it necessary to describe my feelings on the very important subject.

Last night we all took showers after the ballgame and then I played bridge for about an hour and then went to sleep. It's very cold here at night and although I have five blankets I still can't keep warm. Our soldiering is mostly for parades. We have parades and dress rehearsals every day and the regiment really looks good. I can just picture this outfit in the States as it is one of the most famous Divisions in the European war. Today we are having a rehearsal for a Division parade. The first Division parade so far.

I had to buy some clothes and a battle jacket. This takes the place of a blouse. It looks like a blouse but it's made of OD material. All the men have the same jacket and we all look pretty good dressed up and wearing all our ribbons of which I have very few. Well darling, that's all for now.

◆　　　◆　　　◆

Japanese continue to retreat from Chinese coast.

June 25, 1945   Germany

Dear Roz,

At last we are on the way back. I've just completed about a 5 day train ride in a 40 and 8 and ended up near Le Havre. I imagine that we will remain here about 10 days or so and then take the boat back to the States. By this time next month I expect to have my family with me. I couldn't write darling as the mail was stopped. Making as large a move as we did was a *little too much for my APO as they had to move too. However, I expect the mail to go out again soon. Also, I haven't received any mail for the same reason. I know that I should have plenty of mail on the way to me. Perhaps I'll be lucky and get about ten at a time.*

Dad in uniform.

Darling, now that I know that I'll be seeing you I can't begin to tell you how impatient I am. I'm sure that the newspapers published that the 4th Division is on the way home. You probably knew it before I did. Only a few men have been taken out of our outfit for having over 85 points. Those men were transferred to the 19ᵗʰ Division who are still way back in Germany. I know we will be home first. Also, we still haven't received the official credit for our last two combat stars. I know it's only a matter of an official order as the Stars and Stripes published those authorized. Oh yes, I have been put in for three bronze stars. If they go through I'll have 15 points for that and 10 more points for the two combat stars. Without these I've only 78 but so far no officer I know of as yet has been reassigned. I don't know when all this takes place. They seem to suggest that the division will be processed when we are home.

◆   ◆   ◆

Back Home in the United States

Japan is moving towards a democratic government to replace the totalitarian regime established for the war. Six political parties may take part. Diet chamber to be reorganized. Forced military training will be ended. All this is a plan by Emperor Hirohito to have home grown democracy in place before Allied troops land and impose their will.

August 23, 1945   USA

Dear Roz,

Yesterday I wrote my first letter to you in ages. It was very hot today and we have lots of work to do getting in shape. Now the men are almost all back and of course it will be necessary to process all men ready for discharge. All men with 85 points or more will be discharged in a few days but of course nothing definite has come down on Infantry officers. The Air Corps is discharging all those with 45 points or more. You probably have read about it in the newspapers.

I'm almost sure that as soon as the war with Japan is officially over the War Department will adopt a more positive position and state definitely what's to be done with officers. I know you don't take this news too badly as I'm almost sure that it will only be short time until we know definitely where we stand.

Love, Dave

GIVE HER PERMISSION TO LIVE

Dear Dad,

I'm sorry to have to bring these words of yours up now but it's important. Dad, I have a special favor to ask of you. I think you will understand. Since you passed away in December Mom has missed you terribly. It has been hard for me to witness the deterioration in her body and spirit these last few months. I believe she has lost the will to live and she sometimes says she wants to be reunited with you and hold your hand again. I know how much you miss her too, but we are not ready or prepared to have her go yet. Please, give her permission to live awhile longer and allow her to enjoy some more precious time here with her family, who also love her. She always listened to you and did whatever you asked. There's a chance she will do as you wish one more time.

> Dear Roz,
>
> Darling, from your letter you sound pretty blue. Please try and buck up. I'm here and you're at home and I want you to appreciate all the luxuries home has to offer even though I can only be with you in soul only. I don't want you to wear a hard look. I'd rather have you smile and be gay for our little son, as I know you are.
>
> Luxemburg   December 25, 1944

Before you died, and even on that very day, Mom had enough energy and strength to climb the stairs to your bed caring for you whenever you called. She was not very strong but nothing stopped her from following her heart and doing whatever it took to comfort you. It was right after your funeral that I noticed she began to have some trouble walking and getting up from a chair. Within a week she took a fall, which wasn't too bad or serious, but during the trauma she had completely forgotten how to walk. She spent many weeks in the rehab center learning how to place her hands on a walker so she could get up from a chair, and learning how to lean on the walker frame as she moved her feet. I was sad to watch her learn how to open a door while holding onto the walker without falling.

Dad and Mom in the later years sitting by the town dock in Port Washington, NY.

She finally did regain enough dexterity to leave rehab and return to her assisted living facility, The Bristal, which she calls her five star hotel. For several months she seemed to do better, gaining some weight on her frail body, and improving her walking skills. But there were many troubling signs. Her short term memory became very poor and she has very little interest in socializing with the other residents or taking part in activities at her residence.

A week ago she came to our home for a few days and enjoyed looking at old photographs and spending time with her great-grandsons. When it was time to take her back to The Bristal she didn't want to go but also didn't want to burden us by staying in our home. Several times she cried, as if she could not find a place for herself here without you. We could not convince her that she was welcome to live with us. It's as if she doesn't think she deserves to be happy, and in fact, welcomes unhappiness instead. She said, "Too much of a good thing is no good. "

The other day, while alone at The Bristal, Mom fell and severely broke her hip. Yesterday she had surgery to repair it. My worst fears for her seem to be on an accelerated schedule. If she is to walk again, and all that implies, we need some drastic intervention now. She must know that you are patient to wait for her to join you and that you want her to enjoy some more time with us. I know she senses you with her and will hear your message if you send it with truth and love. The words you wrote to her in 1944 are perfect:

> Darling, from your letter you sound pretty blue. Please try and buck up. I'm here and you're at home and I want you to appreciate all the luxuries home has to offer even though I can only be with you in soul only. I don't want you to wear a hard look. I'd rather have you smile and be gay for our little son, as I know you are.
> Love, Dave

Dad, I know you will understand. Thank you for this gift.

Love, Rich

◆　　◆　　◆

Dear Dad,

Several weeks have passed since Mom broke her hip. I've seen her gain physical strength and even walk several steps with her walker. She is eating again by herself and the hue in her eyes has improved, indicating to me that the crisis has passed.

I wish the same could be said about Mom's mind. Her forgetfulness has its good days and those in which she remains somewhat confused. The only message I hear consistently from her is that she yearns to join you and hold your hand once again.

I now know that it's entirely up to her how her health progresses and whether she can find happiness again without you.

We all shine our love onto her and attempt to give her reasons for wanting to live. She smiles when I hold her and sweep gentle kisses across her brow, but when the room is quiet and the air is dark, I suspect the tears come and she softly calls to you.

I know I must be more accepting of what is to come, whatever, and whenever that is. I am grateful and blessed for the time I have had with her and must be open to what the future brings. I could not have had a finer mother and I'll say you picked wisely when you courted Roslyn Cohen.

Dad, we are taking good care of Mom and you must be happy to witness the love and care she is getting. I pray there will be more sunny days for us to show her our love, and fill up our hearts with her spirit.

I love you both,

Rich

Richard Leitman with Michael Hollander

COMING FULL CIRCLE

There once was a time,
a long time ago it seems,
when he held my hand to
cross the street;
yesterday I held his.

There once was a time,
a long time ago it seems,
when I rested my head in his arms;
yesterday it was the gentle strength of my shoulders
that comforted him.

Life goes full circle,
and the young and the old
walk together through time.
I am so proud because once upon a time,
a long time ago it seems,
a baby boy was born
who now is a man...
      following his dreams.

- Dena Dilaconi

4.

Finding My Father Through His Letters

The journey I began months ago on an uncertain winding route brought me to some extraordinary vista locations. I'm now standing on a scenic overlook taking in the view laid out before me. In American Indian lore, the four directions of the compass hold special energies and are home to four arch-types; King in the north, Warrior in the south, Lover in the east, and Magician in the west. From my vantage point high above the countryside, I too can visualize the spirit energies residing in the four directions of the compass. Looking out towards the east, my heart becomes aware of the deeper LOVE that I have discovered for my father. My anger has subsided and I see the issues that at one time brought up anger in me with a new perspective.

I've gained the ability to see our differences through his eyes and they no longer generate the same charge in me. Learning about his life by studying his letters to my mother has illuminated a new perspective for me when viewing his actions. I've learned that I can disagree with him while maintaining love and respect for him. He, like the rest us, was influenced by his history of life experiences. These worked to shape his outlook on life and his future. His letters, unintentionally, served as a camera into his soul, a means for me to learn how he thought, how he felt, and more importantly, how he loved. I have been blessed by the spirit of the lover in the east that brought my father deeper into my heart.

The greatest insight I gained about my dad through reading the letters was how strongly he loved my mother. I never saw him as a romantic, and never related to the strong love my parents had for each other. When my father bullied my mom I couldn't understand her willing compliance to his harsh words. I never got that she was totally in love with this man throughout their 67 years of marriage, since I projected my anger towards him onto her. I imagined her love for him being diminished with each abusive command, each selfish demand, and each outburst. I saw her hiding in her own shadows to escape his arrows, as I used to do when I felt his arrows coming my way. What I didn't see or hear were their intimate words of love they shared or the physical expression of their romance carried out in the privacy of their bedroom. When I recently told Mom that I never saw Dad's romantic side, she responded, "You weren't supposed to see it."

The letters opened up this personal side of their relationship to me. They taught me that she understood the trauma he went through in the war and the subsequent scarring of his mind, and she was willing to overlook his faults while seeing the inherent beauty in her husband instead. When I see her now and her eyes are red from crying I know she misses her lover and her best friend. I know she loved him for better or worse and chose to focus on the glorious aspects of their relationship. Listening to Billie Holliday or Frank Sinatra recordings now take on special meaning for me. They are singing to my parents about the love they shared for each other, a love that began in another era and lasted until today, and that brings tears to my eyes.

Looking towards the south, home of the WARRIOR, I can visualize a symbolic fortress my dad built for himself on the edge of a forest, beside a cold and blue-black lake that plunges to endless depths. This was a fortress surrounded by iron gates, designed to keep intruders out, but functioning more to imprison its willing occupants. As Robert Bly's wild man in *Iron John,* Dad spent much of his life shaking the bars of the cage that entrapped him, searching for the key to unlock the chains that tormented him.

Dad fought every demon that crossed his path but never learned that happiness would come when, and if, he directed his sharpened sword inward to confront the enemy that lurked in the darkest shadows, found only within his own mind. He protected his family and home by confronting the enemy, whether approaching from society in the form of change, or sent by fate, head on with a clenched fist and a mighty roar. He was a brave man and never let fear get in the way of him beating the enemy down.

During Dad's lifetime, change usually came in the form of more personal freedoms that society was finding acceptable. These included freedoms for expressing oneself more openly in sexual matters and for allowing people to take on less traditional roles in society. I don't think Dad trusted his children, his wife, or himself with these greater options which were suddenly thrust upon his world. He didn't like to lose control, especially in setting the rules his family was to follow and the new societal norms were a direct assault on his authority.

As most children, I always thought that my Dad was disinterested in, and unaffected by things sexual. I was surprised to learn, by reading his letters to Mom, that Dad was a very normal sexual man. The constant bombardment of sexual content in the media had to have had a tempting effect on him too, and yet he needed to present a stoic, puritanical face for his children's sake. He would set the example of correct behavior once again, rejecting the changes and fighting them whenever he had the chance.

The opportunity for conflict usually presented itself when one of his frequent visitors walked through his front door carrying with them some symbol of the outside world that would represent all of society's evils. It was not unusual to hear him lash out at someone carrying a personal water bottle or a cell phone, or a boy wearing long hair, sporting a shaved head or wearing an earring.

Dad was quick to take on all challenges, but couldn't see the greatest contest needed to be fought inside himself. The Nazi's were no match for Dad but he forgot to protect his own little boy who cried out, begging to be held and comforted, and loved by the only one who could do it, David Leitman. Like the army, Dad had his own rulebook that he had written himself. It covered any potential circumstance that might arise but the author of this manual was not familiar with the little boy. It had been too long since they had met and the author had seen too much of life's darkness in the war to hear his cries.

It doesn't surprise me that Dad was blind to his little boy's deepest needs since he was never comfortable with the energy of the west, the MAGICIAN. Dad knew only one way to do things, and that was the first idea that came to him and it was based on experience and observation. He didn't question his decisions, and didn't seek alternate methods, analyzing the options before him. If it worked in the past it was right for now and in the future.

The magician, with his creative ability, was always available but Dad didn't see him because he had no need for him. He was too busy defending his lakeside home from the changes and new ways that never seem to tire of sneaking around in the nearby forest, waiting for the moment when the warrior's guard was down to pounce in the darkness of night on the warrior's home. Instead of welcoming the magician Dad saw him as an enemy that needed to be conquered, and he was very good at protecting his home from the evil magician.

Dad had built a second house in the north where he was KING, and what a powerful king he was. He had no trouble writing mission statements for his warriors. I was an easy task for his sovereign spirit to distinguish things black from those white, good behavior from evil, or which fork to take when the road split.

His warrior trusted the wise king, never doubting where his loyalty belonged. If the king loved you, the warrior would be on duty for your protection. When the king saw you as a threat, the warrior was ready to take up arms. When Dad saw the Parisian street walkers as threats to his family, he was on highest alert to subdue any temptation out to bring him down. When the snipers were in hiding, watching for the right moment to pick off his men, the king knew what backup artillery to call for, and what counter measures were required to protect his men. How fortunate they were to be serving under 1st Lt. David Leitman. They trusted him when he gave an order; if he led them in a charge they would never think of questioning his decisions.

Even as a child I knew Dad could protect me from the outside world, and I believe he would have had I not been afflicted with my own childhood shadows. I feared Dad's reaction towards me if he knew about schoolyard bullying I received, or my belief that personal failure was no further away than the next exam. I worried he would love me less if he saw me for who I was and not who he wanted me to be. So I kept my anguish to myself and sought protection by hiding in my room, blanketed in shame.

Memorial Garden for Dad.

Looking down again from the scenic vista point I see the road I recently traveled and the many alternate routes that lie ahead. I know the choice is mine whether to take the super highway and race from one lofty goal to the next, or to choose the winding two-lane that runs through the smallest of villages and rolling farm country. I know now that I will choose to take my time, partaking in what has been created for me to experience, and to stop long enough beside each lake to see my reflection, and to walk barefoot on the rocks in the meandering stream to learn the lessons that unfold along the way.

I choose this path knowing full well that Dad will be with me, watching to see what he missed when he had the chance. Why do I know this? Because I have felt his presence grow as I spent more and more time with his letters and speaking to him through mine.

The other day Marlene and I went to eat in a restaurant we used to go to with Dad and Mom and his nursing aide. I became nostalgic when I saw the table in the corner where the five of us used to sit. One time Dad said he wanted clams on the half shell. We went to this particular restaurant because I thought they served raw clams. When Dad found out they only served baked clams he became agitated and complained bitterly.

Since clams were forbidden by the kosher dietary laws I never ate them. Now in my saddened, nostalgic mood I experienced the need to be close to him at that moment. Amazingly, I suddenly heard myself tell the waiter to bring me an order of Little Neck clams on the half shell. I couldn't believe it. That was the first time in 55 years that I had eaten them. In my childhood, he would take me to Lundy's in Brooklyn for clams as a special treat. I must admit they were good and they didn't make me sick, as I had been certain they would, and they did make me more connected to Dad at the moment.

Another thing I was compelled to do was plant a memorial garden in my front lawn in his honor. He died in December and as soon as the New Jersey weather warmed I dug a large hole and planted a beautiful white birch tree, chosen for it's small, spirit-like leaves which dance in the breeze, and its captivating while bark that peels in paper-thin strips. I added some small accent bushes, said a prayer asking for good luck and for the deer to dine somewhere else, and I sprayed them with an obnoxious smelling repellant. I just hope Dad doesn't think I'm spraying wolf urine on his memory. When the weather warmed I added some annuals. I know he smiled when I wood-burned his name on a piece of bark, hung it on a branch of the birch tree and posted a small American flag in the soil. Lying in the soil is a piece of driftwood with wood-burned lettering that reads, *David Leitman Memorial Garden 1919-2008*. Names of other deceased relatives are also hung on the branches. When I pull into the driveway from now on I think of him.

The last time I went to the house where he died to pick up some of his items, I found several worn and tattered large American flags that he proudly flew by the front entrance of his home. What will I do with them? I don't know yet but I'm sure he will guide me when the time comes.

So what did I learn from my journey through his letters? What insights did I gain about this man I call my father, and about myself? I attempt to explore this is the following analysis.

Integrity

My father certainly was a man of integrity. You could trust him to be honest. He said what he believed, he did what he said he would do, he acted as he thought he should, and his standards were set high. Numerous examples are found in his letters that clearly show how important honor was to him. He touched no woman other than Mom. He treated German civilians with sufficient respect and he obeyed the orders of his superiors. I never knew him to be untruthful or dishonest with other people. I learned this trait from him, although I don't claim to live up to his high ethical standards. When I do fall short I am aware of it, acknowledge my fault, and try not to punish myself over it.

Memorial Garden with wood-burned driftwood.

I wonder, though, whether I still am seeing him through the innocent eyes of a son who idolized his father, or the eyes of an elder in his own right. Surely no man's integrity is without fault. I challenge myself to come up with examples where his words didn't match his actions, where he failed to live up to a promise or where he let someone down. The one thing that continually comes up is his rough treatment of others, the disrespect he showed to those he professed to hold dear, including Mom and his children. It was as if a switch went off inside of him every now and then, changing him before our eyes.

One of the difficult things I had to deal with when he passed away was the belief that he could suddenly know or sense everything I was doing, and as his son, my actions were dishonoring his name. This would surely result in his anger and disappointment with me. I've come to terms with this now and accept myself for who I am, a good man with some flaws. When confronted by a difficult situation and seeking guidance or moral support, I continue to ask myself, "What would he do?"

Generosity

Generosity came naturally to Dad. When a package arrived from home he shared the cookies and canned food treats with men he fought with. When his officer's whiskey ration came, his men took part in the enjoyment of this bounty. He shared army foods with the civilians whose home he was temporarily occupying. He gave another soldier a personal wristwatch to use. If he saw someone in need, and thought he could make a difference, he never hesitated to try. What he had, he shared. He sent money home faithfully and made it clear he wanted Mom to buy new things for herself and her infant son. He lived his life this way and was always alert for someone who needed a "Care" package, as he called it, or even a job. I admired this trait in him and strive to live up to his standards.

I consider myself to be fairly generous with my time and physical possessions, but once again I don't believe I always live up to his standards. There are many times my heart tells me to give but my brain finds a reason to hold back. My want may be to turn out to support a friend's project or function but my body says stay home and rest; he really doesn't need me the be there. Dad set an example that I was fortunate to experience firsthand. Witnessing unselfish behavior is beautiful, especially when the person you are observing is your own father.

Spirituality

I never envisioned Dad as being a very spiritual person. If he believed in God he didn't demonstrate it. He wasn't apt to see spiritual energy in nature or art, and he scoffed at the value of formal, organized religion and prayer. His letters often speak of his wonder at being so fortunate on the battlefield, despite the odds against him. He attributed his good fortune to luck rather than some divine presence looking out for his wellbeing. I never remember him seeking heavenly support in times of worry or stress; rather he looked inward for the strength and the guidance he needed. He could not connect this inner power to a force greater than himself.

I have a much more spiritual nature than Dad. I too, have lost the need for organized religion and have difficulty finding its relevance, although I did experience that for many years in the past. I've just become discouraged with religion's concentration on ritual and it's seemingly lack of concern for people of other faiths. Too many wars have been fought because one group of people wanted to convert the world to their way of thinking, and it's still going on. I think we would be better off without this deadly competition and seek out God on our own.

I'm not claiming to be right, and I don't look negatively on those who find comfort in an organized faith, but it just doesn't work for me at this time in my life and I want to live in my truth. I can feel the presence of God's energy in everyday experiences and I am most connected to this feeling when alone in the woods, watching the snowfall covering the landscape, or listening to the birds singing out their morning cheers.

I know there is a spirit greater than myself that is the source of any power I possess. I believe Dad's soul now lives in a heaven, whatever and wherever that is, and that he hears and sees me now. I have no doubt that he knows what I have written to him in my letters in this manuscript, and in fact, he helped me to write it. Even now my fingers are moving over the keyboard without much thinking, as if guided by his hand. I am but a medium for him, a mechanism for him to tell us his story, one that he could not express when he was living amongst us.

I expect he will stay with me for a while and help me select some new roads to travel, the diverse paths I can see from the scenic overlook. I hope he directs me down the path where I not only see spirit around me, but learn to find comforting peace through it when I need it the most. I hope that when Dad's soul takes up residence on this earthly soil once again, he will find that connection to spirit, so that his next journey will be more beautiful.

Intelligence

How fortunate I am to be blessed with the ability to think, learn, reason, and sort my way through life in a way that makes sense for me. I thank Dad for providing some good genes, and for showing me a lifestyle wherein education and learning are essential ingredients. Dad enjoyed learning, read many books and was attracted to the Discovery Channel on TV.

The army recognized this in him and sent him to Officers Candidate School. He took those studies seriously and knew how to put his book learning into practice. His platoon had relatively few casualties due to his expert leadership. He knew when to send out scouts, when to move his troops forward and how to protect them from enemy fire when they rested.

He never went to college, yet his letters were beautifully written and well organized. His choice of words read like poetry, even when written from the front lines after a long day of marching through frozen snow or deep mud, while attacking and pushing the enemy back. I wonder how much more he could have contributed to society, had he been given the opportunity to advance his education as I did. He saw to it that I was trained in a good profession and encouraged me to stick with schooling until I earned my Ph.D. in chemical engineering. He taught me the joys one could find through learning and how it could serve me in achieving my life goals.

In some respects I think Dad was making sure that my brother, Mark, and I had a chance to experience the part of life he missed out on. He made sure we got our educations and it gave him great joy to follow our careers; mine in engineering, and Mark's as an ophthalmologist. Dad seemed to live through our accomplishments and worried over our obstacles. He always seemed more interested in what was going on with me professionally than with my family or social life. He was known to brag about promotions at work but I can't remember him praising my social accomplishments, or my home projects to anyone. What impressed him was that I had risen above the blue collar status and had thus made it in American life.

How did he react to my sister's accomplishments? My sister Susan never worked outside the home and Sally, educated in computer technology, became a school teacher. It is my suspicion that he did not take women's roles in business too seriously, and therefore, their professional accomplishments were of lesser importance to him. It would be interesting to know what they think of my assessment and one day I may discuss it with them. It is true, however, that in the final years of his life, he got great enjoyment from the college and career accomplishments of his two granddaughters, Randy and Julie. It was clear, though, that the internal battles were raging on in his mind; praise for the accomplishments, criticism of the freedoms they took advantage of. Nevertheless, it was obvious he had begun a softening of his views.

Social Graces

I don't know how to say this gently; Dad was not blessed with a whole lot of social skills and he was not always easy to get along with. In order for me to better understand him, and thereby find clues to my own behaviors, I find it necessary to detail some of his specific, shall I call them, personality flaws, which were responsible for the barrier I erected to shield and protect me from his barbs. This barrier made it impossible for me to get close to him and learn who he was until he passed away and I found myself compiling this book.

Richard and his wife, Marlene.

How unfortunate that I could not, or would not, attempt to write it sooner, when he was alive. I had great fear of venturing into the shadowy places and my anger was always on alert to act as an early warning alarm if I ventured too close to him.

Dad was a classical bully. He could out-shout anyone and knew all the unfair punches, the way to make one feel insignificant and unworthy. He never used physical force with his children, his wife, or anyone else but he could be abusive, never-the-less.

He was not tolerant of people with different ideas, lifestyles, and interests, and sometimes people of different races or ethnicity. Combine this with a bully tendency and the atmosphere could become charged rather quickly. Dad never restrained himself from telling dinner guests that their children were idiots for picking the wrong school or for playing the wrong sport. His politics were well known and guests learned not to offer liberal opinions in a discussion. You could be criticized for marrying too soon, or too late, or for selecting the wrong mate. There were no boundaries and no easy retreat once the gates were opened and his warrior was set loose. Of course, thirty minutes later he may have forgotten what he was so angry about and would act as if nothing out of the ordinary had happened, but by this time the damage had been done. Having been witness to many such exchanges when I was a child I learned not to speak at all about anything that could, in any way, be controversial, and if perchance I wound up the target in one of his battles I became instantly silent, or sheepishly agreed with him until the fire was extinguished. When I was a bystander to one of his onslaughts, my defense of choice was to retreat into a distant corner deep within my own self and block out as much of the vitriol as I could.

Another response of mine was to take on a personal vow to become the opposite, strive for tolerance, and always attempt to make people feel good. Unfortunately, I have a tendency to take this reaction to an extreme. I sometimes find it hard to be honest, when honesty is called for, and have to force myself to be up front, choosing my words very carefully to make an impact but cause minimal upset.

The puzzle I needed to address is why Dad thought he needed to behave so crudely to other people. Again I looked to the letters for evidence and discovery.

What I found was a man totally at ease with the world and greatly in love with a woman who could do no wrong. No matter what he went through or was feeling, when it came time to write to Mom he was in total control of his words and thoughts. The letters actually only contain a hint of his behavior to come.

I think Dad was a victim of circumstances. He was an officer in a brutal war and was used to men following his orders. Towards the end of the war his tolerance for the hardships of front line combat began to wear him down and he began to complain of orders he didn't agree with, fearful that a bullet with his address was overdue. He was weakened from the cold and rain, and constant attacking. He wanted to scream out, "I've had enough," but wasn't allowed that privilege. He wanted to tell his superiors to get the hell out of headquarters, take up a rifle, and help him fight, or to at least give him and his men a rest. Frustration built, whiskey became a distraction, and directions were given to his men to move forward with a little more bitterness. The pattern began to set. His fear of winning the current battle, only to be sent to the Pacific theatre, became the tipping point. What should he have hoped for – with peace in Europe could come more of the same or worse in the Pacific. He admitted in one letter, towards the end of his duty on the front lines, that his supervisor told him he complained too much. This starts to sound a little more like the dad I knew.

When he was finally released from the army, his newly formed habits remained. His worn out body attempted to adjust to civilian life, and his temper was now more volatile. He still found that whiskey took the edge off hardship and he resorted to indulging more often, especially now that he didn't have to depend on a rationed supply.

Roslyn Cohen, the object of Dad's affection.

He loved his family but his wife also had unfulfilled needs that had to be attended to. He had a young son who didn't know him and cried when he attempted to pick him up. Everything just lead to more frustration. The pattern was set for his future behavior. He soon gave up the whiskey but the damage has been done. The infantry officer still gave orders in the civilian world. The more he was ignored the more he fought back. Thusly, the father I knew was born.

Other possibilities and influences were also possible. I am aware of a familial tendency on his side of the family towards anger and a strong need for control. Were these traits always hiding out within his mind, waiting for the nurturing and training a wartime experience can so efficiently provide?

There is also evidence that Dad was already very sensitive to real or perceived harsh treatment by others. As he envisioned life at home when he returned, he writes of Mom's criticism towards him as an expected component. He expected her to find fault with his habits and to complain of a lack of attention on his part. I think I'm fair when I say that Mom was not overly critical of Dad and, if anything, tolerated much abusive behavior from him without so much as a complaint.

Am I certain of the validity of this analysis? Of course not. But it makes sense to this wounded man, his son, from what I can put together from his own words in his letters. Perhaps, Dad may also have been afflicted with a medical condition, either physical or mental. We will never know because he would not admit to having a problem and would not undergo an examination or treatment.

The personal price I paid for victory over the Nazi's and their monstrous machine was losing a piece of my father. That was a big price to pay, but I understand winning the prize was necessary.

Special Acknowledgement

I am especially indebted to The Mankind Project (MKP) for teaching me the skills, and giving me the platform in which to explore my relationship with my father. Were it not for MKP I would have said good-bye to a man I was acquainted with for 65 years but didn't really know very well, and more importantly, barely acknowledged for the strong, caring and devoted father he was. I can now look back at what I consider to be mistakes he made as a father and human being with sorrow, but the anger I lived with most of my life is no longer in the driver's seat.

I have been active in MKP for nine years doing my personal growth work and supporting other men in doing theirs. I believe that the world would be a safer, happier place if more men and women explored just a piece of their own shadow, that part of themselves that they hide, deny and suppress, as I had previously done. Learning to control one's shadow and directing the energy into a more positive direction can change the way one experiences relationships and one's role in life. The alternative is to yield power to one's darker side and act out in ways that can be harmful to oneself and others, always unaware of the source of one's intense emotions and remaining powerless to change.

For more information about The Mankind Project see its website:

<u>www.mkp.org</u>

APPENDIX A

Dear Norm, Steve, and Jennifer,

Know that your grandfather was a very unusual man and lived a life you and I have never had to experience. I have come to realize that he is an unsung hero, who lived the early years of life in the service of his country with honor and bravery, never wavering from the principles he believed in. He was forced into a situation he did not ask for, but like so many of his generation, he carried out his duties with dignity. We have much to be proud of in him.

I prepared this book based on excerpts of letters he wrote to your grandmother, Roz, during his years in the army. I included his writings about unusual things he saw and did as well as those more mundane subjects such as how he washed his clothing, how the weather effected him, what his daily life was like and what he did for fun. When you read these exerts I hope his experience comes alive for you as it did for me when I read it. I hope you can feel what this twenty-five year old boy was feeling, and what he was thinking at the time. Picture yourself in his place, more distant from home than he ever imagined he could be, with a young family at home. Imagine what he must have been envisioning, wondering if and when he would be called upon to fight our country's battle in Europe. To put his letters in a proper time perspective for you I have provided a summary of some important event which took place on each day corresponding to the date on his letter.

Richard's family; (left to right), back row-Steven, Garrett, Andy, Daniel
Center-Marlene with Sammy, Jenny, Tyler
Front-Richard, Gabi (Norm's girlfriend), Norm

Do not be fooled into thinking this is just a mild version of a World War II novel. This is about your own grandfather, a very real person, and a man whose blood runs in your veins. He is part of your history so I ask you to be reverent when you read his story. And one more thing, be grateful that you and I did not have to follow a similar path, giving up five years, and placing our lives at risk on the battlefield in service to our country. We can find less dangerous and forgiving ways of choosing to serve.

Love, Dad

Michael Hollander

Michael Hollander is a friend and fellow traveler

A poet

A seeker

A warrior

As Strong Jay, as Jaguar, as lover and as a pollinating bee

He comes to this project with compassion and vision and art

Asking questions and seeking answers

A muse to the captain of this life affirming ship

Anything more and anything less

would be a lie.

Michael lives with his wife Carol in Skillman, NJ